Dedicated to the memory of my father,
Tom Wainwright

Printed in England by Flexipress Printing Ltd., Ormskirk, Lancashire.
Tel. 01695 576839 I www.flexipress.co.uk

About This Book

During the life of a busy industrial centre like St Helens, events that were once the talk of the town can quickly be forgotten – displaced by the news of the day and the passing of time.

"The Hidden History of St Helens" takes advantage of the recent expansion in the volume of historic newspapers that are now on offer to researchers. Many titles are available via online subscriptions, although, at the time of writing, only a limited number of St Helens' newspapers are digitally accessible.

Apart from making a personal visit to the British Library, longstanding newspaper titles such as the St Helens Reporter and St Helens Newspaper are exclusively obtainable from the St Helens Archive Service collections at Eccleston and Newton-le-Willows libraries.

The St. Helens Reporter

WITH WHICH ARE INCORPORATED

THE ST. HELENS STANDARD & THE ST. HELENS CHRONICLE, ESTABLISHED 1865.

FRIDAY. DECEMBER 16, 1921.

OXFORD ... PICTUREDROME.

If you have not used the microfilm readers and are a family history researcher or are otherwise interested in the history of St Helens, do book a slot. There are incredible discoveries just waiting to be made! Newspaper cuttings books – as well as many other records – are also available from St Helens Archive Service at the Gamble Building.

Much of the content of this book has been sourced from newspapers stored on microfilm at Eccleston Library and the author would like to thank their ever-helpful and cheerful staff for their co-operation.

About The Author

Stephen Wainwright is a social historian and avid newspaper researcher who has been documenting the heritage of the Lancashire town of St Helens for twenty years.

Stephen publishes a number of websites and Facebook pages that are devoted to aspects of the town's history.

'Sutton Beauty & Heritage' covers in depth the present and past of the Sutton district of St Helens; *'George Groves The Movie Sound Pioneer'* is the official website for the St Helens man who gave birth to talking pictures and *'St Helens History This Week'* features three weekly articles devoted to events from 50, 100 and 150 years ago.

The latter articles are also accessible via a matching Facebook page of the same name – and *'Stories From St Helens Heritage'* features three weekly articles on the social media platform concerning facets of the town's history.

Contents

The Amazing Story of the "Great Doctress" Madame Enault

"I Am Not Going To Be Cured, It Is Only A Farce"

Picture this astonishing St Helens scene. You are sat in a gilded carriage on a fairground surrounded by hundreds (if not thousands) of almost hysterical folk and a mini-brass band.

The mob cheers and the musicians strike up as a glamorous woman yanks out your teeth and holds each blood-soaked molar up to the mob as if it were a trophy!

Or perhaps the *"Great Doctress"* performs some miracle remedy on your innocent but ailing body? Cancer is cured, paralysis is healed, deafness is treated and hundreds of bottles of cure-all medication called malachite are sold to gullible believers at two bob a time.

So-called "quack" doctors are routinely portrayed in fiction as men – but during the 19th century there were a few female versions that were often called "doctresses".

These unscrupulous individuals promised all sorts of fake cures and undertook simple procedures, such as tooth-pulling and cyst removal.

This is the story of the most outrageous and callous quack of them all – a woman known as Madame Enault, who spent several weeks in 1879 conning the poor people of St Helens.

Although aspects of this tale are amusing – at its heart is theft. And not just of poor working-class folk's hard-earned cash – but of desperate people's hopes and dreams of relief from debilitating conditions.

The authorities in St Helens did nothing to stop the Frenchwoman's criminal activities – indeed night after night the police were on hand to assist her entourage in controlling the boisterous crowd!

The con-woman calling herself Madame J. Enault first appeared in St Helens at the end of August 1879 after spending seven weeks deceiving the sick in Warrington.

Sat in her gilded chariot driven by three jet-black horses, the doctress would, each late afternoon, be driven through the streets of St Helens from the Royal Raven Inn to what locals called the fairground, near Salisbury Street.

The glamour of show business was an important aspect in relieving the poor of their cash – and Madame Enault certainly looked the part.

Dressed in a purple robe covered in golden embroidery and what were described as spangled ornaments, the doctress carried a tiara on her head from which gold chains hung down and handsome-looking Chinese slippers were worn on her feet.

"THE WONDERFUL DOCTRESS"

Even some reporters were taken in by the showmanship. The St Helens Examiner newspaper was initially highly impressed by the reports they'd received and on August 30th 1879 published this account of Madame Enault's grand arrival in the town under the headline *"The Wonderful Doctress At St Helens"*:

On Monday afternoon no little excitement was created in the neighbourhood of the Raven Hotel by the arrival of the celebrated French doctress from Warrington. The reports of the cures that have been effected at Warrington, and which have been circulated for a radius of several miles round, caused crowds of people of both sexes to congregate near the Raven for the purpose of getting a glimpse of her.

It was some time before she made her appearance outside, but this had not the effect of decreasing, but rather of increasing, the crowd of spectators eager to see her. About three o'clock the lady entered her gorgeous carriage, and drove round the town, accompanied by a band of six performers, and afterwards took up her stand in the fair-ground, where she gave signs of her skill both in surgery and dentistry.

Her dental manipulations were performed with remarkable dexterity; and, judging from the appearance and remarks of her patients, it may fairly be assumed that the disagreeable operation was accomplished with little or no pain. Cases requiring considerable surgical skill also received her attention, and several wonderful cures are said to have been effected.

Many thousands of people for several nights collected in the fair-ground to witness her surprising performances; and, judging from the quickness with which she disposed of her medicine, she will, no doubt, reap a good harvest during her stay in St. Helens.

The tiny bottle containing Madame Enault's "malachite" medicine

The cure-all medication called malachite or *"Indian malachite"* cost 2 shillings (10p.) per bottle. When many poor people were then only earning around 20 shillings a week, that amount was not insignificant.

Madame Enault sold huge quantities of her worthless potion and was said to place orders with manufacturers for tens of thousands of little green bottles.

I expect the St Helens Examiner came to regret their gullibility in publishing their gushing report – however, their longer-standing competitor, the St Helens Newspaper, had not been taken in.

Its outspoken proprietor / editor Bernard Dromgoole had clearly been observing events in Warrington with a more critical eye than his competitor.

Seven days prior to the Examiner's article being published, the Newspaper had described how the wife of a well-known St Helens man had travelled to Warrington to see whether the doctress could heal her sick son. A cure was promised but at the huge cost of £10, with the money to be paid in advance.

The mother agreed to Madame Enault's price but not her terms, stating she would only pay when a cure had been affected. In their report the Newspaper disparagingly described the doctress as the *"miracle-worker"*, *"magician"* and *"wizard"* and the cure-all malachite medicine as *"golden ointment"*.

THE GREAT DOCTRESS

Within days the medicine show had relocated to St Helens with ten rooms occupied at the Raven. So many were needed because the showwoman's entourage included her husband and fourteen children. There were also the seven musicians in her band, although the stated number of musical accomplices varied slightly by newspaper.

On September 6th 1879 the St Helens Newspaper issued this challenge to Madame Enault:

> We have recently published several statements made to us by persons who have paid their money, in instances large sums, to the Great Doctress, and who declare they received no benefit in return. The Doctress who is on a visit to this town, while professing the Medical Art, has surrounded herself with the tinsel and gewgaws [worthless trinkets] of the Showman and the Mountebank [charlatan], accompanied with the sounding trumpet and tinkling cymbal. In this country these meretricious accompaniments are considered to betoken the impostor and the humbug.

> However, Madame Enault says she was induced to come to St. Helens on reading a short paragraph we published in reference to a youth who was taken to her from this town to Warrington, and for whose cure she demanded ten pounds, which sum the youth's parents were unwilling to part with, until the cure was effected.

> Madame has again and again referred to this case, and each time declared she can cure the youth. Well now, to put the matter to a fair test, the proprietor of this paper will deposit ten pounds in the hands of the Mayor, or any other Magistrate in St. Helens whom Madame Enault may appoint, which sum shall be paid to her as soon as she has consummated the cure of the youth in question, and we further undertake to procure the publication of the fact of the cure in twelve newspapers.

> ...Let Madame Enault also deposit ten pounds in the same magistrate's hands to be, in case she fails to cure the said youth, paid over to the Cottage Hospital.

Soon after making the challenge, the St Helens Newspaper told its readers that Madame Enault's response had been to demand more money – £100 in fact – for the cure of the lad.

The paper then went on to list a number of individuals who had complained of being tricked by the doctress – some during her stay at Warrington and others while practising at St Helens.

A farmer living near Nutgrove and suffering from deafness had travelled to Warrington to receive treatment. He paid the woman a total of £1 5 shillings and received a small bottle of malachite and a promise of a cure within fifteen days – but had not improved a jot.

A miner who had lost his eyesight paid the charlatan five shillings. The Newspaper wrote: *"She did nothing for him but take his money, and tell him to come again in three months."*

A woman from Peel Street in St Helens (which used to be near College Street) suffered badly from rheumatism. She managed to raise some money to pay Madame Enault for a consultation and medicine. A total of nine shillings was handed over but she had showed no improvement.

These were typical cases with poverty and desperation their hallmarks. Some could not afford the bills of genuine doctors or had tried conventional medicine without success and the talk of miracle cures drew them to the doctress like a moth to a flame. Sadly many got burned.

Bernard Dromgoole was editor of the campaigning St Helens Newspaper

SWELLED FEARFULLY

The Newspaper also described how the son of a coal miner living near Pilkington's glassworks had visited the fairground to have an extraction.

The tooth was broken and his face had *"swelled fearfully"* and the lad was left in such pain that his mother had sat up with her son all night to comfort him.

However, in summing up, the Newspaper felt the people of St Helens were beginning to wise up to Madame Enault:

> The fame of the Great Doctress is already on the wane, while the great number of those who, in their simplicity, have sought her aid – and have found that they have been deceived, and relieved of their money only – is every day on the increase, and the crowds who went nightly for the fun of seeing the molars of their neighbours extracted with wonderful rapidity, if not always with equal skill, are daily growing less.

That might well have been the case, although the woman still had many supporters in St Helens. One speciality of hers was treating hearing complaints – and I expect the doctress "cured" many deaf people by simply removing earwax.

If you were not aware that a build up of wax could naturally occur in your ear, you would have been mightily impressed with Madame's ability to restore your hearing and happily sing her praises. The so-called malachite medication sold by the doctress may also have had a positive placebo effect for some takers.

On September 13th 1879 under the headline *"The Great Doctress At St Helens"*, the St Helens Examiner published this letter from a correspondent adopting the pseudonym *"A St. Helener"*, which refuted the accusations of fakery:

Sir, – The greatest excitement which has operated upon the nerves of the people of St. Helens for the last two or three months is, you will agree with me, due to the marvellous displays of skill which the great medical phenomenon has so unremittingly exhibited daily since her appearance in this part of the country. Many are the remarks that have been made concerning her.

Some are of such a character which, if they were not counteracted by some favourable to the doctress, would cause that lady to take up her traps and try her luck in some other portion of the globe. But, happily for the lady, she has many admirers, who place implicit confidence in her skill and ability. This may readily be proved by a visit to the fair ground, where she is kept in a constant state of bustle and activity removing the disagreeable stumps from the mouths of those who are unfortunately afflicted with them.

We all know there are some ever ready to raise a paltry objection against what they term some new-fangled notion or patent, or something, in fact which is out of the ordinary every-day occurrences. St. Helens has been no exception in this respect, though allow me to say that I think the majority of the people of St. Helens have some faith in the efficiency of the "malachite" and its inventor.

THE FEMALE QUACK

However, Madame Enault left every town with far more victims in her wake than satisfied customers. In the summer of 1880 the Sheffield Independent exposed the doctress as a money-grabbing fraud. At that time the woman they called *"The Female Quack"* was in the Yorkshire town attended by crowds of *"infatuated disciples"*.

As part of its campaign against Madame Enault, the Independent of July 28th described the doctress's doings in St Helens during the previous year:

> She arrived there towards the end of August last from Warrington, which town she left in a sudden and mysterious manner, much to the bewilderment of a considerable number of uncured patients, who subsequently arrived in accordance with instructions they had received to "come again next week." At St. Helen's Madame conducted her operations much in the same way that she is doing at Sheffield. There were the same daily performances on the gorgeous carriage, and similar gaping and deluded crowds.
>
> Unfortunately, as remarked by a St. Helen's journal, the only persons who followed her from Warrington and the adjoining districts were the poor people, who had parted with their money under the promise that they should be cured in fifteen days, and in other short periods, but who now found that the only thing of which they had been relieved was their money, while, as far as their ailments were concerned, they were no better, and in some cases much worse under her treatment.
>
> Ugly rumours soon began to be circulated, and the popular confidence in her received a severe check by her non-acceptance of a challenge, publicly made by a local newspaper proprietor. The non-acceptance by the doctress, gave courage to a number of Madame's dupes to state their experiences, and a number of statements, all proving the grave nature of the system of imposture that was being carried out, found their way into print.

Being female and foreign certainly boosted the allure of Madame Enault. She claimed not to be able to speak English and in public always relied on the services of an interpreter.

However, one newspaper claimed that the doctress could speak the language well and the translator was simply a gimmick employed to enhance her mystique among her gullible followers.

Certainly women had a history of making impressive miracle cure workers. In September 1852 it was reported that crowds of desperate people had invaded the secluded village of Wing, near Leighton Buzzard, praying that a doctress who had taken up residence might cure them of their afflictions.

It was claimed that as many as 200 people a day from all over England were travelling to Wing to plead with the woman for help. However, the only ones who probably benefited were the inn-keepers, shop-keepers and cottage-owners who rented out a huge number of rooms to the desperate travellers and sold them goods – and the railway company that took them there in the first place!

THE "WISE WOMAN OF WING."—A CLEVER DOCTRESS.—We learn from the *Stamford Mercury* that a doctress, who has been very successful in some of her cures, is attracting crowds of ailing persons to the secluded village of Wing. The village is now completely full of lodgers, and "respectable people too—not the poor, ignorant, and vulgar." It is quite a common thing for 200 people in one day to make application to the woman. The Midland Railway must be gainers by the doctress, for scarcely a day passes but fifty or sixty people alight at the Manton station, and no less than three licensed vehicles are generally employed to convey patients from the station to the village and back. People from almost all quarters of England have visited her, and Scotland and Wales have contributed their portion of the "poor, ignorant, and deluded people." We are assured that last week she had upwards of 300 patients in her books, and that two persons who went to visit her

The Londonderry Standard September 23rd 1852

A GILDED AND DECORATED CHARIOT

In November 1879 the British Medical Journal published a report on Madame Enault's activities in Birkenhead. At every town she employed the same *modus operandi* to work her scam.

So we can safely assume that their detailed description of how she operated on the Wirral also occurred during her three to four week stay in St Helens. The BMJ wrote:

> Her diagnosis would seem to be extremely rapid; for we are told that she can invariably "tell at a glance" what to do with her patients and what they require. Madame Enault takes her "rides abroad" to heal the sick. This is done in true Dulcamara style – a large carved, gilded, and decorated chariot, drawn by three horses abreast, fantastically caparisoned [bearing rich decorative coverings] receives the lady, as well as eight bandsmen, who are disposed of in the back part of the chariot.

> Attired in ruby silk and cloth of gold, a tiara of pearls and silver on her head, and attended by M. Duflot [assistant doctor], she drives to the ground selected for her operations, where she covers her gorgeous attire with a professional mackintosh apron with pockets, arranges instruments, lint, and other necessaries, and then announces her willingness to extract teeth without fee or reward.

> On the occasion described, we are told that for more than an hour she was extracting teeth as fast as people could open their mouths to receive the forceps. All this time an enormous mass of patients are waiting their turn, including poor creatures afflicted with deafness, blindness, rheumatism, tumours, and various enlargements of the head and neck. Now comes the tug of war, or rather the means of providing its sinews.

> Madame begins a speech in French, which is interpreted sentence by sentence as she goes on. In it she vaunts the "Indian Malachite", contained in small bottles, as a cure for toothache, inflammation of the lungs, loose teeth, headache,

neuralgia, dizziness, cuts, burns, scratches, rheumatism, earache, and hoc genus omne [that sort of thing]. Nor does she content herself with simply vaunting its virtues; she borrows a knife, cuts her finger, places on it some lint steeped in "Malachite," and in a few minutes shows the cut to be quite healed.

She then proceeded to make an apparently lame man walk; removed a tumour from a man's head, after an application of "Malachite," to the intense admiration of the crowd, who, it seems, were full of tales of wonderful cures, effected by Madame Enault. And now came the moment to reap the harvest produced by all these gratis wonders.

Hundreds of buyers are eager for a bottle of "Indian Malachite," at the low price of 2s; and, to show the immense extent to which this so-called remedy is sold and these poor people are duped, the manufacturers of the bottles in which it is put up state that they have delivered upwards of fifty thousand to Madame Enault during the last few weeks.

Madame Enault was a callous confidence trickster of the highest order. She claimed to be the daughter of a French doctor and a native of Rome with a long list of qualifications.

At a time when many universities were not allowing women to study medicine, the doctress boasted of having graduated from colleges in Italy, France, Belgium and Philadelphia and claimed to have spent 18 years in public practice.

A SUCCESSFUL QUACK DOCTRESS.

Attention is called in the *North British Mail* of yesterday to the antics of a French female charlatan, who has succeeded in betraying the citizens of Glasgow during the last fortnight. This woman, says our contemporary, made her appearance in the city the week before last. Spangle and pretence had never failed to demonstrate the existence of superstition, and with an unswerving reliance upon the soundness of her assumption, this woman drove with spangle and pretence to a vacant plot of ground in New City Road, and there declared that she, the person with the mountebank's dress, proprietress of the flaring brass band and the glass-encased car, was the most wonderful physician and surgeon of the present day, and offered to prove her words on the bodies of as many as would submit their lives and limbs to the experiment. The result proved that the woman had correctly estimated the mental calibre of those to whom she addressed herself. People who had lost all faith in the power of

Sunderland Daily Echo Sept. 7th 1880

However, everything about the woman was bogus. One English newspaper wrote to a French university from where the doctress claimed to have graduated. Somewhat predictably, the reply was received that they had never heard of her.

The vast majority of patients supposedly treated by Madame Enault were the poorly educated and gullible poor who found qualified doctors and dentists expensive. Many turned to unqualified quacks or visited the so-called "lightning tooth extractors" for cost-effective solutions to their simple health needs.

Such nomadic dentists often set themselves up in the marketplace of towns and whipped out their patients' teeth for a bob each.

In March 1906 an eight-year-old boy called Joseph Johnson died after having two teeth pulled in St Helens market place by a lightning tooth extractor. Blood poisoning set in after the stumps of the teeth had been left in the boy's mouth.

But to a doctress like Madame Enault public tooth pulling was simply the hors d'oeuvre to a meal of far richer pickings – the appetiser that allowed her to charge the gullible for fake remedies and sell thousands of little bottles of her magic malachite potion.

"IT IS ONLY A FARCE"

Occasionally, a more intelligent individual would be her victim and not stand for being duped. Richard Nicholson of Chorley Street, off Duke Street, in St Helens was one such person – a man clearly of some education who provided this remarkable testimony of his experiences to the St Helens Newspaper:

I, Richard Nicholson, mason, living in Chorley street, St. Helens, am partially deaf, and have been for over eight years, caused by a lengthy immersion in water while rescuing a gentleman from drowning at Moseley Hill. Hearing of the arrival in this town of a doctress who was said to be famous for curing deafness, I tried to obtain an examination by her with the desire to be operated upon for my failing. I left my work early on Tuesday afternoon, and went down to the fair ground, while the doctress was operating, and managed to get into the carriage. I attempted to explain the nature of my ailment, but the doctress, without doing anything for me, sent me off the coach.

Being anxious to have my hearing restored, I again made another attempt on Saturday last, and, with the assistance of a policeman with whom I am acquainted, I got near the carriage and spoke to the assistant doctor, who stands near, and explained to him the object of my visit, and my wish to be operated upon.

He took me and seated me on a box underneath the carriage, and after examining my ears, and after considerable 'messing,' he put something into my ears. I felt him do it, but he then said "Come now, go into the carriage quick." I got up and made for the carriage, but owing to the crowd I could not get up then.

I felt a sort of tickling in my ear, and put my finger into it and drew out a piece of prepared substance, fleshy-looking, and what was evidently a prepared polypus, which he had put in. I replaced it in my ear, and then told the doctor what he had done, but he told me to go up and Madame would remove the obstruction to my hearing.

I said, "What she will remove is the stuff you have put there." His face changed colour, but he did not reply. It was then my turn to go up, and I said to the constable, "Brodley, I am not going to be cured, it is only a farce." But still, being anxious to be cured, and hoping that the doctress might do me some good, I went up.

Madame then looked in my ears and did not send me down as on previous occasions, but got a piece of cotton wool and put some malachite on it and placed it in my ear.

After rubbing about the outside of my ears a little she made me sit down in the carriage for about half-an-hour. She then got me to stand up, and having removed the cotton wool she took an instrument and extracted the prepared polypus.

The latter she held up and displayed to the multitude which surrounded the carriage. I then said to those in the carriage that the stuff which she was showing was the same as the doctor had placed in my ear.

The interpreter spoke to Madame, and then motioned to me and told me to be quiet. He asked me could I hear better, and I said any man can hear better after having wool taken out of his ears; but I said the noise was in my head, as before, and I was no better.

He then shouted to the crowd that I said I was much better, and that Madame had done me good. I told him that he was telling lies, and that I was no better. I was then bundled off the carriage, and the "doctor" calling me to him as I went off, put a bottle of stuff into my hand, and gave me a look as much as to say, "Go away, and don't say anything."

I went away, and on looking into my hand I found the bottle and a half-crown piece.

Richard Nicholson, 48, Chorley-street, St. Helens.

MADAME IS GONE

In their edition of September 16th 1879 announcing the doctress's exit from St Helens, the Newspaper stated that one reason being given for Madame Enault's sudden departure from the town was that the Frenchwoman had received a threatening letter. However, the missive was of a legal nature and not of a violent one.

A person from Sutton had paid a large sum to be cured of rheumatism and as the promised cure had not materialised, a letter had been sent threatening court proceedings for the recovery of the money. The Newspaper added:

SEPTEMBER 16, 1879.

E. **DEPARTURE OF THE DOCTRESS.**

The Great Doctress is said to have left St. Helens, but her loss is to be mitigated by the host of the "Black Bird" supplying her unfailing green bottle. Various reasons are alleged for her rather sudden departure; the latest is that she had received a threatening letter. If we are correctly informed, the threatening letter is from the friends of a person in Sutton, who paid a large sum to be cured of rheumatism. The cure was promised, but not performed, and a letter was sent threatening proceedings for the recovery of the money.

Many cases of disappointment are still reaching us.

A man named William Johnson, from Manchester, for swelling on the side of the face and neck, cure promised; money taken; no relief afforded; man worse. Second visit, asked if he had any more money, and when, he said he had not, told to come again in three months.

Young lady from Eccleston went to have her tooth operated on. Paid 35s.; seven teeth

St Helens Newspaper Sept. 16th 1879

Many cases of disappointment are still reaching us. A number of persons from Cheshire have also come to the town, and demanded the return of their money, under a threat of legal proceedings. A number of persons have been about Raven-street yesterday and this morning, but all the help and information they can get is, "Madame is gone."

The Sheffield Independent also provided more examples of the poor being conned during the doctress's stay in St Helens. They described how Madame Enault had examined a Prescot lad suffering from what was reported to be hip disease and promised him a cure for £6. That was then a considerable sum.

However, his friends clubbed together and managed to raise half the required amount. The lad's sister was in domestic service at Huyton and she persuaded her employer to advance her three months' wages so she could give her brother the outstanding cash. The newspaper wrote that the £6 was taken to the doctress, who relieved him of the money but...

...that was the only relief the lad had experienced. He was no better than when he first consulted the wonderful woman.

Madame Enault claimed that she made the rich pay for the poor, as her tooth pulling was often undertaken without charge. However, that was not always so if the doctress thought she could fleece someone of a considerable sum.

A young woman from Eccleston paid 35 shillings to have seven of her teeth removed but six were broken and she required medical care from a genuine physician for some time afterwards.

Most of those duped wrote off their misfortune of meeting Madame Enault to experience, although a small number did receive redress. In one instance a St Helens woman suffering from rheumatism was promised a complete cure from her debilitating condition.

Thirty shillings was paid over but no improvement was made. So her son – who held a good job as a managing foreman at a St Helens works – took out a summons against Madame Enault and the court ordered that the 30 shillings be refunded.

It was after this episode that the doctress came to the conclusion that she was played out at St Helens and early one morning left the Raven with her troupe for Wigan. However, the authorities there refused to rent her any part of their market or fairground and so Madame Enault travelled instead to Birkenhead.

On September 23rd 1879 the St Helens Newspaper reprinted this short piece from a Liverpool paper:

A female doctor and dentist, who carries on her vocation in an open carriage, and is accompanied by a band of musicians, has been attracting large crowds in Conway street, Birkenhead. On Monday night, as the carriage drove away, and the crowd, as has been their wont, surged after it, a woman, named Mary Carey, of George street, Birkenhead, was knocked down and had her leg broken. She was conveyed to the Birkenhead Borough Hospital.

Immediately after the reprint of the article the Newspaper posed the question: *"Where was the Malachite?"* Apparently, the magic mixture was not very good at fixing broken legs!

During 1880, Sheffield, Glasgow and Hull were amongst the towns that the doctress is known to have visited. But her stay in Glasgow was fairly short after a local paper called the North British Daily Mail exposed what they called her *"fraudulent career"* in England.

IMPUDENT FRAUD

Sarcastically referring to the woman as *"this benefactress of the poor and friend of the afflicted"*, the Mail on September 10th 1880 wondered why had it been for the press and not the authorities to hold the woman to account:

One of the most impudent frauds that Glasgow has ever witnessed has at length been put an end to. On the face of it the pretence of selling a drug for two shillings that would cure paralysis was falsehood, fraud, and wilful imposition. No doubt many credulous fools thought that the claim to the possession of this virtue might be well founded; but were the authorities for one day among the credulous?

It surely was never for a moment fancied that the miraculous cures of the paralytic performed by the woman in public, and on the strength of which she sold her drugs, could be real? But with a supineness that would require a good deal of explanation the police, instead of lodging her in the cells, were actually in attendance to procure for her well-regulated audiences whom she might gull. It is humiliating to think that an impostor like her could do this, and it is the reverse of creditable that the authorities allowed her to do it.

After Hull the newspaper trail of the doctress goes cold. Perhaps Madame Enault decided to ply her callous trade to the gullible and desperate sick in other countries?

The common factors in each case are interesting. With the possible exception of Wigan, the authorities in each town freely allowed the Frenchwoman to dupe their citizens. As the North British Daily Mail stated above, the police even provided free protection – as opposed to investigation and prosecution.

Offering free teeth pulling and other simple treatments for the masses gave her many supporters – but it took local newspapers to hold the doctress to account and drive her from their midst.

The St Helens Newspaper of Hardshaw Street – under its proprietor and editor Bernard Dromgoole – could be highly outspoken. Occasionally they got things wrong and were sued for libel.

But while other newspapers in the district were far less critical – and even supportive of the doctress – the Newspaper's campaign against the charlatan limited her time in St Helens and the distress that she was able to cause.

The Children Begging and Selling
On The St Helens Streets

"The number of children in the streets was quite scandalous"

During the 19th century many young barefooted children tramped the streets of St Helens until late at night, begging from strangers or selling them matches or newspapers. Large families were the norm and to some parents their youngsters were a financial burden that could be eased if they brought home some cash.

Some kids were given a sales or begging quota for the night and were frightened to return home without reaching it – fearing a beating would be their reward. Others took the coppers they received straight to their boozing parents in the beerhouse. Often poverty would be the root cause – but there was also much exploitation.

On May 15th 1869 the St Helens Newspaper published this extraordinary letter written by a woman using the Latin pseudonym 'Materfamilias':

In the midst of the heavy soaking rain of Friday evening, a shivering, bare-footed, little bundle of suffering humanity, came to my door to beg. It was a little girl of only five years of age, and, on questioning the child, who, despite her misery and her rags, was pretty and interesting looking, I found that she had walked from St. Helens, a distance of some two miles, in the drenching rain; that her mother sends her out regularly to beg, wet or dry; that her name is Annie Kearney; that her father is dead, and she lives on Smithy Brow, with her mother and brothers and sisters.

Now, either her mother is a depraved, cruel, and thoroughly worthless woman, or she is suffering from some disease which prevents her earning a livelihood and supporting her little ones, at least so as to keep them from such utter misery as that of the poor child I have described. In any case this should not be allowed to go on. The writer would be sorry if this letter brought any undeserved trouble on the woman. If she is utterly abandoned and bad, the children should be taken from her; but if she has anything in her favour she should be relieved, and suitable employment given to her and her children. For the credit of St. Helens, if for no better motive, a disgraceful trade such as this seems to be, that of systematically training up children to beg, and under the most miserable circumstance, ought to be put an end to.

One problem for the authorities was that parents would often deny sending their child out to beg. In the St Helens Petty Sessions on August 1st 1870, a girl called Ann Buckley was charged with begging on Croppers Hill. A constable said she had been going from house to house with another girl – but her parents simply denied sending her out and it could not be proved otherwise.

Both mother and father had criminal convictions and checking census records, the girl from Blackbrook appears to have been only six. So the child was cautioned by the Bench and discharged from the court but I expect would have soon been sent out on to the streets again.

Children only slightly older than Ann could be imprisoned for begging, with this example described by the St Helens Newspaper in January 1871:

A little fellow named John Feigh was charged with begging in Waterloo-street on Saturday night. It was stated that the child's father was a notorious character. An elder brother of the prisoner appeared before the court and said that his father was an "odd character". The prisoner was sentenced to seven days' imprisonment.

So that is a child sentenced by St Helens magistrates to serve a week in Kirkdale prison in Liverpool either because his father would not provide for him or – more likely – because he'd sent him onto the streets to beg.

The boy's Dad was Thomas Fay (or Feigh) who had over thirty convictions to his name. The age of the child was not stated in newspaper reports but I would estimate John Feigh as being in the region of eight or nine.

MATCH SELLERS

As well as the child beggars on the streets there were many sellers of matches or other items – as well as newsboys attempting to offload their "Echo's", or other titles. The authorities did permit such selling, although very young children were not supposed to be out working on the streets late at night.

> electric machinery, amounted to about £200.
> ST. HELENS MAGISTRATES AND STREET SELLING BY CHILDREN.—At St. Helens Police Court yesterday, before Mr. B. A. Dromgoole and Dr. M'Nicoll, Mary Heslin, of John-street, Greenbank, was charged with cruelty to her daughter Rose, by causing her to sell matches in the streets at ten o'clock on Saturday night. Police-sergeant Hudson proved the case, and stated that the girl was without shoes or stockings and was badly clad. He had cautioned the defendant about similar conduct previously.—The magistrates remarked that the mother was guilty of cruelty to her child, and they had considered

Liverpool Mercury Sept. 15th 1894

On September 14th 1894, Mary Heslin of John Street in Greenbank was charged in St Helens Police Court with cruelty to her daughter Rose by causing her to sell matches at 10 pm.

The Liverpool Mercury wrote:

> Police-sergeant Hudson proved the case, and stated that the girl was without shoes or stockings and was badly clad. He had cautioned the defendant about similar conduct previously. The magistrates remarked that the mother was

guilty of cruelty to her child, and they had considered whether to take the child away from her and send her to some institution where she would be better cared for. As the mother had promised not to send her out again, however, they would be satisfied with the imposition of a fine of 6s., including costs, on that occasion.

On May 17th 1895 a miner called John Marsh and his wife Mary from Doulton Street in Eccleston were charged with causing their 10-year-old son to be selling matches at midnight. PC Bramwell told the court that the boy was very poorly clad and had neither shoes nor stockings on his feet.

He was crying and told the officer he dared not go home as he had not sold all of his matches and his parents would likely thrash him.

In court it was revealed that John had been selling matches on the streets for as long as fourteen hours – with the boy's mother admitting sending her boy out at 10am. She told the Bench that she had to do something to maintain her children, as her husband was out of work.

Clearly the "something" did not involve either adult going out selling. The magistrates said they considered the case a disgraceful one and fined both parents 15 shillings and costs, or 14 days imprisonment if in default.

HEARTRENDING SIGHT

Of course, St Helens was not alone in having children out on its streets begging and selling. The St Helens Examiner described on September 16th 1882 how Liverpool Corporation was asking Parliament for powers to control the city's children that infested their main thoroughfares.

Then in January 1883, the Examiner quoted barrister and future MP Robert Pierpoint speaking at a church tea party in Warrington:

He thought there could not be a sight more heartrending to either man or woman than the sight that one might meet with in any large town in England – to see the little waifs and strays of life eking out a miserable existence in the streets, perhaps selling newspapers, or pretending to sell matches. It was a terrible thing to think that these children had no prospect before them.

But children also sold matches within pubs – which could present their own dangers. One of the nicest-named drinking houses in St Helens was the Old House at Home in Bridge Street. I expect the pub sold matches to its own customers and it seems the landlord's dog did not appreciate competition from boys!

The St Helens Examiner described what happened on February 18th 1888:

At the Town Hall, on Friday, William Cook, landlord of the Old House at Home in Bridge-street was summoned for keeping a dangerous dog not under proper control. A lad named McIntyre said he went into the Old House at Home on the 4th inst, selling matches, and was bitten in the leg by defendant's dog. The boy's mother said when her son came home on the day named, he was limping and she poulticed his leg. He stayed in bed next day through the wound. Evidence was given by three witnesses to the effect that the dog was not dangerous, but the Bench made an order to have the dog placed under proper control.

As well as dog attacks, children selling matches also had to look out for older kids stealing their takings.

On March 1st 1886, two Parr lads – John Mulligan (15) and Thomas Haverty (14) – appeared in court charged with stealing 7½d off Dennis Wynn. The St Helens Examiner described the latter as an *"intelligent-looking little fellow of seven years"*.

Dennis's older brother had earned the money by selling matches on the street and the boy was taking the cash home for him. The Bench declared the robbery a *"bad and abominable transaction"* and fined each prisoner 20 shillings or 14 days in prison.

In the 1891 census the Wynn family were living in Barber Street in Parr and at the time of the case, Dennis's older brother – who had been selling the matches – would have been either eight or eleven.

Then on March 17th 1888, the Examiner wrote of another similar case of theft:

Before Alderman J. C. Gamble and Alderman T. Cook, at the Town Hall, on Monday, Jesse Dingsdale, a boy residing at 10, Bridge-street, was charged with stealing 4d. and a box of matches from another boy named Philip Francis Flood, of 64, Phythian-street, on Saturday night. The complainant stated that he was selling matches in Ormskirk-street, when the prisoner and another lad named Devlin asked him to go into a shop for a halfpenny "Play up Rec's" card. Complainant added that he refused to go in, and the prisoner knocked him down, took fourpence in copper and a box of matches, and then ran away. After some further evidence had been given, the Bench ordered the prisoner to receive six strokes with a birch rod.

STREET ARABS AND GUTTER CHILDREN

Not all children on the St Helens' streets during the 19th century were beggars or sellers. Many spent their days loitering and were often referred to as "street arabs". The derogatory epithet was, of course, because of the nomadic nature of some real-life Arabs.

Although adults could also earn that nickname – mostly the wanderers were nuisance kids with nothing to do apart from hang around the town and cause mischief.

Out of 4.3 million children of primary school age in England and Wales in 1870, two million did not attend school. That was partly because it cost money to have an education, which poor parents could not afford.

Older children were allowed to work – but there was too much supply for the needs of employers and so unemployed kids would simply gather on the streets.

With no parks or amenities of any sort, anti-social activities like stone throwing were popular. As a result, adults often saw these street children as pests with little compassion shown.

In 1869, under the headline *"Street Arabs"*, the St Helens Newspaper published this letter from someone adopting the pseudonym *"An Eye Witness"*:

Sir, When passing St. Mary's Lowe House Church on Sunday evening my attention was called to some children who had assembled in the open space in front of the building amusing themselves by swinging upon both entrance gates, some walking round the iron railings, and others were throwing stones at the notice board and into the streets, the latter being dangerous to persons passing at the time, many remarking how strange it was that such like scenes should be allowed to take place within the grounds of a church. Such, however, should be stopped, and I trust the Rev. Mr. Ullathorne will call the attention of the officials of his church to locking the gates after the services of the

Correspondence.

STREET ARABS.

TO THE EDITOR OF THE ST. HELENS NEWSPAPER.

Sir,—When passing St. Mary's Lowe House Church on Sunday evening my attention was called to some children who had assembled in the open space in front of the building amusing themselves by swinging upon both entrance gates, some walking round the iron railings, and others were throwing stones at the notice board and into the streets, the latter being dangerous to persons passing at the time, many remarking how strange it was that such like scenes should be allowed to take place within the grounds of a church. Such, however, should be stopped, and I trust the Rev. Mr. Ullathorne will call the attention of the officials of his church to locking the gates after the services of the day are over, that children or other persons cannot enter to amuse themselves, or do damage to others.—Yours respectfully,

AN EYE WITNESS.

St. Helens, May 3, 1869.

St Helens Newspaper May 8th 1869

27

day are over, that children or other persons cannot enter to amuse themselves, or do damage to others.

Such scenes within the St Helens district would have been quite common at that time. What offended the letter-writer was that they were taking place on a Sunday on church property.

In the following year, the Prescot Reporter complained about *"dirty, ragged and most impertinent boys and girls"* making the entrance to Prescot Town Hall a *"little Pandemonium"*. It seems they were doing little more than running up and down the town hall steps and making a loud noise.

On August 12th 1871, under the headline *"What Shall Be Done With The Gutter Children?"*, this more sympathetic missive was published in the St Helens Newspaper:

In perambulating the town of St. Helens, I see numberless, almost unclothed, children. Their daily employment appears to be either stone-throwing – a dangerous pastime – or squatting in the gutters. I naturally think to myself: What will these children become? It is easy to solve the question. Will they not be likely to feel the great stream of crime rushing on to misery and death? And yet we jog on as comfortably as though we had performed our duty; we sleep soundly while mischief is spreading over the town; we are deaf while ignorance calls for help! We record with thankfulness the efforts made by denominations, and the work carried on in endowed schools – but do any of these bring in the gutter children? Emphatically – no? Whose work is it to do so?

Does it belong to the Corporation? If it does, such a body will require a traction engine of 200-horse power to drag it along. Don't tremble over the difficulties. It is by steady plodding that the mountain is levelled to the plain. Don't fear a small addition to the rates; it will repay you with compound interest. – **NON-CLERICUS**. St. Helens, Aug. 2, 1871.

Essentially, "Non-Clericus" was referencing the new Elementary Education Act. This required what were then called board schools *(which became council schools in 1902)* to be set up where existing provision was inadequate. The schools remained fee-charging but poor parents could be exempted.

However, the churches were generally hostile to the concept of educational establishments that they did not control and there was the question of additional funding needed to finance the schools. Non-Clericus's solution of a rates rise was certainly not one that everyone approved of.

St Helens did have its own Ragged School in Arthur Street, which used to be near Westfield Street. This had opened in 1861 to provide free schooling for the destitute street children of St Helens.

However, it was only able to accommodate a small number of kids and it was not until 1880 that school attendance between the ages of five and ten became compulsory. So given the choice of going to school or not, many kids (and their parents) would say "Not".

Ironically those children who started work at a tender age *could* receive better schooling than those who had not. One hundred and fifty years ago it was quite permissible for children as young as eight to be employed in workshops.

However the Workshops' Regulations Act of 1867 restricted 8 to 13-year-olds to half-time working and stipulated that child employees must attend school for 10 hours a week.

Although bear in mind that most adults then worked 70 hours a week – so half-time attendance was what we today would consider full-time employment. Also fines for breaching the Act were low and there were lots of loopholes, with coalmines amongst many other workplaces, including shops, that were excluded from its provisions.

On October 28th 1869 trade union organiser William Pickard complained about this sad state of affairs to a meeting of miners in the White Lion in Church Street in St Helens, saying:

> It is pitiful to see that in the year 1869 there is no compulsory education clause nor hours of labour clause applied to our children. The child might be made to work from four in the morning until four the next morning with interference. If he abused his horse, dog, or cat, he would be summoned and punished, but he might work his child to death without coming within reach of the law.

Some of the children in this 1920s photo from Parr Street are barefooted

NEWSBOYS

I expect many readers were paperboys or girls when they were young. Most would have used their bikes to deliver their newspapers with the cash that was earned serving as pocket money – to be spent, perhaps, on the latest chart hits. It was very different in the 19th and early 20th centuries.

The newsboys that populated the streets of St Helens were some of the poorest kids in the town and they looked the part with little in the way of warm clothing on their skinny bodies.

The cold nights were, of course, the worst time for them and on March 20th 1886, the St Helens Examiner revealed that some temporary help was being made available:

Last week a kitchen was opened in a shed behind the Raven Hotel, St. Helens, where the newsboys of the town are nightly regaled with a substantial supper at the expense of Mr. Jos. Bennett, of the Raven. Mr. Bennett intends to continue his generosity as long as the cold weather lasts. Cast-off clothing or other articles of attire will be gladly received and distributed by Mr. Bennett.

In 1885 the auctioneer and estate agent Joseph Bithell Leach began his annual New Year's Day treat for the newsboys and other poor children of the borough, distributing free food to them on the first day of each year. For many it would be the only substantial meal that they would receive until January 1st rolled round again.

VERY POORLY CLAD

One might not have thought that many newspapers could be sold late at night – but unsold papers needed to be offloaded. On September 7th 1894, miner Thomas Burns from Cyril Street in Eccleston *(off Doulton Street)* appeared in St Helens Police Court charged with causing his two children to be selling newspapers in the street at 10:40pm.

One boy, Henry, was only five years old and the other child, William, was eleven. Constable Wilson told the Bench that both boys had been very poorly clad and upon taking them home their parents admitted sending them out to sell papers. The magistrates imposed a fine of 5 shillings including costs.

At the same hearing a Peasley Cross man was fined after committing a similar offence. Magistrate Bernard Dromgoole declared that the Bench wanted both cases to serve as a warning to other parents. Children, he said, were not permitted to sell papers, matches or anything else late at night, adding:

> The number of children in the streets of St. Helens was quite scandalous. He had personally observed many children earning coppers, which he knew went to purchase drink for their parents, while the children were again sent into the streets, shoeless and ill-clad, to get more money. The state of affairs in St. Helens in that respect was perfectly scandalous.

In 1912 the St Helens Chief Constable Arthur Ellerington launched the Police-Aided Clothing Scheme for Destitute Children. This was otherwise known as the 'Clog and Stocking Fund', which provided free footwear and clothing to the poorest children in the borough.

In its first seven years, about 6,000 barefooted youngsters in St Helens were helped through the issue of 17,000 articles of clothing. These comprised 5,000 pairs of clogs, 5,000 stockings, as well as jackets, vests, shirts, skirts and underwear.

This support along with an expansion in welfare payments and social services helped to reduce the amount of child poverty and exploitation in the town.

However, the depression years of the '20s and '30s meant that it would take more years before barefooted children begging or selling on the streets of St Helens became a shameful relic of the town's past.

The "Colorado Millionaire" Conman

"It was a dear day when I and mine first saw you"

This is the Wellington Hotel in Naylor Street in St Helens near the old market. In 1910 the landlord of the hostelry was one of a number of local businessmen taken in by the extraordinary fraudster known as the *"Colorado Millionaire"*.

Licensee James Scowcroft was so sucked in by James Smythe's scam that he ended up penniless in America from where he sent a despairing letter back home.

But men were not the only victims of Smythe's lies. The "Colorado Millionaire" was also a bigamist who treated women shamefully.

James Henry Smythe was born in Durham in 1865 but was brought up in Pemberton after his parents relocated to Wigan. After initially working as a pit pony boy and then as a railway porter, Smythe married Margaret Smith in 1887 at St Catherine's Church in Wigan.

His mother-in-law loaned him the considerable sum of £90 to start up a stationery and fancy goods business at Seaforth. However, a mysterious fire soon occurred and the business closed with the loan never repaid.

In 1898 after obtaining money from his wife, Smythe travelled to Boston in the United States where he remained for two years, working as a fireman and janitor at a hotel. During this period his wife Margaret was left with no income and she became financially dependent upon her mother.

When Smythe returned to England he visited his wife in Wigan and she discovered by means of a blotting pad that her husband intended to illegally marry a young American lady.

Mrs Smythe wrote to the woman to inform her that her intended spouse was already wed – but she would not believe her. In 1908 the conman returned to the States and bigamously married a Miss Topham and she had three children by him.

During this period Smythe obtained large sums from several gentlemen by fraud, including one of £4,000 – that's about £500,000 in today's money.

In early 1909 he came to St Helens and took up residence initially at the Fleece Hotel. This was not the same Fleece that closed in 1986, as the original Church Street hotel was demolished in 1931 and a replacement building was constructed.

THE FAKE RUTH MANCHESTER MINE

After a few weeks, Smythe relocated from the Fleece to the Wellington Hotel where he ingratiated himself with its landlord,

James Scowcroft. Eventually, he induced the former manager of the Sefton Arms to give up his licence at the Wellington and take his family to America as secretary of the Ruth Manchester Mine Company. Smythe was said to have received a considerable sum from Scowcroft, to whom he gave in exchange 2,750 worthless shares in his bogus firm, promising him a salary of £1,000 a year.

That was then a huge amount and a photograph of the Colorado conman, published in the St Helens Newspaper, shows him as a distinguished-looking, well-dressed middle-aged man. It is not difficult to imagine his victims being taken in by the smooth-talking swindler who showed his victims bogus bank drafts and share certificates to add credibility to his claims.

During his period in St Helens, Smythe made a couple of short trips to the States. At one point, he despatched across the Atlantic a telegram to Scowcroft confirming his new position as secretary / manager of the Ruth Manchester Mine Company.

That was after supposedly negotiating Smythe's appointment with the firm's directors at the promised salary. By this time Scowcroft had already quit his tenancy of the Wellington and gone to live in Cowley Hill Lane pending his emigration to America.

Just before Smythe's arrest in September 1910, the conman received this letter from Mr Scowcroft, who was now in America with his family but realising that he had been fooled:

My dear Smythe. I suppose you are quite pleased with yourself. You must be fully aware of my predicament. I have had a letter from Mrs. Smythe appealing for money, and she says you have not been there since I left. Let me have an explanation, and, for goodness' sake, be truthful for once, and say just how things are. It was a dear day when I and mine first saw you. We have paid for it. Drop the mask. I have taken no steps against you as regards Boston and made no inquiries. You had perhaps better cable me what to do. If it is fraud, and I have been had, I will rise again and make the best of it. I have had to pawn all I had.

The Mrs Smythe mentioned in the letter was not Margaret in Wigan – but the bigamous wife in Boston with three kids. The St Helens Newspaper reported that Smythe had cruelly deserted her and the children *"leaving them to starve on the streets of Boston".*

When finally arrested in New Brighton, the 45-year-old was living with a Miss Davies who he claimed to be his niece. She was only 18 years of age and was believed to have given birth to a child.

THE GREAT MINING MAGNATE

Headlines from reports in the St Helens Newspaper of September 1910

On September 27th 1910 the St Helens Newspaper described the shock in the town as its residents learnt of the fraudster's activities within their midst:

The principal topic of conversation in the town during the past few days, has been Smythe, the "Colorado millionaire," who has victimised so many people in St. Helens and district, who were filled with an abounding faith in the Ruth Manchester Mine in far away Nevada. Every day fresh stories come to hand of business men who were, apparently, only too pleased of the opportunity of showing their complete trust in the great "mining magnate," and it is said that a Rainford farmer is the loser by a considerable sum in consequence of having come across Smythe.

The farmer was duped by having initially invested in a small number of mining shares and then at the end of the next quarter, Smythe handed him a cash dividend.

That gave the farmer the confidence to make bigger investments in the fraudulent concern. Others were conned in similar ways or were persuaded to allow Smythe to have goods on credit for which they were never paid.

COLORADO SMYTHE.

Amazing Career of Bogus Millionaire.

(From Our Own Correspondent.)

ST. HELENS, Friday Night.

An astounding story of fraud was told at St. Helens to-day when James Henry Smythe, who for the past eighteen months has posed in that town as the "Colorado millionaire," was charged with obtaining goods to the value of £264 by false pretences from a local draper. There were five other charges of obtaining sums of money ranging from £5 to £100. Smythe pleaded guilty to all the charges, and the story of his career was truly remarkable.

London Daily News - October 1st 1910

James Smythe finally faced the music at the end of September 1910 – although not for what he had done to the Scowcrofts and other victims in the USA and Canada. When he appeared before St Helens magistrates, Smythe was charged with fraudulently obtaining £339 from Henry Thewlis, £100 from William Crompton, £37 from Joseph Wilcox, £5 from Lawrence Wall and £20 10s off William Bolton.

They were all St Helens businessmen from whom Smythe had taken money or goods. For example, Henry Thewlis kept a draper's shop in Church Street and told the court that he had known Smythe since June 2nd 1909. The conman had then entered his shop, saying he was staying at the Wellington Hotel and wished to purchase some goods.

However, he claimed to have been short of ready cash at the time and so worthless shares were offered instead. Henry Thewlis knew the landlord of the Wellington well and James Scowcroft was able to provide him with an excellent reference for Smythe. The other duped men told similar tales of how they were tricked.

BOGUS LETTERS

Chief Constable Arthur Ellerington explained to the court how upon his arrival in St Helens, Smythe had claimed to be very wealthy with interests in Colorado copper mines.

The Wigan Observer of September 27th 1910 wrote:

Far from this being the fact, Smythe was, Mr. Ellerington said, only a paperhanger, a native of Pemberton, and had not a cent in the world except £1 11s. 6d., part of a loan he had recently obtained, and was not known at any of the banks the names of which he had given to his dupes. The Chief Constable stated that some 18 months ago prisoner turned up at St. Helens, and took up his abode at the Wellington Hotel, representing himself to be a wealthy man.

By means of bogus letters, bogus share certificates and agreements which he produced, relating to mines in the West and Colorado, and saying that he was over here to obtain controlling interest in the mines by purchasing shares secretly, so as to prevent the running up of the shares by the Stock Exchange, he got into the confidence of Mr. Scowcroft, who then was proprietor of the Wellington Hotel, and who introduced Smythe to Mr. Thewlis.

The Chief Constable added that when arrested by the police and returned to St Helens from New Brighton by train, the conman had come clean, saying:

I have not bought a single share. I have not obtained advances from the banks at Denver, nor transacted business through the National Provincial Bank, Manchester. I am the company, and the whole thing is bogus. I told lies when first I came to St. Helens, and I had to tell others to back them until up they got to such a colossal heap that I felt during the past few weeks that the end must come. I wanted money. I grew desperate. This is how I got it, and there you are.

For several years Smythe had stayed at the best hotels in England and America. During that period his claims to be a wealthy man who possessed the power to enrich others gave him great respect. But it was all a fantasy and all things must end.

Now, Smythe had to face reality and rough it in prison. The St Helens Newspaper's headline to their report was *"Short Shrift For Smythe – Two Years Hard Labour For Amazing Swindler".*

Considering all that the man had done, I expect his victims considered the sentence to be lenient. However, Smythe felt hard done by and in March 1911 submitted an appeal, claiming the St Helens magistrates had exceeded their powers.

The conman had pleaded guilty to six charges of obtaining money by false pretences and had been awarded six terms of imprisonment of either three or six months' duration, with each sentence to be served consecutively.

Magistrates do not possess the power to impose prison sentences on defendants longer than six months. But the consecutive sentencing allowed the court to construct a total incarceration period of 24 months.

However, Smythe's legal advisers reckoned that the magistrates were also limited to passing no more than two consecutive sentences on an offender. So, on March 16th 1911 an application was made to the King's Bench Divisional Court to consider the legality of the sentence. In their report on the proceedings on the following day, the St Helens Newspaper added these comments about Smythe's fraud:

> Smythe had been living upon the fat of the land. People almost tumbled over each other to make him loans, and even when it was proved that he was an audacious swindler, a local tradesman was heard to say, "Well, if he came out to-morrow I would lend him a fiver," so great was his confidence in him.

SMYTHE'S SENTENCE.

REDUCED BY HALF.

HIGH COURT PROCEEDINGS.

St Helens Newspaper headline from May 19th 1911

Two months later at a further hearing, the court ruled that the magistrates in St Helens had erred in their sentencing. Smythe's prison terms for charges 3 to 6 were ruled invalid, leaving just the sentences of six months each for the first two charges to be consecutively served. That meant that the Colorado millionaire would soon be released from prison.

Mary Price – The St Helens Poisoner

"I'll make the old b_____ remember it this time"

There are two perspectives that can be drawn from the conduct of arsenic poisoner Mary Price. The first is that the little Irishwoman from Greenbank in St Helens had taken enough brutality from her husband.

So, the 49-year-old with six children drank to make her harsh life that bit more tolerable and sought revenge on her spouse by putting some arsenic in his tea.

Mary was not well educated and, perhaps, not fully aware of the potential consequences of her actions. However, these proved far more serious for her than for her bully of a husband who only suffered a few days' stomach ache.

The second scenario is that she was a wicked, drunken woman who attempted to murder her hard-working man who had been extremely fortunate not to lose his life. The latter was the court's view, leading to a stern judge at Liverpool Assizes imposing a sentence of death upon Mary Price.

Standing at just 4ft 11ins, the middle-aged woman from Bath Street, off Liverpool Road, must have seemed an unlikely poisoner when she made her first court appearance in St Helens on September 23rd 1852.

Mary was charged with having administered arsenic with intent to kill her glassblower husband and 16-year-old son Edward. The latter appears to have been an unintended victim of the tea poisoning.

and of 348 Irish cases, and of £57. 7s. 1d. in cost.

ATTEMPTED POISONING AT ST. HELEN'S.—On Monday, Mary Price was charged at the St. Helen's Police Court, with having, on the 13th instant, administered arsenic with intent to kill her husband, William Price, and her son, Edward Price. The evidence showed that her husband, who had had a quarrel with her on the previous Saturday, returned home on Monday the 13th inst. drank some tea which he found made for him, and was soon afterwards seized with violent illness. The son, who also drank some of the tea, was likewise seized with illness. The tea had been made by the prisoner's daughter, who had placed it near the fire, and had then left the house, where the prisoner had gone and come from time to time. The prisoner had purchased some arsenic of a druggist; and the tea and the matter vomited by her husband were analysed, and found to contain arsenic. Several threatening expressions had also been used by the prisoner respecting her husband. The prisoner, who appeared to be very much affected, was cautioned, and, making no statement, was afterwards committed to take her trial at the next assizes.

FIFTEEN HUNDRED MILES IN A THOUSAND HOURS. — To-day, at 11 o'clock, James Jones, the pedestrian, will

(Manchester) Guardian's report from September 25th 1852

ANGRY WORDS

William Price told the hearing held in St Helens Town Hall that he'd arrived home from his work at Pilkington's glassworks about 11:15pm on the previous Saturday night. He said he found his wife to be drunk and they exchanged angry words.

According to his testimony, Mary then left the house and did not return for two days. The 47-year-old added that on the Monday morning at 6 am, he left to go to work, leaving his young daughter in the house.

When William returned home from the glassworks at about four o'clock that afternoon, he described finding a teapot standing on the oven and the tea things set on the table – but his wife was still absent.

He said he poured out a cup of tea for himself and noticed it was very black but assumed that was because the pot had been left standing for some time.

Being thirsty, he quickly drank the first cup, which made him feel nervous – as he put it. So William told the Bench that he stood at his front door for a few minutes to take in some fresh air before pouring out a second cup of tea.

He drank half of it but began to vomit heavily and suffer cramps. William and Mary's son, Edward, gave evidence that he'd also drunk some of the tea and had immediately vomited.

Their daughter Elizabeth told the court that her mother had returned home at about 7am on that Monday morning after her father had left for work. She remained in the house most of the day but had gone out at intervals.

Elizabeth added that at 3pm she made her father's tea, put the teapot near the fire, left the house and did not return until about seven o'clock.

INFESTED WITH BUGS

Next to give evidence was a druggist called John Hibbert. He stated that Mrs Price had visited his premises in Church Street at about 10:30am on that Monday morning. She claimed her house was infested with bugs and asked Mr Hibbert for some arsenic to destroy them.

The pharmacist said he had mixed a quarter of an ounce of arsenic with a quarter of a pound of soft soap and gave it to the woman.

Dr Robert McNichol of St Helens was next in the witness box. He described attending William Price at his home in Bath Street and found him displaying symptoms of poisoning – although his patient was fully conscious and standing up. Samples of the tea and the man's vomit were conveyed to Dr Brett of Liverpool who gave evidence that there had been sufficient arsenic in the drink to destroy life.

A witness told the court of hearing Mary Price say: *"I'll make the old b_____ remember it this time, if I never did before."* Other witnesses stated that the accused had returned home at seven o'clock on that Monday evening and asked several of her neighbours if anything had occurred.

Upon being told that her husband and son had been poisoned, she said her husband must have done it to himself. In court Mrs Price was described as having been much affected by the evidence and, as expected, the St Helens magistrates remanded her in custody to take her trial at the next assizes.

Those hearings were held every quarter at the combined prison / court at Kirkdale in Liverpool and Mary had nearly two months to wait to discover her fate.

"POISONING AT SAINT HELEN'S"

Mary's trial at Liverpool Assizes took place on December 11th 1852 and with St Helens newspapers not published until the following year, we have to rely on the Liverpool Mercury for a detailed account of the proceedings. Their article was published under the headline *"Poisoning At Saint Helen's":*

Mary Price, aged 49, was indicted for having, at Eccleston, feloniously and unlawfully administered to her husband, William Price, two grains of white arsenic, with intent to murder him. The prosecutor in this case is a working man in the employ of Messrs. Pilkington, glass manufacturers, St. Helen's, and the prisoner is his wife. On the night of the 11th of September, William Price, the husband, returned from his work, and found his wife in a state of intoxication. Some words ensued between them, and the result was that the

44

prisoner left her home that night, and was not seen again by her husband until the following Monday night.

The prosecutor returned home about four o'clock on the Monday afternoon, and found his daughter, Elizabeth Price, a girl of seven or eight years of age, in the house. The tea-things were set at this time, and the teapot was placed on the oven. Price poured out a cup of tea from the teapot, and observed it was of a very dark colour. He drank the tea, and found it to have a very nauseous taste, and a curious sensation of the throat followed.

His head also became giddy; but he recovered by standing for a short time at the door. He then returned in, poured out a second cup of tea, and drank half of it. After drinking part of the second cup he became very sick. He subsequently became worse, vomited much, and suffered from cramp, and showed other indications of having taken some virulent poison. A medical man was called in, and Price was unwell up to the following Friday.

Ann Marsh, who resides at St. Helen's, stated that she gave the jug containing the contents of the teapot to Mr. McNichol, surgeon, St. Helen's. On Monday, the 4th of September, she heard the prisoner threaten to do for her husband, for his usage of her. She was then the worse for liquor.

Mary Fields stated that on the evening William Price was taken ill, shortly after he had drunk the tea, the prisoner came into the yard and asked was there anything to do. Witness replied, "Yes, your husband and son are almost dead." Witness said "Some one must have put poison in the tea;" and the prisoner said, "It was not me; it must be Mrs.

Smart that has done it." After his lordship had summed up, the jury, without leaving the box, returned a verdict of guilty. The prisoner having been called on in the usual manner, His Lordship said:

"Mary Price, the jury, after a very careful examination of this case, have come, I am sure not without very painful feelings, to the conclusion that you are guilty, and I concur with them in that opinion. You see now to what dreadful consequences the habit of drunkenness leads. I frequently have had reason to make the observation before; but it is seldom I have had such practical proof of the fearful consequences of this habit. You involve yourself in dissensions with your husband; by it you become reckless; you are lost to all feeling, to all shame, to everything like humanity. (The prisoner here made some charges against her husband.)

"Your exclamations against your husband now will not at all deter me from discharging the painful duty that remains to me, or at all shake my confidence in the inference drawn by the jury from the facts that have been established. How ill you are prepared to bear the consequences of your own act. You should have reflected beforehand, and have considered that if you brought your husband to a violent death, you infallibly would forfeit your own life; and if you endangered his life by an attempt to destroy it, your life would still be forfeited to the law, although possibly the full penalty should not be exacted.

"And I think by good fortune, rather than any feeling of mercy or compassion on your part, your husband's life was spared; that he had not sufficient of the noxious ingredient administered to cause death was not because you had not intended to produce it, but because he happily escaped the

46

peril. I think, therefore, I may with safety recommend to her Majesty to commute your sentence. If it be so commuted you will have to thank her Majesty, through her secretary of state, for extending clemency to you; because, in my judgment, morally, the crime you have committed is as great as if you had actually effected the dreadful purpose you had in view. Judgment of death will be recorded against you, and it remains with her Majesty to say in what form it will be commuted; probably by ordering the heaviest secondary punishment which can be inflicted." – The prisoner was then removed from the bar. Whilst she was being removed she continued to utter threats against her husband.

Note, how without retiring from where they were sat in the courtroom, the all-male jury had according to the judge, made a very careful examination of the facts! Justice was then quickly dispensed and six other cases were also heard in the same courtroom at the Liverpool Assizes on the same day.

One concerned Thomas Laidler from Manchester who was convicted of manslaughter. The 40-year-old had killed the woman that he'd been living with by beating her on her head and chest while she lay sick in bed. For that crime he was handed just four months hard labour and not sentenced to death like Mary Price, who had only given her husband several days of stomach ache.

There is no doubt that women convicted in 19th century courts could be treated much more harshly than men. The judge was heavily critical of Mary's drinking and considered it the root cause of her sad situation.

Even sixty years later when the St Helens Chief Constable presented his annual report for 1917, he stated that all the licensees in St Helens had had their attention drawn to the *"desirability of discouraging, in every possible way, drinking by women."* That was despite only eighteen women having been convicted of drunkenness during the whole of that year.

DISSENTIONS

The judge's simplistic view was crystal clear. Mary was a drunkard and her condition caused rows or "dissentions" with her husband, which led to her poisoning his tea in revenge. As Mary's counsel chose not to put his client in the dock, we only have a few pointers to the abuse that she appears to have endured.

The testimony of Ann Marsh having heard Mary threaten to *"do"* for her husband, for his *"usage"* of her speaks volumes. "Usage" or "ill-usage" was a term then commonly associated with wife beaters.

> Whereas the said Mary Price hath been duly convicted at this Session of administering poison — with intent to murder and had sentence of death — recorded against her for the same But Her Majesty having been graciously pleased to extend Her Royal Mercy to the said offender on condition that she be transported beyond the Seas for the term of her natural life and such condition of mercy having been signified to this Court by the Right Honorable Spencer Horatio Walpole one of Her Majesty's principal Secretaries of State This Court hath allowed to the said offender the benefit of a conditional pardon
>
> And it is therefore ordered by this Court that the said Mary Price be immediately transported beyond the Seas for the term of her natural life. —

The official document that commuted Mary Price's death sentence

The judge suggested that Queen Victoria would likely show mercy to Mary Price and commute her death sentence. This she did and a public hanging was replaced by transportation "beyond the seas" for the remainder of Mary's natural life.

However, transportation was being phased out during the 1850s and so Mary's passage to Australia did not take place. It was instead replaced by life imprisonment and was served initially at Millbank Prison in London and then in Brixton Prison.

Mary Price was finally released on licence in 1864 after serving twelve years in gaol.

The St Helens Fairs, Menageries
And Freaks Of Nature

"Fat women were shown, mammoth specimens of humanity so ponderous that one wondered what they were intended for"

The first weekly St Helens market is believed to have originated in 1780. With the creation of Market Street some two decades later, its junction with Church Street became the congested site for market traders to sell their wares.

Entertainment would often be provided for shoppers and once the market relocated to an open field in New Market Place *(where Church Square Shopping Centre now stands),* the barrel organs and other amusements followed.

In 1896 James Brockbank, a local historian and shoemaker, published his 'History of St. Helens' and described the entertainment on offer in New Market Place during the earlier part of the 19th century:

> It was in this square that Van Amburg, with his performing lions, used to electrify the people of those days by making them jump through hoops, and opening their capacious and formidable jaws, and thrusting his own head therein. Fablo Fanque with his circus, Old Smalley and his "Thespian Temple," with the players, kings and queens parading the stage in front. It was in this square the bi-annual fair used to he held; when the itenarary [sic] vendors and purveyors of toys, toffee, gingerbread and nuts, migrated and crowded with shows, swings, hobby horses, boxing booths, conjuring shows, circuses and theatres, in fact, everything under the sun that belonged to such old fashioned gatherings.

Space again soon became an issue and by the 1860s a field near Salisbury Street became known as "the fairground" – hosting occasional circuses, open-air meetings as well as the St Helens Fair. As Brockbank described, this came to town twice a year during much of the Victorian era, usually on Saturdays, Mondays and Tuesdays during April and September.

The three-day event was often controversial due to reports of drunkenness and licentious behaviour. The latter appears to have been little more than young couples enjoying a kiss and a cuddle on fairground rides – especially the dangerous swingboats.

But the St Helens Newspaper thought such behaviour while in motion quite shocking! On September 19th 1868 the paper wrote that no good came of such gatherings and criticised fairgoers disregard for decency while riding on the swingboats:

> There is not much circumspection amongst the giddy creatures of both sexes who abandon themselves and their hoarded coppers to the jollification of the fair, but decidedly the species of amusement which is most destructive to morals, and most disgusting to the sensible adult, is the swing boat. In this gilded thing a crowd of lads and lasses take their seats, huddled together in the most indiscriminate manner, and while the suspended boat sways up and down, the most shameful conduct goes on unchided.

WONDERFUL BEARDED WOMAN

However, the Newspaper had no worries about the exploitation of the human curiosities that were always on show at the fair – including the *"wonderful bearded woman"*. They wrote that she would charm the rough fellows in the crowd by allowing them the *"pleasant and harmless little liberty of tagging at the hirsute appendage to test its genuineness"*. The exhibition also included a fully-grown freak of nature of just thirty inches height.

There were plenty of other "freaks" on exhibition at the Spring Fair of 1870. The St Helens Newspaper of April 30th described how these had included a man with three legs and a bison with six legs – *"both genuine cases, of considerable interest to a physiologist"*.

Two children were also sadly on show. An eight-year-old grotesquely fat girl was exhibited along with a boy several years older – *"so diminutive that she might have nursed him as a doll"*.

Other attractions that the *"dense throng of carnivalists with apparently plethoric pockets"* had patronised included a waxworks, peepshow and a circus. Much gingerbread was then made in Ormskirk and several vendors were always in attendance at the fairs to sell their wares to the St Helens' public.

The Newspaper also described the brutal boxing ring, which was another staple attraction of the fair:

> The tent where the manly art of self-defence is ridiculously caricatured, was there as usual, and the rostrum was graced as of old by the gentlemen who show the same family likeness to each other that is to be found amongst bull dogs. What crowds paid their pennies to watch the "mills," [fights] and how they relished the pummelling they witnessed! It was usual for a few local "gentlemen amateurs" (the politic phrase of the bullies) to commence the sport by exhibiting the training they have received in the sparring-rooms of the coal and chemical districts around. The "professionals" avoided encountering each other, and always induced members of the audience to become antagonists, as the most effective way of showing their skill. It was the habit of the sparrers to bet on the length of time the amateurs would last the rounds, and as the race thus became against time, the punishment was of the most remorseless character. Some of the locals were so punched and pounded that they carried away black eyes and swollen faces as mementoes.

In their descriptions of the fairs, the Newspaper regularly commented on their level of patronage as being directly linked to the state of trade in the St Helens district. At times of recession, people were out of work or on short time and had no money to spend on such ephemeral pleasures.

ROARING TRADE

However, the Spring Fair of 1872 had been a *"perfect hive of business, and itinerants drove a roaring trade"*. This had been another event where human exploitation had been a central part of the carnival experience.

The level of obesity in St Helens was then a fraction of what it is today and so grossly overweight individuals were the star attractions in the *"caravans of curiosities"* that were on show.

St. Helens Fair.—The spring fair of St. Helens opened on Saturday and closed on Tuesday. These fairs may be accepted as a very safe criterion of the state of trade generally, for when it is depressed they make but a melancholy attempt at liveliness. On this occasion the fair ground was a perfect hive of business, and itinerants drove what may be called in more senses than one a roaring trade The pence and shillings of the working classes converged from all directions on the rendezvous, and were deposited there to an aggregate that would be perfectly astonishing if given in figures. The usual amusements—or rather amusements of the usual class—were present in unusual profusion, and no one speculator in caravans of curiosities had to lament slender patronage. Fat women were shown, mammoth specimens of humanity so ponderous that one wondered what they were intended for. if not to be exhibited at a penny a head. Circuses and

The St Helens Newspaper April 13th 1872

The St Helens Newspaper described this sad exhibition on April 13th 1872:

Fat women were shown, mammoth specimens of humanity so ponderous that one wondered what they were intended for, if not to be exhibited at a penny a head. Circuses, and menageries were there too, flanked by professors of magic, and exhibitors of mechanical contrivances. One genius filled his master's coffers by drinking burning naphtha and walking barefoot on red hot bars. There did not seem to be any deception in his performance, and no one appeared to envy his salamander qualities. The fair of itself would not be objectionable, but for the impetus it gives to intemperance, and the herd of vile beings who hover in its train.

MENAGERIES IN ST HELENS

At well as these twice-yearly fairs, travelling animal shows would make regular appearances in St Helens. These varied from a showman exhibiting one or two performing animals to fully-fledged circuses and massed menageries.

On May 12th 1870 the St Helens Newspaper described a small-time exhibition of underfed bears that would likely have been trained to dance and perform tricks:

> On Thursday two performing bears and their custodians visited the town, and the antics of the peripatetic bruins afforded, of course, considerable amusement to the juveniles. The quadrupeds, it is scarcely necessary to add, seemed better taught than fed.

An example of a much bigger event was held on March 15th 1869 when Manders' Grand National Star Menagerie toured the town *"in triumphal procession"* before making its way to the fairground.

An advertisement placed in the St Helens Newspaper two days earlier had described how an African man known as Maccomo would lead the parade in a golden chariot hauled by elephants and camels.

Also in the procession would be *"fifteen immense caravans drawn by fifty powerful draught horses"*. More elephants and camels would haul other carriages and wagons, along with bulls, mules and grey horses. It promised to be quite a spectacle and an enclosure 170 by 64 feet would house these and many other animals for the townsfolk to inspect.

The zoo would feature male and female zebras, a family of monster polar bears *("just added, at an enormous expense")*, a mandrill or blue-faced gorilla, a *"full-grown ourang outang"*, Royal Scotch lions and a *"magnificent group of variegated lemurs and Tasmanian devils"*.

At ST. HELENS, on MONDAY, March 15

OLD ENGLAND'S BRIGHTEST STAR!

MANDERS' GRAND NATIONAL
STAR MENAGERIE,
A spacious enclosure 170 ft. in depth by 64 ft. in width,
WILL BE EXHIBITED AT
ST. HELENS on MONDAY, THE 15TH INST.
When the patronage of the Public is earnestly requested.

The Menagerie will enter the Town in
TRIUMPHAL PROCESSION,
ABOUT TWELVE o'CLOCK,
Headed by MACCOMO, THE AFRICAN, in his
GREAT GOLDEN BAND CHARIOT.
Drawn by Elephants, Camels and Dromedaries;
THE GRAND DRAGON CARRIAGE,
Drawn by an Elephant and Brahmin Bulls;
THE STATE HARNESS WAGGON
Drawn by an Elephant and Two Dromedaries;
THE MOTHER O'PEARL BAROUCHE,
Drawn by Four richly-caparisoned Piebald Mules;
THE GREAT MANDERNETHECA,
Drawn by 12 Splendid Grey Horses;
THE RESIDENTIAL SALOON
Drawn by Four Magnificent Horses, with Silver
Trappings; followed by

St Helens Newspaper March 13th 1869

A big attraction would be a baby elephant called Tinky. At just 30 inches tall, this would contrast with a huge elephant 9 feet high and 9,000 pounds in weight.

Visitors were also promised a giant elephant playing the piano and trombone and a *"Lilliputian elephant dancing a hornpipe"*.

If that wasn't enough, there were five hundred living specimens of natural history to view. The price of admission was one shilling, with children under ten charged a tanner.

On May 31st 1870 Howes & Cushing's Great American Circus and Menagerie appeared in St Helens. In their advertising they claimed to have performed in front of Queen Victoria, as well as the Duke of Cambridge and in America in front of Presidents Grant and Lincoln. The Mayor of Shrewsbury also somehow got in their short list of celebrity attendees – not quite as impressive though!

The menagerie's procession toured the main streets of St Helens at 1pm, which must have been quite a sight. As well as many beasts on show, they promised:

"...richly attired Moors and Turks, and their Ladies of the Harem, attended by a band of Amazons clad in the most gorgeous steel armour, richly set with costly jewels."

What was described rather oddly as a morning performance took place at 2pm, with an evening show at 7:30pm. The animals included elephants, camels and packs of performing wolves, bears and monkeys. The price of admission ranged from 6d to 2 shillings for first class seats.

However, transporting a large group of animals into St Helens could prove problematic and cruel. On December 30th 1869 the Liverpool Courier described how bad weather had hampered Edmond's menagerie from making a midnight flit from their base in Liverpool to St Helens:

Between five and six o'clock [A.M.] the menagerie was fallen in within the Old Swan-road in a terrible pickle. The ascent from Liverpool had taken four or five weary hours, and the procession was a most melancholy one. By this time the slight fall of rain on the frozen roadways had made progress impossible. The heavy vans had to be dragged, as it were, up an incline of ice, and the horses – magnificent animals though they are – were of no more use in the ordinary teams than so many kittens. They stumbled and fell in a heap at almost every step, and the elephants and camels, who look so stately when drawing the cars on occasions of triumphal entry, were not of the slightest use in such an emergency.

They had no shoes to be "roughed," and their broad, fat feet sprawled and slided about on the slippery surface – the animals being evidently in considerable terror – in a manner which was only saved from being painful to witness by being utterly ludicrous. The only way get on at all was by yoking the horses twenty or thirty in a team to a single van and hauling it some distance, the process being repeated van by van.

Nearly an hour and half was thus taken up in getting over half a mile of ground to reach a blacksmith's forge at the Old Swan, where a general halt was made that all might take a rest and the horses have their shoes "roughed," so as to get over the slippery roads with more certainty and celerity. Ultimately the procession of caravans, favoured by the rapid thaw, dragged its way through the muddy quagmire between the Old Swan and St. Helens, and reached the latter place in the course of the day, after a journey long to be remembered.

However, terrified animals taken unwillingly from their natural environment also knew how to cause terror to humans.

The St Helens Examiner described one such incident in Earlestown on April 5th 1890:

On Tuesday Wombwell's menagerie visited Earlestown, and at night a startling incident was witnessed during the exhibition. Madame Leo, one of the artistes, described as a snake-charmer, had a terribly narrow escape from losing her life. The show was packed with a very large audience, and the lady was going through her performances with several cobras. She put a very large one round her neck, when it suddenly tightened its embrace.

The woman finding its toils becoming unpleasantly tight, endeavoured to free herself, but not succeeding she screamed for help, and immediately fell to the ground. Assistance was quickly rendered, and the cobra was with difficulty taken from her throat. She was picked up and assisted from the arena, the ringmaster (Mr. Taylaure), after allaying the excitement among the audience, explaining that she had a marvellous escape. Enquiries made elicited that the cobra in question was only added to the collection on Monday last, and was of an Indian species.

Later that same year a circus lioness caused panic after escaping from a goods van at Widnes. The beast then walked boldly along the railway line and gave a porter at Halebank station the shock of his life after suddenly appearing next to him on the platform!

Despite the fact that the lioness made no attempt to attack any of those that it passed, the animal was sadly shot in the neck and then battered to death by a heavy hammer.

MONSTRE FETE

1890 was also the year that Charles Liptrot of the Salisbury Hotel & Music Hall in St Helens held what was described as:

"The most extraordinary programme of special attractions, ever brought together at any Fete ever held in Lancashire".

That was a bold claim but there were dozens of performers at the eight-day event that took place over Easter in Dentons Green. The fete was held on a field in between the Lingholme Hotel and the Gerard Arms in Dentons Green Lane.

The admission price at 6d a day was quite low, with children under 12 only paying half-price.

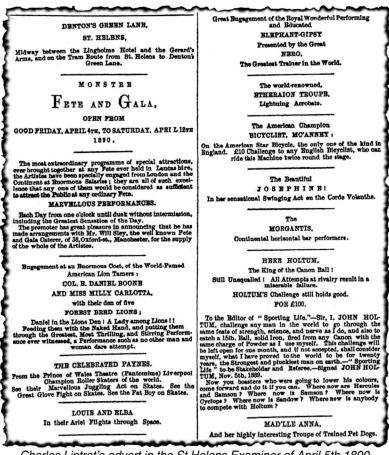

Charles Liptrot's advert in the St Helens Examiner of April 5th 1890

This is part of Liptrot's lengthy advert for his "Monstre Fete":

The artistes have been specially engaged from London and the Continent at enormous salaries; they are all of such excellence that any one of them would be considered as sufficient to attract the Public at any ordinary Fete. – Marvellous performances. Each day from one o'clock until dusk without intermission, including the Greatest Sensation of the Day. – Engagement at an enormous cost, of the world-famed American Lion Tamers; Col. E. Daniel Boone and Miss Milly Carlotta, with their den of five forest bred lions; Daniel in the Lions Den! A Lady among Lions!! Feeding them with the naked hand, and putting them through the greatest, most thrilling, and stirring performance ever witnessed, a performance such as no other man and woman dare attempt.

Great engagement of the Royal wonderful performing and educated elephant Gipsy. Presented by the Great Nero, the greatest trainer in the world. – The American Champion Bicyclist, Mc'anney on the American Star Bicycle, the only one of the kind in England. £10 Challenge to any English bicyclist, who can ride this machine twice round the stage. – Herr Holtum, The King of the Cannon Ball! Still unequalled! All attempts at rivalry result in a miserable failure.

Lion tamers Edgar Boone and his wife Milly Carlotta

Col. E. Daniel Boone – the monstre fete's headline act – traded on an alleged ancestry with the famous American pioneer of that name. Despite the claim in the ad that he was American, researchers believe that the lion tamer actually came from Norfolk – and not Kentucky!

Born Edgar Daniel Boon, he simply added the "e" to his surname; adopted the rank of colonel and claimed a false family link with Daniel Boone. But he does appear to have been a lion tamer that spent much time in the States and in the 1900 US census Boone's occupation is stated as "Tamer of Wild Beasts".

There was a lot of promise in Charles Liptrot's advert for his monstre fete – but would the acts deliver and would the people of St Helens turn up? This is how the St Helens Examiner reviewed the shows on April 12th 1890:

GALA AT ST. HELENS. The eight-days' "monstre fete and gala" at Denton's Green, St. Helens, promoted by Mr. Charles Liptrot, of the Salisbury Hotel, was commenced on Good Friday and proved a most gratifying success, on the opening day. Fortunately the extensive undertaking was favoured with the finest weather that could be desired, and it was estimated that nearly 10,000 persons passed through the turnstiles during the afternoon.

The attractions offered for the interest and amusement of visitors, were certainly far superior to anything of the kind ever before attempted in the district, and the success which has rewarded the efforts of Mr. Liptrot has been thoroughly well-earned and deserved. The gala has been held in a field adjoining the Recreation Football ground, and was within easy access of all parts of the town, as the tram lines to Denton's Green passed within a short distance of the ground. In addition to the engaged artistes, there were many attractions in the shape of swings, shooting galleries, nut, gingerbread stalls, Aunt Sallies, &c.

On the opening day Miss Alvira went through a series of performances on a rolling globe and she was succeeded by the Maleons, grotesque flying ring performers, who delighted the onlookers. Mdlle. Anna, with a troupe of trained pet dogs, next engaged attention and the American champion bicyclist, McAnney, went through a number of clever tricks.

Mdlle. Josephine followed with a very clever wire performance and a great amount of interest centred in the feat of Herr Holtum "the king of the cannon ball," who, standing about six yards from the mouth of a cannon, caught at the second attempt a cannon ball weighing about 15lbs., as it was fired from the cannon. A performance by the Eatheron troupe of "lightning acrobats" was highly appreciated, as were also the clever feats by the flying gymnastics Louie and Elba, who went through a performance on the trapeze.

One of the most exciting and successful feats was next performed. Colonel E. D. Boone and Miss M. Carlotta entered a den of five lions, and daringly put the animals through some startling movements. In the evening a somewhat similar programme was gone through. The whole of the performances were extremely successful.

The new steam trams have done an extensive traffic on the Denton's Green section, the gala being the great attraction, and keeping many people in town during the holidays who would otherwise have journeyed to other places. A large number of people from the surrounding country districts have also visited the gala.

Mitchell's fair on Barrack's field at the rear of Lowe House church in 1914

During the early years of the 20th century before Silcock's became synonymous with funfairs in St Helens, Mitchell & Sons was the main provider of amusements in the town. Events were often held on Barrack's field *(aka Volunteer field)* near Lowe House church and the Volunteer Hall.

The annual Lowe House Carnival took place there and on May 16th 1917, the St Helens Reporter described how lions were involved in the carnival's fair:

Amongst recent arrivals has been Manders' American menagerie, where real lions ramp and rage, and where a real man goes into their cages and makes them go through [the] most terrifying evolutions. Mr. Mitchell has won the hearts of the children by extending invitations to several schools to come to the fair on certain afternoons "free, gratis and for nothing". They came in droves with their teachers, and had the time of their lives.

I've mentioned boxing booths at fairgrounds as being staple events. These continued well into the 20th century and could be used as a means of settling scores.

In 1934 the Daily Herald's St Helens correspondent published an account of an unusual bout that had taken place at Silcock's Fair in Gerards Bridge. The fight was between two Eccleston lads – Chris Sephton of Dodd Avenue and Thomas Moore of McFarlane Avenue, the latter being two stones lighter than his opponent.

The Herald's article was published on February 20th 1934 under the headline *"Fought For A Girl – But She Vanished":*

They were old pals, Tom Moore and Chris Sephton, of Eccleston – bosom pals for years. But a girl intervened, and now, after fighting for her, they don't know precisely where they are about it. They happened to walk round Silcock's Fair here a fortnight ago and met a girl. Both fell in love with her, and they could only think of the traditional way out. They were Lancashire men. They would fight for her. They hadn't to leave the fair to do it. "Here's a boxing booth," said Moore. "I'll fight you for her." The result was a draw. Then last night they again met in the ring. Neither knew whether the girl was present or not. Len Johnson, the boxer who refereed, had the onerous task of finding the bridegroom. He gave the laurels to Chris Sephton on points. They shook hands. The crowd cheered. But nobody could find the girl!

I'd like to conclude this chapter with a mention of the Prescot Fair. Although I'm sure pleasure fairs did take place in that district during the 19th century, what was known to locals as Prescot Fair was more of a market where animals, flowers and other commodities were bought and sold.

What was particularly interesting was the traditional means in which the fair was launched – or proclaimed – at the start of each season. Under the headline *"A Venerable Nuisance"*, the St Helens Newspaper of June 8th 1872 described the unusual ceremony:

On Thursday afternoon the ancient custom of proclaiming the fair at Prescot was observed. The proclamation was read as usual from the Town Hall steps by the beadle [church official]. After the proclamation came the "perrying" of coppers from the windows of the Town Hall. For numbers, dirt, and rags, the crowd of children assembled on this occasion has not been beaten for many years. The children rolled over each other while scrambling for the coppers, like bundles of rags falling into a marine-store dealer's cellar. The sight was suggestive, if not edifying and gratifying.

The Newspaper went on to explain that those involved in the ceremony – including the vicar of Prescot – felt the longstanding proclamation should be abolished. Although, I expect the poor, ragged children did not share that opinion!

The Brutal Gang of Highway Robbers

"After being beaten and cruelly treated, [he] was robbed of his watch and the post bags, and left weltering in his blood."

The brutal highway robbery of the St Helens to Prescot mail cart in 1836 was the last in a series of thirty-five such raids by the same ruthless gang of robbers. The men's crimes had taken place in Lancashire, Cheshire and Shropshire over a period of three years and were described as the worst such robberies for a century.

ROBBERY OF THE ST. HELEN'S AND PRESCOT MAIL —We mentioned last week the robbery of the Prescot and St. Helen's mail by five ruffians, who dragged the conductor from his seat, and so maltreated the poor fellow that he has kept his bed ever since. The bag was found by the pupils of Plumb's House, whilst taking their customary walk on Saturday last, in a pond about a mile from the spot where the robbery took place. The bloated appearance of the bag, partly concealed under water, together with the sequestered situation of the place, led the young gentlemen to suspect something foul and tragical. Their fears were, however, soon relieved by their teacher dragging to land a bag of opened letters and newspapers, the former of which had been carefully opened at the seal with a penknife or some sharp instrument. It is hoped this circumstance will serve as a clew to their apprehension.

Preston Chronicle March 26th 1836

The savage assault in the Rainhill / Whiston district had left the driver of the mail cart *"weltering in his blood"*. As a result of the investigations made into the daring attack, a number of men were handed death sentences and others were transported to Australia. However, at least one completely innocent man might well have been amongst them.

With St Helens and Prescot newspapers not published until the 1850s, accounts in other papers are our only record of what took place. And so I begin this story with the Chester Chronicle's brief report from March 18th 1836 of how the horse-driven post van had been waylaid:

On Wednesday evening, about half-past seven o'clock, the mail cart which runs between St. Helen's and Prescot was stopped when within three miles of the latter place, by five ruffians who, after severely beating the driver, broke open the box of the cart, and decamped with the whole of the bags. A reward has been offered by [the] government for the apprehension of the robbers.

Eight days later the Preston Chronicle stated that the men had dragged the driver from his seat and *"so maltreated the poor fellow that he has kept his bed ever since"*.

The paper also reported how a group of schoolboys and their teacher had since recovered one of the stolen postbags about a mile from where the robbery had taken place.

Plumb's House Academy was a private boarding school for young gentlemen – located near Holt Lane in Rainhill. Every Saturday their teacher accompanied the lads on a nature ramble but on the last occasion they'd seen something in a pond that initially caused them considerable concern.

The Preston Chronicle wrote:

> The bloated appearance of the bag, partly concealed under water, together with the sequestered situation of the place, led the young gentlemen to suspect something foul and tragical. Their fears were, however, soon relieved by their teacher dragging to land a bag of opened letters and newspapers, the former of which had been carefully opened at the seal with a pen-knife or some sharp instrument. It is hoped this circumstance will serve as a clew [sic] to their apprehension.

CONFESSED

Five men were soon arrested and one, James Maguire, confessed to the gang being responsible for numerous highway robberies.

The Manchester Courier described the resulting court case on April 9th 1836:

On Wednesday last, the small court at the New Bailey [Manchester] was crowded almost to suffocation by persons anxious to hear the examination of the five Irishmen who have been in custody upwards of a fortnight, charged with various highway robberies in this county, as well as in Cheshire and Shropshire. Mr. Thomas [police officer] read his minutes of Maguire's confession on this subject.

He said that he and the other prisoners, with the two men not in custody, stopped the mail cart between St. Helens and Prescot. Thomas (the man not in custody) struck the postman with a stick, and Owen McDaniel, alias John Rooney, also struck him; Thomas took from him two leather bags containing letters and newspapers, and his watch, and Holland took another bag.

The watch was pawned by Thomas in Manchester. William Collinson, the driver of the mail cart, said that about twenty minutes past seven in the evening of the 9th March, he was going from St. Helens to Prescot, when five men sprang out of the hedge, struck him several blows with heavy bludgeons, and stole from him four mail bags and his watch. He was left insensible on the ground, and the horse was driven back towards St. Helens.

The Courier praised the actions of the police and the co-operation of a Manchester pawnbroker, saying:

"The public are indebted for the breaking up of a gang, such as has not been heard of in England for the last century." That might have been so – but more than 700 people each year were then convicted of highway robbery.

As one of the gang's most brutal crimes had taken place in Shropshire, the magistrate sent the five men in irons for trial at Shrewsbury, accompanied by a large escort of police officers.

On August 1st 1836 at Shrewsbury Assizes, Patrick McDaniel, John Mulholland, Edward McDaniel, Lawrence Curtis and Owen McDaniel were sentenced to death. None of their victims had died but the law then allowed for capital punishment in the most serious of cases of highway robbery.

Two of the men were reprieved from the gallows with their sentences commuted to transportation to Australia. However, the other three were hung within a fortnight.

In describing the ghoulish public event, the Manchester Courier reprinted this article from the Salopian Journal that bore the headline *"Execution Of The Irish Highway-Men"*:

On Saturday last, at 12 o'clock, Patrick McDaniel, alias Patrick Donelly, Edward McDaniel, alias Edward Donelly and Lawrence Curtis, alias James McGuire underwent the sentence of the law, over the lodge in front of our county gaol. The number of persons, of all ages and both sexes, who came to Shrewsbury from all the adjacent parts of the county to witness their execution, was unparalleled.

The Roman Catholic clergyman resident in Shrewsbury (the Rev. Eugene Egan), with a coadjutor (Mr. Coglan), attended upon them with assiduity, and accompanied them to the foot of the scaffold. In answer to several questions put by Mr. Egan on ascending the stairs leading to the fatal platform, the wretched culprits acknowledged, unhesitatingly, that their lives were justly forfeited to the offended laws of their country, and also for that offence of which they had been convicted, and they hoped for the forgiveness of all whom they had injured.

Patrick McDaniel, with a firm step, ascended first to the platform of the drop, and addressing the unprecedentedly large assemblage who covered the area in front of the gaol, and crowded all accessible places within sight of the scaffold, he exclaimed: "There are three men in Liverpool gaol; they are innocent – I am the man who committed the robbery. No Englishman was there." The executioner then proceeded to perform his last duties, and the drop fell under the three unhappy men, who thus terminated a life stained with crime.

PHRENOLOGICAL GALLERY

However, there was more ghoulishness on show than just the swarms of people who went to watch the hangings. A man called Bally from King Street in Manchester took casts of the three dead men's heads as soon as their bodies were brought down from the scaffold.

These were then placed in his "phrenological gallery" which had the purpose of allowing people to study aspects of skulls that supposedly displayed criminal traits. This pseudoscience is the origin of the expression "You want your bumps feeling!"

Patrick McDaniel's gallows confession to a robbery in which three others had been convicted was music to the ears of a man called Elson. He was the father of one of the accused who had been moved from gaol in Liverpool to Chatham in Kent awaiting transportation.

The trio had been found guilty of committing a highway robbery on the road between Rochdale and Middleton. Mr Elson Snr had been convinced of his son's innocence in the crime and had travelled to Liverpool and Dublin and other places searching for evidence.

He had also journeyed to Shrewsbury and was with a small group that had been allowed to interview the three doomed men, who each signed a full confession to the crime in prison prior to their hanging. The Manchester Guardian campaigned for the trio's release, citing a mass of evidence. However, a victim of the robbery believed the right men had been convicted and the Government stubbornly refused to release them.

But returning specifically to the robbery of the mail van in the Whiston / Rainhill area, three of the five men involved had been brothers. As we have seen two of the McDaniels – Edward and Patrick – were hung and seven months later their brother Thomas was also brought to book.

Under the headline *"The Robbery of the Prescot and St. Helen's Mail"*, the Chester Chronicle on March 3rd 1837 wrote:

We gave an account in February last year, of the robbery of the man who carries the mail-bags between Prescot and St. Helens; and it will be seen from the following particulars, which we copy from the Manchester Times, that one of the persons supposed to have been concerned in that robbery has been apprehended, and that he proves to be Thomas McDaniel, the brother of the Irish highwaymen executed a few months since at Shrewsbury.

He was examined on Wednesday week at the New Bailey, Manchester, when the following facts were established:- Mr. Thomas, the deputy constable, stated that in Feb., 1836, a person named Collett, carrying the post bags between St. Helens and Prescot, was stopped on the road near Prescot, by some highwaymen, and after being beaten and cruelly treated, was robbed of his watch and the post bags, and left lying in the road weltering in his blood.

The post bags were afterwards recovered, and Collett with care and attention was restored to health. His watch was soon afterwards discovered to have been pledged at the shop of Mrs. Fisher, pawnbroker, 201, Allport Town, Deansgate, and there was evidence to prove that the prisoner was the person who pledged it. John McWhirter and Richard Fleming, the two Irish officers, stated that they apprehended the prisoner in consequence of information forwarded to them at Trim, in the county of Meath.

He stated his name first to be McCormick, but afterwards, on being asked if he was not Thomas McDaniel, he replied "I am, and I'll be hung." He afterwards stated that he could have kept out of their hands, but he always knew he should be taken and "hung, as his brothers had been."

NORTHERN CIRCUIT.—LIVERPOOL, MARCH 29.
CROWN SIDE.
(Before Mr. Baron Alderson.)
Thomas M'Daniels was indicted for a highway robbery on the road between St. Helen's and Prescot, on the 9th of March, 1886. The prosecution was instituted by the Post-master-General.

William Collett deposed that between seven and eight o'clock on the evening of the 25th of March, in the last year, he was driving the mail-cart from Prescot to St. Helen's He had got about half-way on his journey, and was within. two miles of St. Helen's, when four or five men rushed out upon him from behind the bridge, and while one seized his horse three others dragged him backwards out of the cart. As he fell he received a very heavy blow from one of the party over the left eye-brow, which cut it severely, and filled the eye with blood. The sight of that eye has remain-

The report of the Morning Post from March 31st 1837

But Thomas McDaniel was not executed, as he had feared. Instead at Liverpool Assizes on March 29th 1837 he was sentenced to transportation beyond the seas for life and ordered to work in his new Australian home in chains.

Seven Strange St Helens Characters

Over the years the town has been blessed – and sometimes cursed – by many characters of one sort of another. In the main these have been harmless individuals who provide proof to the saying *"it takes all sorts to make a world"*.

Often amusing, sometimes sad and a damned nuisance at other times, here are the stories of seven such persons who brought colour to the courts of St Helens:

a) <u>Bridget Kildare and Elizabeth Tither</u>

"Notorious local characters and incorrigible rogues"

On August 3rd 1891 Bridget Kildare and Elizabeth Tither appeared together in St Helens Police Court to face separate charges of drunkenness. By then the two notorious ladies had between them been convicted **354 TIMES** – and they had many more court appearances to come!

Their offences were usually drunkenness, sleeping rough or indecency – which often meant soliciting men for sex to pay for their drink and their lodgings.

No punishment, no matter how harsh, deterred Bridget and Elizabeth from reoffending. Local newspapers referred to them as females of *"considerable notoriety"* or *"notorious local characters"* and they were often laughed at in court.

On May 17th 1884, the St Helens Examiner wrote:

At the Town Hall, on Tuesday, Bridget Kildare was charged with indecent conduct on the previous evening; and she was committed to prison for one month with hard labour. It was her 136th appearance, and the police records show that during the last twenty-five years she has spent over twenty years in prison.

When Bridget appeared in the Police Court on June 8th 1891 charged with disorderly conduct, she was reported to have excitedly asked the St Helens magistrates to sentence her to 12 months in prison – but they refused to oblige and only gave her a month. She had seemingly become institutionalised and preferred the ordered harshness of prison life to being on the outside.

During her lifetime Bridget had at least 207 convictions with – as far as I can tell – her final appearance being in St Helens Police Court in December 1892. With no probation or support service for individuals like Bridget, life was a revolving prison door.

She had no cash to pay fines or find sureties to guarantee her good behaviour and so gaol was her inevitable destination upon being arrested and appearing in court.

Prison records show that Bridget Kildare had been born in 1847 in Blackburn and she never married. At what point she came to St Helens, I don't know. But by August 21st 1875 the St Helens Reporter was able to call her *"A Very Old Offender"*.

That was after Bridget had been charged with sleeping in an outhouse at Eccleston. Upon the Bench being told that this was the prisoner's 70th appearance before them, she was sent to prison for three more months.

In April 1878, Bridget was found guilty at Kirkdale Assizes of being an *"incorrigible rogue"* and given six more months in gaol. Her charge had been:

> Having, at Eccleston, on the 1st February, 1878, she then being a common prostitute, unlawfully wandered in a certain street called Liverpool Street, and behaved in a disorderly manner.

The Kirkdale Gaol and court complex in Liverpool

Elizabeth Tither was also declared a rogue at the same hearing and handed the same sentence. I don't think she and Bridget were close friends as such – but their paths very often crossed. Their cases are so similar that I have combined their potted histories within this section.

Born in 1841, court documents state that upon appearing at the assizes in 1878, the charge against Elizabeth had been:

> Having, at Windle, on the 31st March, 1878, she then being a common prostitute, did unlawfully wander in a certain street there called Raven street, and did then and there behave in a riotous manner, she the said Elizabeth Tither having been once previously convicted of being an idle and disorderly person, and afterwards convicted of being a rogue and vagabond.

For that offence in Raven Street, off Church Street, Elizabeth was given six months hard labour. At that time the woman had 51 convictions in the St Helens courts to her name but within the next ten years she would acquire 80 more. This we glean from this report in the Runcorn Examiner of December 10th 1887:

Elizabeth Tither, of St. Helens, has won fame as one who has been convicted no less than 120 times. Brought before the magistrates, on Monday for being drunk and disorderly, she said: "Give me three months this time, please." She evidently likes the inside better than the outside of a gaol, and was quite disappointed when they gave her fourteen days only.

It was a common practice for drunks chucked out of pubs to seek revenge by breaking a window using the nearest object to hand – or to foot, as in Elizabeth's case.

In February 1888, she used one of her boots to clobber the glass in the front door of the Liverpool Inn in Liverpool Road after the landlord had ejected her.

The St Helens Examiner described what happened on the 11th of that month:

At the Police Court, on Saturday, before Mr. Sinclair and Alderman Cook, Elizabeth Tither, a middle-aged woman, who had been 123 times convicted, pleaded guilty to wilfully breaking a plate-glass window, value £2 15s, in the door of the Liverpool Inn, the property of Lieutenant-Colonel T. C. Wilcock. William Humphries, manager, stated that he refused to supply the prisoner with liquor because she was drunk, and as she refused to leave the house he put her out. She attempted to break several windows, but he prevented her, and she seemed to be going away. Eventually, however, she returned, took off a boot, and smashed the window in the door. Prisoner said that the manager kicked and struck her. The magistrates committed her for two months with hard labour. Prisoner (to Humphries): "When I come out I'll break two or three – not only one; you'll see."

Whether Elizabeth realised her threat I do not know – but she was clearly an alcoholic who saw prison as an opportunity to dry out. In January 1891 after St Helens magistrates had sentenced her to 28 days, she exclaimed: *"Oh, it'll keep me sober, thank God".*

by the officials of the **London** and **North-Western Railway Company.**

A RIVAL TO BRIDGET KILDARE.

In our last issue we reported that the notorious Bridget Kildare, of St. Helens, had been convicted at the local Police Court, for the 180th time. On Monday, at St. Helens Town Hall, Elizabeth Tither, another well known female, was placed in the dock for drunkenness. She informed the Bench that she went to the police station and asked to be locked up, but the officers would not take her into custody. It appeared she was disorderly outside the office and was then placed in the cells. It was her 144th appearance, and she was committed to prison for 28 days.

GALA AND SPORTS AT ST. HELENS.

A gala and sports on a most extensive scale

Report from the Runcorn Examiner of March 29th 1890

Then on November 21st of that year the St Helens Examiner reported that Elizabeth *"who had been in prison times innumerable for being drunk and disorderly"* had seven days earlier been released from gaol.

However, the woman was already back in trouble but was blaming prison for causing her problems with her health.

The Examiner mockingly wrote:

Oddly enough, she pleaded, this time, that going to prison had "so ruined her constitution that she could not stand any drink." The drink of course has not injured her. How would it be to give her "another month" in a brewery by way of restoring her constitution?

77

Towards the end of the 19th century attitudes were beginning to change. It was realised that social difficulties could be the root cause of crime and sentencing offenders repeatedly to gaol for relatively minor offences could be counter-productive and an extremely expensive way for society to manage their behaviour.

On February 26th 1898 the Liverpool Weekly Courier referenced the case of Elizabeth Tither in discussing the problem:

> Social problems in abundance are presented to readers of police court cases, and, it may be their very plentifulness that prevents attempts at solution. Here is the case of Michael McHugh, who was charged at the Manchester Police Court with attempting to pick pockets. He is fifty-four years of age, but he told the court that he had "done thirty-five years and hadn't taken more than £5 altogether."

> There is also the case of Elizabeth Tither, of St. Helens, whose convictions have reached into the three figures, and who has appeared periodically before the magistrates for the last twenty years. We do not know that there has been any suggestion made, with a view to obtaining judicial leniency, that either of these "well-known" characters is suffering from hereditary taint. Few people, as a matter of fact, would trouble to dive down to the root-cause of their wrong-doing. But there is far more likelihood of hereditary mental or physiological "twists" to be discovered in the two persons mentioned than in the case of Lord William Nevin, just sentenced to five years' penal servitude.

By the 1890s St Helens had its own Police Court Missionary who was a forerunner of the probation officer and initially provided by the Church of England.

Previously Bridget Kildare and Elizabeth Tither had received no support upon their discharge from prison – and so, as stated, would soon return to gaol. But changing societal attitudes and the creation of a system of basic support for offenders came far too late to assist our two St Helens' ladies.

Bridget Kildare appears to have died in 1897 and Elizabeth Tither followed two years later. By then the pair had notched up 400 convictions between them, with Bridget convicted at least 207 times and Elizabeth on 193 occasions – although none were for violent acts or anything really serious. They did not even have any convictions for theft, as far as I can tell.

Both women were only in their mid-fifties when they died. After living lives of drunkenness and enduring harsh prison life for so many years, it is perhaps surprising they lived as long as they did.

b) John Jones – "The English Home Ruler"

"You are a lot of villains; you have robbed
and plundered me for five or six years"

Oxford Street houses pictured prior to their demolition in the 1980s

Assuming that the house numbers have not changed over the years, the home of John Jones at number 64 Oxford Street in St Helens can be seen on the photograph on the previous page where the car is parked on the left hand side of the street.

The self-proclaimed *"English home ruler"* was a regular in St Helens Police Court where he showed little respect to the magistrates – and, in fact, to anyone else in authority!

AN "ENGLISH HOME RULER" AT ST. HELENS.

EXTRAORDINARY SCENE IN THE POLICE COURT.

At the St. Helens Police Court, this day, before Messrs. J. C. Gamble and C. J. Bishop, a middle-aged man named John Jones, fish-dealer, who lives in Oxford-street, St. Helens, and is a well-known character, appeared to answer a summons charging him with using profane language in the public street on the 14th inst. Defendant said he was not guilty ; he knew his Bible too well for that. Police-constables 1,231 and 1.251 gave evidence, and a written statement of the language used was handed to the bench. It was a gross attack upon all religious societies. Defendant asked the constable if he did not say that religion, law, and politics was a three-card trick, to which the officer replied, "No ; he was not talking to me." Defendant said he was talking to them all, and saying that he had learned the three-card trick, which was religion, law, and politics since he was five years of age.

Liverpool Echo March 19th 1883

Indeed the insulting behaviour of the highly-opinionated fish hawker resulted in harsher sentences for what were usually minor offences that Jones had committed.

During the 1880s the prospect of home rule for Ireland was a controversial issue that was splitting the Liberal party. It was a sensitive subject that needed careful consideration and discussion. But John Jones preferred to yell at people about it from the bedroom window of his Oxford Street home!

On March 24th 1883 under the headline *"An Oxford-Street Celebrity"*, the St Helens Examiner wrote:

On Monday, at the St. Helens Police Court, John Jones a resident in Oxford-street – who is well known to the inhabitants of Cowley Hill on account of his somewhat noisy endeavours to instruct them in his own peculiar theories of religion and politics, generally using an upstairs window as his rostrum – was charged with having used profane language on the 14th inst. A police officer spoke to having heard the defendant use profane language, and then a sheet, on which the language used was written was handed up to the Bench, who seemed to think that it fully sustained the charge.

The defendant: "Didn't I tell you that religion, laws and politics were the three card trick, and that you couldn't play the three card trick on me?" He (defendant) then explained that an officer had come with a summons for his son for having played at pitch and toss, and he would not take in the summons, because he was not responsible for everything that his family did.

He also told the officer that he had known the three card trick ever since he was three years of age, and that he was an English Home Ruler. That charge, he added, was an old grievance that the police wished to bring up, but they couldn't come that over him; he had learned knowledge, tactics, stratagems, money, diplomacy, etiquette, technicalities, wash and humbug.

Defendant then referred to Moses and the prophets, and shouted out in an excited manner, that the "parsons had tied the knot and the lawyers couldn't undo it," and was proceeding to say more when he was stopped by the magistrates. On being asked if he was guilty, he said "Not guilty; I know the Bible too well for using bad language." – He was fined 5s and costs.

John Jones' pitch-and-toss playing son Richard was only fourteen at the time and so the man who claimed to possess knowledge and diplomacy was very much responsible for him.

And a few weeks later, the boy, with several criminal convictions to his name, would be sent to prison for a month for stealing pigeons.

On May 8th 1883 the Liverpool Daily Post wrote how Jones Snr had also been back in court:

At the St Helens Police Court, yesterday, before Dr. Twyford, Mr. Richard Pilkington, and Alderman Harrison, John Jones, who styles himself as "The English Home Ruler," and who has frequently figured in the St. Helens Police Court, was placed in the dock charged with committing a breach of the peace on Sunday night.

When called upon to plead, prisoner commenced to shout and rave at the top of his stentorian voice, "Do as you have a mind. If you want me to plead you must send me before a jury. None of your three-card tricks; you have played it now for five or six years. You are a lot of villains; you have robbed and plundered me for five or six years." The prisoner used very bad language, and said there was a plot against him at the Town Hall.

While he was raving about his three-card trick, "Theology, law, and politics," Police-constable McHenry stated the case. He said that prisoner had a crowd round him, and was ringing a bell. Prisoner (interrupting) said it was a political procession. To apprehend him on Sunday too!

At the close of prisoner's harangue, Dr. Twyford said after that exhibition the bench felt bound to bind him over to keep the peace for three months, himself in £40 and two sureties of £20 each. Prisoner said they had better let him go and join Davitt in America.

Michael Davitt mentioned above was a well-known Irish republican leader who is known to have secretly visited St Helens on at least one occasion. But it wasn't to see John Jones!

The outspoken fishmonger often had summonses issued against him for committing one offence or another. And so Jones would keep a wary eye out for the unfortunate police officer given the task of serving the summons on him.

However, even completely "innocent" bobbies suspected of being delivery boys were given a rough ride by the "English Home Ruler". On September 6th 1884, the St Helens Examiner described how the then 53-year-old had turned violent and attacked a policeman who had simply been walking on his beat down Oxford Street:

At the St. Helens Town Hall on Monday, before Mr H S Hall, Mr J C Bishop, and Alderman Harrison, John Jones, of Oxford-st., known as the "English Home Ruler," was charged with assaulting P.C. Ewan on the 24th July. It appeared that on the date named the constable was passing along Oxford-street when, without any provocation, the prisoner rushed at him, kicked him violently on the shins, and knocked him to the floor. The officer regained his feet, however, and attempted to take his assailant into custody.

The latter thereupon shouted to his wife, who came running out of the house with a poker in her hand, and with that weapon she dealt the constable a violent blow on the hand, smashing one of his fingers. The prisoner again struggled hard, and catching the officer's hand between his teeth severely bit it. Between the two the constable was so severely thrashed that he had been off duty for 35 days.

It was stated that after the prisoner and his wife had made their way into the house they threw pots, a bell, and other articles at the constable, who fortunately escaped any further injury. The prisoner said he only threw the articles out of the window in a "Jerusalem style," and added "I could have hit the officer like fun if I had wanted, but I did not want to do so."

Superintendent Johnston said the prisoner had been frequently convicted for various offences; and the Bench, remarking that it was a very bad case when a constable was attacked and beaten in that manner without any provocation, committed him to prison for two months with [hard] labour.

POWERFUL-LOOKING WOMAN

As for Ellen Jones, the *"powerful-looking woman"* was fined 20 shillings for her part with the poker. Aged thirty-three, she was twenty years younger than her husband and sounds like quite a character in her own right. Unfortunately, this is the only occasion that Mrs Jones figures in this narrative.

Then in November 1884 – not long after John Jones' release from prison – he was in trouble again for hawking fish without a licence and for using abusive language to John Coughtrey, the local inspector of nuisances. The St Helens Examiner wrote:

Inspector Coughtrey deposed that about 11 o'clock on the previous Wednesday morning he saw and heard the defendant crying fish for sale in Cooper-street. He asked him if he had got a toll ticket, and he replied "No, and I don't intend to take one." He then began to use very abusive language, and called Inspector Coughtrey a thief and "a Corporation robber." The defendant had not got a ticket, and was hawking fish without having paid the toll.

Mr. J. O. Swift (who appeared on behalf of the Corporation) drew attention to the previous bad character of the defendant, and remarked that the defendant had made a practice of abusing not only Inspector Coughtrey, but other officials employed by the Corporation.

Under those circumstances he (Mr. Swift) must press the case, and ask the magistrates to inflict the full penalty. The Bench said the defendant would be fined £2 and costs or one month's imprisonment for hawking without having paid the toll; and for using bad language to Inspector Coughtrey, he would be further fined 10s. and costs or otherwise 14 days imprisonment.

It was a common practice for babies to sleep in the same bed as their parents and many infants were accidentally smothered through what was called "overlaying". In July 1885 the inquest was held on Randolph Jones, the five-week-old son of John and Ellen Jones, who had died in that fashion.

The infant's father had absented himself from the inquest, seemingly because police warrants had been issued against the fishmonger for other matters. The coroner heard that Mrs Jones had awoken one morning and found the lifeless body of her son in bed, with the child's head resting under her husband's shoulder.

The coroner remarked that these cases of overlaying were of too frequent an occurrence, not only to himself but to his colleagues all over the country. He could not take evidence from a wife that would incriminate her husband or vice versa, and unless there was the independent testimony of a third party, a charge could not be proved against a parent.

And that's where reports on John Jones fizzle out – apart from a case in 1887 when he was prosecuted for shouting the *"most foul and disgusting language"* at the magistrates' clerk who he happened to see in the street while flogging fish!

Perhaps his baby's death led the English home ruler to temper his ways a little and demonstrate real diplomacy and knowledge?

c) **Bridget Ward**

"It's a nice thing to have a poor woman lek me, that
has six little childer to contind wid, kicked."

Bridget Ward lived in the Irish quarter of St Helens within the
Liverpool Road district known as Greenbank. She described
herself as a tailoress and made regular appearances in court for
relatively minor offences – often through rowing with her
neighbours or the police. And she wasn't quiet in court either!

On April 26th 1869, Bridget was charged in St Helens Petty
Sessions with assaulting a police officer. The case was in
connection with an incident in Liverpool Street on the previous
Sunday that lasted from late morning until three in the afternoon.

Constable Michael Darmody told the court that the row had led to
over 1,500 people occupying the road, making it completely
impassable.

Liverpool Street in the Greenbank district of St Helens

The trouble had begun when the officer attempted to take Bridget's
son, Patrick Ward, into custody. PC Darmody accused the young
man of disorderly conduct and said he had been forced to use his

baton on him after he'd resisted arrest. That act had upset his sister, Mary Fitzgibbon, who helped her brother to get away.

Their mother Bridget Ward then got involved in the scuffle and claimed that Constable Darmody *(who she sometimes referred to in court as McDermott)* had kicked her. The St Helens Newspaper quoted her like this:

> Mr. McDermott gev me a kick on the leg, which I can show yer honours. Its a nice thing to have a poor woman lek me, that has six little childer to contind wid, kicked in this way. (Turning fiercely to the officer.) A nice thrick of you, Mr. Dermody, but God will meet you yit for it. It was all out o' spite agen me and my childer.

The magistrates thought the evidence against Mrs Ward on this occasion had not been very strong and so decided to dismiss the case against her.

In November 1870 Bridget was back in court charged with having committed a breach of the peace at midnight by *"cursing, swearing, and creating a noise"*. The St Helens Newspaper remarked that she presented rather a *"wild appearance, with her bare arms and dishevelled hair"*. Fancy having bare arms in court!

The paper added that Mrs Ward denied the charge of blaspheming but did admit making a noise. She claimed that as she was passing the corner of a street, some men who were fighting had jostled against her and knocked her down.

Bridget's story might have been true but unaccompanied women on the street at midnight were not considered respectable – and this was her twelfth time in court since May 1868.

She had no chance of being believed and was ordered to pay bail in the sum of £10 and find two people willing to risk £5 each as sureties to guarantee her future conduct.

Then on July 1st 1871 under the headline *"An Old Familiar Face"*, the Newspaper described how Bridget Ward had made her fifteenth appearance before the St Helens magistrates – although the irascible Bridget disputed that figure:

> Bridget Ward, a well-known woman, was charged with committing a breach of the peace. Police constable 845 said that [at] one o'clock that morning he found the prisoner making a great disturbance in Sandfield-crescent. Prisoner: What time did you say it was? Officer: Ten minutes to one. Prisoner: Eh, dear me. For shame of your face. It was not 11.
>
> Bridget made so many objections to a conviction, and said so much in support of her own innocence, that Police Constable Murney was requested to tell a little tale he was acquainted with. The officer stated that when she was brought into the police station she got a brush handle, and tried to swing it so that its course would be intercepted by some policeman's head. The witness disarmed her before she could realise her benevolent plan, and then he began to remonstrate with her but she was unappeasable, and in her fury she caught his tunic in her teeth and tore it pretty considerably. Prisoner: I will not deny that I am very passionate.
>
> Supt. Ludlum: The coat will have to be made good. Prisoner: I am a tailoress myself, and I will mend it for him when I get into the station. Supt. Ludlum, in reply to his Worship, said this was her fifteenth appearance in court. Prisoner: It is only my thirteenth. His Worship: You have kept a close account. You will have to find sureties to keep the peace for one month.

Bridget certainly had difficulty getting on with her neighbours and, of course, claimed that they were the ones causing all the trouble and not her! Countless squabbles were played out in St Helens' courts during the 1870s because it only cost a few shillings to obtain a summons.

"I'll 'ave thee up in court", must then have been a popular refrain in the town when neighbours got involved in disputes.

"MURDHERED"

On June 22nd 1872 the St Helens Newspaper gave this comical account of Bridget's court claims to be the "murdhered" victim of her neighbours' violence:

A woman named Bridget Ward, who resides at Greenbank, and has been "murdhered" at least a dozen times by her neighbours, appeared alive and hearty before the court, under the following circumstances:-

Last week some near neighbour – a Mrs. O'Donnell or McDonnell – made herself the instrument of the latest "murder" of Mrs. Ward. The latter recovered locomotion in all her members in a wonderfully short time, and proceeded to the office of the magistrates' clerk where she deposited 5s. 6d., together with a circumstantial account of the tragedy, and of everything else except what was wanted.

The clerk has long got over the suspicion that it is the ghost of a murdered woman which comes to him for revenge, and he extracted from her, without the slightest nervousness, all he wanted to know. The accused woman was served, but did not appear, in answer to the fist of justice, at Petty Sessions on Monday.

A warrant was issued for her apprehension, and a police officer took her into his keeping that evening. On Tuesday morning she was brought up for trial, but – with a repetition of the see-saw motion which is so common in those cases – Mrs. Ward was not to be seen, or spoken to, or heard of and the prisoner was released.

This morning Mrs. Ward presented herself for an explanation, and would've made it appear that her absence on the previous day was due to a misunderstanding had an officer not confounded her on the spot, by proving that he had given her notice on Monday evening.

The magistrates then refused to allow her to air her eloquence any further and she terminated the interview with the following astounding statement:- "It is no justice to take my money, after this woman killing me, and breaking every tooth in my head."

d) Annie Murphy – "Gentle Annie"

"I had nowhere to go, and no money for lodgings; you can lock me up"

Born in 1874, Annie Murphy was another character that made regular court appearances. Often these were for minor offences, such as *"lodging out"* or *"wandering abroad without visible means of support"*. It might be a free country but you could be imprisoned for making the streets look untidy by sleeping in public spaces.

You didn't even have to be in the land of Nod to get arrested. At 1:30am on February 24th 1918, PC Heaton was on duty in Corporation Street and spotted Annie Murphy sitting quietly on a seat in Victoria Square.

She had not been able to obtain lodgings for the night and wasn't doing anybody or anything any harm – or even moving about. But she was still charged with wandering abroad without visible means and sent to prison for 14 days with hard labour.

Of course, it was Annie's bad record that led the magistrates to impose a custodial sentence for such a minor offence. It had certainly not been her first time in court! Annie's previous convictions were generally petty – but did include several thefts.

One of these from 1914 involved stealing 8s 5d from the offertory box of Sacred Heart Church in Borough Road. That was considered sacrilege and she received six months hard labour.

Annie's police record from that time reveals a wide range of offences committed over a fifteen-year period – ranging from prostitution to giving a false alarm of fire.

She was by now serving her 15th prison term and had 58 summary convictions that had been dealt with by local courts. Sometimes she called herself Annie Percival and at other times Anne Hackett.

Annie Murphy, 40. Hawker   ...   .
14 days, Manchester Police Court, 16th December, 1901 (stealing watch from person)
2 mos., Liverpool Police Court, 8th September, 1902 (stealing 13/-)
3 mos., Salford Police Court, 30th March, 1904 (rogue and vagabond)
B.O. Salford Sessions, 18th April, 1905 (rogue and vagabond)
3 mos., Ashton Police Court, 19th October, 1905 (stealing bed quilt)
28 days, and 2 mos., (consecutive), St. Helens Police Court, 22nd November, 1909 (prostitution, assault)
28 days St. Helens Police Court, 12th January, 1911 (stealing cloth)
28, 28, and 28 days, (consecutive), St. Helens Police Court, 13th February, 1911 (stealing shawls, etc, 3 convictions)
28 days, St. Helens Police Court, 25th April, 1911 (stealing bottles, etc.)
1 mo., Manchester Police Court, 16th September, 1911 (stealing brushes, etc.) as Annie Percival
2 mos., Manchester Police Court, 25th January, 1912 (stealing corsets)
3 mos., St. Helens Police Court, 16th August, 1912 (lodging out)
3 mos., Manchester Police Court, 12th September, 1913 (giving false alarm of fire) as Annie Percival
2 mos., Oldham Police Court, 7th January, 1914 (wilful damage) as Annie Percival
2 mos, Liverpool County Police Court, 17th March, 1914 (stealing 6/9) as Anne Hackett
58 summary, prostitution, drunkenness, wilful damage, etc., since 1899

Annie Murphy's record of imprisonment between 1901 and 1914

LODGING OUT

On March 30th 1918 the now 44-year-old was back before St Helens magistrates after the police had again discovered the woman in Victoria Square. This time it had been at 11:30pm and she had been sat in the doorway of Dr Frank Bassett's surgery minding her own business.

Annie had only been released from prison earlier that day and was charged this time with "lodging out". She told the Bench that she'd rather go back to prison than be sent to the workhouse and the magistrates decided to oblige her. They sentenced her to 28 more days in gaol, extending Annie's long list of convictions.

"Wanted God's Fresh Air – An Old Offender Sent To Prison", was the headline to the St Helens Reporter's account of Annie's court appearance on July 17th 1918:

> The only case before the St. Helens Police Court on Wednesday, was one in which an old offender, named Annie Murphy, was charged with lodging out. P.C. Johnson proved the case, and Supt. Dunn informed the Bench that prisoner had been before the Court five times during the past twelve months, and 67 times altogether. The Chairman (Mr. J. A. Collins) told the prisoner she seemed to have a very bad record. Prisoner: Yes, according to them who gave it to me.
>
> Mr. T. Edmondson, J.P.: You could easily get something to do if you wanted to work. There is plenty of work for you. Prisoner: Yes, but I don't want to be deprived of God's fresh air altogether. You won't see me here anymore. I walked to Prescot yesterday in all that thunder and lightning. The Chairman: And you walked back again? Prisoner: Yes, what else was I to do? The Chairman: Well, you have been here so many times and made so many promises that your case seems hopeless. You will have to go to gaol for two months

with hard labour. The Clerk (Mr. T. A. Turton): And if you come here again.... Prisoner [interrupting]: You are not the magistrates. The Clerk: You will probably be sent to Liverpool and to prison for a long time.

Annie made her 69th court appearance on January 6th 1919 when charged with vagrancy. She had been discovered by the police sleeping on the cold floor of a lavatory inside the headquarters of the Royal Army Medical Corps in Croppers Hill.

Superintendent Dunn told the Bench that the woman was a regular nuisance and during the past month had been allowed to stay for the night in the charge room of the police station. The magistrates decided that three more months in prison was the answer to Annie's homelessness.

Then on May 6th 1919 she made her 70th court appearance, charged with "wandering abroad" and "lodging in the open air" in Corporation Street. PC Turner gave evidence that he had found the woman on one of the seats in Victoria Square at around half past midnight. The officer asked her what she was doing there and Annie replied: *"I had nowhere to go, and no money for lodgings; you can lock me up"*. And so he did!

The magistrates gave her another 28 days in prison where at least she would be fed, warm and have somewhere to sleep. Then she would be released and the vicious circle of sleeping rough and imprisonment would no doubt resume.

Annie returned to St Helens Police Court on August 4th of that year. However, this time her offence was a tad more serious as she had been lashing out at strangers in the street.

This is the St Helens Reporter's description of her court hearing, under the headline *"Annie Murphy's Offensive Weapon – Striking Passers-By With An Umbrella"*:

An incorrigible woman, according to the police account, Annie Murphy, vagrant, of no fixed abode, was charged, at the St. Helens Police Court, on Monday, with a breach of the peace, and further with assault, the complainant in the latter case being Ellen Jackman. P.C. Cain stated that at 9.45 p.m. on Sunday he was in the Police Office when a man came into the office and complained of a woman outside having assaulted his wife by striking her on the head. He went out and found the prisoner [Annie Murphy] against the Town Hall railings. She struck at him with an umbrella, and called him very bad names. She was violent on the way to the Police Office, and he had to call the assistance of P.C. Pugh.

Ellen Jackman, married woman, 76, Ramford-street, stated that at about half-past nine on Sunday night she was passing the Town Hall along with her husband, when prisoner, who was a complete stranger to her, struck her with an umbrella. She lifted her hand to shield her face, and the blow struck her thumb. Prisoner was striking a second time when witness's husband intervened. Prisoner had just struck two young women who were passing.

The Chief Constable said that Murphy had been seventy-three times before that and other Courts. They could make nothing of her. She had been allowed to remain on certain nights at the Police Office and leave in the morning. Prisoner, who was very garrulous and showed temper in the dock, was sent to gaol for two months at hard labour, when she ejaculated "I'll come out again."

Why Annie was hitting people was not explained but it was likely that she had been turned away from the station and feeling frustrated was lashing out at strangers. Or perhaps it was a deliberate act as a means of getting another night's free lodging at the station? However, she had not been living up to her nickname, which, according to the Manchester Evening News of August 23rd 1926, was *"Gentle Annie":*

Annie Murphy, alias "Gentle Annie," whose address was given as Manchester, appeared for the 88th time before the St. Helens magistrates to-day charged with lodging out. She told the bench that she was a very tired old woman, having walked 28 miles from Manchester to St. Helens to visit her sister, and she now wanted to get to Liverpool, and if the bench would pay her fare she would be glad to go.

The Chairman: "You have told us exactly the same story at least a score of times before." The Prisoner, smiling: "Well. I mean it this time. Pay my fare, and you will never see me again." The Chairman: "See Mr. Holmes, the missionary, and see what he can do for you. You can go." The Prisoner: "Thank you very much."

John Holmes was the probation officer who was then attached to the court – but it seemed his interventions were not able to help the independent Annie. *"You will never see me again"* was her regular refrain but the promise was never kept and she made a further court appearance ten weeks later.

This was again covered by the Manchester Evening News and published on November 3rd 1926 under the headline *"Sleeping Out At 70 – 'Gentle Annie's' 89th Time At Court":*

Annie Murphy, generally known as "Gentle Annie," who is about 70 years of age, gave the St. Helens Police Court her usual ten minutes' diverting interlude, when she made her 89th appearance to-day. She was charged with wandering abroad. The Prisoner: Not abroad, only in Prescot Road. The Clerk: Are you guilty or not guilty? – Seeing that two policemen brought me, we'll say guilty.

P.C. Allen said he found her at one o'clock this morning sleeping in a house which was in course of erection, in Prescot Road. The Prisoner: No, not sleeping. It was much too cold for sleep. I couldn't go much further because of the fog, so I just made myself as comfortable as I could, although the house had no roof on. Continuing, she said she came along quite willingly with the two officers, as she knew she had done nothing wrong.

The Chairman: Was it just an escort you wanted? The Prisoner (blushing): Oh, no, sir. The officer said he had a bicycle, and that he would put me on the pillion and bring me to the police station. I told him it was going to be heavy work, as he would have to do all the shoving. As the magistrates turned to consider the case the prisoner said, "Please do let me go. Nobody wants to be caged in." Mr. Collier (the Chairman): All right. The case is dismissed. The Prisoner: Thank you, sir, and then turning to the officer at her side, "Show me the way to go home."

Annie must have looked a lot older than she was – as records show she was then about fifty-two and not seventy.

On March 5th 1929 she made her 94th appearance before the St Helens magistrates after being discovered at 11:20pm on the previous evening sitting in the doorway of Beecham's pills factory.

The police wanted to take her to a lodging house for the night but she preferred the accommodation provided at the police station at the Town Hall.

It was revealed in court that Annie had spent the last year in Liverpool Workhouse but complained to the Bench that the work had been hard and she had decided to walk to Manchester to see her sister. A magistrate said to Annie:

"You have been going to your sister in Manchester for four years, and we sent an officer to book your fare once." Annie then smiled at the magistrates and said if they would help her again she would return to Liverpool.

The Bench appeared at times during the late '20s amused by Annie's antics and at other times exasperated. It was the latter on this occasion and the wandering woman with a penchant for God's fresh air was told she would be discharged from the court.

But Annie was warned that she would be returned to prison if she came before them again. At that point Annie disappears off the newspaper radar after perhaps deciding she was too old to serve any more prison time.

e) <u>Austin Hull</u>

"I have no peace in St. Helens"

Austin Hull in male clothing and as "Cissie"

Austin Hull was a sensation in St Helens during the late 1920s and early '30s. Often dressed in women's clothing, he also went by the name of "Cissie" and was arguably decades ahead of his time.

Austin was also a small-time criminal – although it's impossible to know how much of the persecution he said he endured drove him to deception and theft.

Austin Joseph Hull was born in St Helens in 1909 to Joseph Stanislaus Hull and his wife Alice, née Halliwell. In the 1911 census the family was living in Grant Street – which used to be near Queen's Park – with the father listed as a coachman and Austin confusingly listed as Augustine.

The boy was registered on his birth certificate as Austin but sometimes would call himself Augustine Joseph or, as stated, as Cissie Hull.

These were the three names listed on his police record of 1931 from which the two photographs on the previous page have been taken. The details were published in the newspaper known as the Police Review as part of an appeal for Austin who was wanted for gross indecency. The record states:

> B. 1909, 5ft. 2in., slim build, c. [complexion] pale, h. [hair] dk. brown, e. [eyes] brown. A colliery haulage hand; native of St. Helens. Pre. con. of larceny and fraud at Brighton. Very effeminate in speech and manner and has lived for some months with a man, at St. Helens, as his wife. Dresses and lives as a female, associates with sodomites and may be earning his living by immoral means. Said to be suffering from syphilis and may apply for treatment at hospitals. Has stayed as a female at Blackpool (as Mrs. Jackson), London and Eastbourne.

The earliest newspaper report on Austin that I have been able to find is a description of the aforementioned court hearing at

Brighton – which took place on January 31st 1930. While dressed as Cissie, the 21-year-old had called at lodgings in Pavilion Street in the seaside town and engaged a room for a week.

The following day Hull left the house without paying his bill and a music case was subsequently missed. Instead of obtaining fresh digs in another part of Brighton, Hull booked in at a boarding house in the same street.

Still adopting the guise of "Cissie", he also left his new quarters suddenly and without paying his bill. Then when the landlady chased after him demanding her money, Hull knocked her down and ran off.

However, a police sergeant later spotted him in another part of Brighton and when asked his name, he replied "Cissie Hull". Detective Lodge told the court that it was not until the police got in touch with their colleagues in St Helens that they realised they were dealing with a man and not a woman.

In court the police asked for a remand in custody as they had more inquiries to make in connection with Hull fraudulently obtaining board and lodging. The Lancashire Evening Post was one of many newspapers that commented how Austin Hull had used a feminine voice to say he was very sorry for what he had done.

There was enormous Press interest in the story nationwide. The Daily Mirror headlined their article *"In Woman's Dress – Surprise For Police After A Suspect's Arrest"*. The Nottingham Evening Post's headline was *"Man's Pose As Woman – Court Story Of Amazing Masquerade – Feminine Voice And Clothes"*. And the Hartlepool Northern Daily Mail captioned their piece *"In Woman's Garb – Police Discovery After An Arrest"*.

THIS RIDICULOUS WHIM

A week later Austin returned to court in Brighton for sentencing after pleading guilty to the charges against him – and was bound over. St Helens Police had informed their Brighton counterparts that they'd previously received complaints about Hull wearing female attire and sleeping at the rear of unoccupied houses in St Helens.

Police inquiries had also revealed that between August and December 1929, Hull had stayed in Blackpool in the name of Miss Norma Jackson of Wolverhampton and had suddenly quit his digs, owing a landlady £9. Then in the name of Miss Micky Taylor, he had incurred a similar debt for board and lodging at Eastbourne.

The Press interest in this unusual case now extended across the Atlantic. The Ottawa Journal concentrated on the knocking down of the cheated Brighton landlady, with the headline to their article being *"Ladylike Clothes But Brutal Still"*.

Other newspapers focussed on its sensationalist aspects. But the St Helens Reporter's detailed account provides insights into the mind of Austin, whose court statement revealed that he was a very frightened young man.

The Reporter's front-page piece was published on February 11th 1930:

The amazing story of sex impersonation by a young St. Helens man, Austin Hull, aged twenty-one, was told to the Brighton magistrates on Friday, when he was charged with stealing a music case and contents, valued 5s. 6d., and obtaining food with intent to defraud. Dressed as a female and speaking and passing himself off as such, he engaged rooms at Brighton, but left without paying his bills. The music case was taken from one of these houses. On one occasion a landlady tried to stop Hull, demanding payment, but he knocked her down and bolted. He gave the name of "Cissie Hull" to the police. It was not until the St. Helens police had been communicated with that it was discovered accused was a man and not a woman.

HULL'S ADVENTURES

In the guise of a woman he stayed at various places, including Blackpool and Wolverhampton, and usually left his lodging without paying his bill. Complaints were first made against him in respect of his appearing in female attire in June, 1929, when, it was stated, he slept at the rear of unoccupied houses in St. Helens. The police endeavoured to trace him, but without success, and on 17th June he left his mother a note saying he was leaving home as the police were after him. According to his parents, accused has always been of effeminate habits and disposition.

From the age of sixteen he had practiced this effeminacy to the extent of masquerading as a female on several occasions. His father would have nothing to do with him while he persisted in posing as a woman. For some time after leaving school he had been employed at various collieries, and was described as a good worker.

WHY HE WORE WOMEN'S CLOTHES

Hull, who pleaded guilty, handed in a long statement, in which he gave as his reason for wearing female attire the fact that seventeen months ago he went on the stage and masqueraded as a girl and found himself successful at it. "But I am going to drop this ridiculous whim now," he said. "I am going to be a man, proud of myself, my parents and my brothers and sisters." He made a dramatic plea to the Justices for leniency. "I have a good mum and dad," he said, "and, two brothers and four sisters, I being the eldest. It is my first offence and it will be my last one.

"I have never been in a prison before, and your one week's remand has been a great lesson to me. During the whole week I have never missed praying to Almighty God that you will not send me to prison, but that but will let me go back to my mum and dad at St. Helens."

At times, Hull continued, policemen in St. Helens had been suspicious of his sex. He was once playing in a street near his home wearing boy's clothes when a policeman told him he would take him to the Police Station if he caught him in trousers again.

"HAVE MERCY"

"I was followed whatever way I dressed," he added. "In future, I am going to dress in the proper way and wear my own clothes. I hope Almighty God will have mercy on me and save me from prison and send me home to my dear mum and dad." The statement concluded, "Merciful Judge, have mercy on me!"

"He has always wanted to be a girl and more's the pity he was not," wrote the mother of the accused in a letter to the Bench. The sudden death of his brother about a year ago seemed to upset him, for since then he had never settled down, and every night he would go to the cemetery. The letter was signed, "His heartbroken mother."

Hull was bound over for twelve months with a warning. "You have behaved in a disgraceful way", said the Chairman, "and the best thing you can do is to go back to your mother." It was stated that clothing and sufficient money for his fare had been sent to him by his mother.

Eighteen months later Austin was back in the news after being arrested in Blackpool for indecency. This was the charge in the Police Review that I stated earlier. The extraordinary allegation was made that Hull had – as Cissie – been living with a man for a lengthy period of time without his partner knowing he was male.

This report comes from the Lancashire Evening Post from September 22nd 1931:

A slim, girlish-looking figure with dark wavy hair beneath a fashionable bowler hat, and wearing a full-length silk dress, black silk stockings, and a leopard skin coat with black fur collar, and high-heeled shoes, caused a sensation at St. Helens Police Court, to-day. Superintendent Cust surprised the Bench when he said: "This woman, your Worships, should appear before you as a man.

He is Austin Hull, of St. Helens. He is 22 years of age, and was at one time employed as a haulage hand at a St. Helens colliery. He is charged with committing acts of gross indecency at St. Helens between July 2nd and July 27th. I ask you to remand him in custody for one week." The Chairman (Mr. W. Collier) asked Hull if he had anything to say, and the prisoner, in a somewhat cultured feminine voice, said: "Not for a week; you can find all about it in a day." The Chairman: You will be remanded for a week. Hull:

You will treat me with leniency, won't you? Prisoner then turned and with a sweep of his silk skirt, left the courtroom.

It was then considered stylish for women to wear bowler hats. A week later Austin returned to court but this time he was dressed in a man's suit of navy blue. Long before the hearing of the case, lengthy queues had gathered outside the courtroom and the police turned hundreds of people away.

The public had all wasted their time in queuing up, as the first thing the magistrates did when the case was called was to clear the court. Only those actually involved in the proceedings – as well as the Press – were allowed to remain to hear the evidence. That often occurred in St Helens when cases perceived as distasteful were heard.

MASQUERADED AS A WOMAN

George Burrows told the court that he had met "the lady" (Hull) last January at Sutton Manor when on his way to a dance in St Helens. Austin had adopted the persona of Norma Jackson and spoke to Hull about dancing and they eventually agreed to spend the night at a cinema.

After some time the couple discussed getting married and "Norma" threatened to drown herself if George did not agree to elope. After some time they decided to live together and resided at several lodgings in St Helens – and at one point the couple went to live in London. Burrows insisted to the court that never at any time did he realise he was not living with a woman.

The magistrates committed Austin Hull to the Liverpool Assizes and on November 14th he faced a charge of having *"masqueraded as a woman for six months"*. The People newspaper (it would not become the Sunday People until the 1960s) wrote about the case in great detail under the headline *"Man's Weird Pose"*.

The paper commented how Austin had walked into the dock wearing *"smart, fashionable female attire"*, which included an ankle-length black lace gown. Asked why he wore women's clothing, Hull replied: *"Because I have no peace in St. Helens. Whatever I wore I would have no peace."*

Asked in court if he had always wanted to pass as a woman, Hull replied: *"Yes, I have, but not for indecency's sake."* After forty-five minutes of deliberation, the jury found Austin Hull guilty and sentenced him to eighteen months in prison. Upon hearing the verdict Austin burst into tears and fainted and had to be assisted from the dock.

Six weeks later on December 29th, the St Helens Reporter described how the British Sexological Society had considered Austin Hull's case and decided to petition for his release. The paper also described how London barrister John Stevenson had sent £22 to the Mayor of St Helens for the benefit of Hull's mother:

"Hull's case was discussed and the money was subscribed to help Mrs. Hull, who is in distressed circumstances," said Mr. Stevenson. "The husband has been taken to a lunatic asylum owing to worries arising from the case. Medical officers in charge of mental institutes, and many other doctors, barristers, and professional men are supporting a petition to the Home Secretary. This man has been more sinned against than sinning," Mr. Stevenson continued. "Hull's mother declares that three years ago, Hull went dressed as a man and on his way to church, was rushed to a police station and stripped because the police suspected him of being a girl masquerading as a man. To quote Hull's own words, 'I have no peace however I am dressed.'"

A report on January 26th 1932 in the Manchester Guardian *(as the Guardian was then known)* stated that Austin was a "medical curiosity". However, the petition does not appear to have helped reduced the length of his prison sentence – although I expect the support from the society that wanted the banning of homosexuality to be balanced with scientific understanding was a boost to the St Helens man's morale.

Little is known about Austin since he served his prison term, although he did return to the news in 1939. The now 30-year-old unemployed clerk of Grant Street in St Helens was charged with *"committing an act of gross indecency"* on January 1st of that year.

That was with Norman Astles from Reay Street in Widnes – who was also accused of indecency with 22-year-old James Ditchfield from Clock Face Road and 30-year-old fitter Ernest Pickering from Gorsey Lane in St Helens.

These were all clearly gay men who had simply had sexual relations at Astles' home. These private acts proved costly to all but Austin Hull, who the jury found not guilty.

Ditchfield was sentenced to three months hard labour, Pickering received six months hard labour and Norman Astles was sentenced to five years in prison.

Austin Hull appears to have died in 1987 when an Augustine Hull passed away in Lambeth. Interestingly the record states *"gender unknown"*, although I expect Austin knew!

f) <u>Thomas Byrne</u>

"If I am not right in my mind, it's probably through the war. Is anyone right who has been in it"?

The mental health trauma endured by those that fought in the First World War was probably the most unrecognised health crisis of the 20th century. Very rarely during the immediate aftermath of the Great War, was a link drawn between an individual's military service and their subsequent suicide, criminality or strange behaviour.

Sometimes those in the dock in St Helens Police Court were given a more lenient sentence because of their war record – but that is not the same as suggesting that their military service might have been the root cause of them breaking the law.

Ex-soldiers and sailors were expected to pull themselves together and only the more serious cases would end up in Rainhill Asylum.

A letter published in the St Helens Reporter on May 30th 1919 provides an insight into the unfolding mental health crisis in which an ex-soldier contrasts two events five years apart and complains how men broken in mind and body were being treated:

August, 1914 – "Your King and Country need you" Town Hall Square, St. Helens:- Hundreds of men, trying to get their names enrolled as England's bodyguard, loitering all over the place, to await their call for enrolment, to be sent to Warrington [army depot] in chars-a-banc, to be made fit and ready to meet their country's foes. No charge is made against them for obstruction or loitering. Old men giving years below their legal age to meet the foe, young, strong healthy men, ready to be trained in the hard school of discipline, who feared no foe, and later, proved their prowess against centuries-old disciplined, yet barbarous and cruel enemies, the Huns. And the Huns had to get out or get under. Our brave soldiers, our heroes, saved this Empire.

May 28th, 1919, Town Hall Square:- The same heroes, crippled, broken, gassed, and maimed. The same Town Hall Square, but not the same spirit that sent these men to be crippled, broken, gassed, and maimed. They form up in an orderly queue, to ask and receive the miserable pittance that is meted out to them for their glorious work of saving this Empire. To-day they are loitering, causing an obstruction, moved on by the police as though they were felons, loitering with intent. This town must understand it is a free town, and its freedom was won by these men who were called "Patriots" in 1914. What is the difference? Are these men, broken in their country's cause, not entitled to justice? This is not Bolshevism. It is pure British thinking, and thinking of this kind has made England what she is to-day. Never forget, England was saved by these broken men, St. Helens men included! God save our King! **A TRUE BRITON**, Sutton.

Thomas Byrne claimed that he had been broken by the war and when in court would offer up his experiences in France in explanation of his anti-social activities. Of course, it is impossible for us to know how much of his behaviour could be attributed to WW1 – but at least we have a much greater understanding of the psychological impact that conflicts have on the mental health of protagonists than they did in the 1930s.

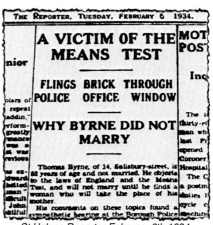

St Helens Reporter February 6th 1934

On April 9th 1930 Byrne appeared in St Helens Police Court charged with lodging out after being turfed out of the lodging house at 14 Salisbury Street. The Salvation Army later took over those premises but they used to be infamous as a place where the homeless paid a penny a night to sleep over a rope stretched across a room.

The Liverpool Echo – under the headline *"A Loquacious Prisoner"* – described how the 49-year-old had walked up and down the dock declaring he had been born British, had fought for his King and country, and that he had only done *"what any human being would do in going to sleep in a boiler house at Lowe House Church, after being turned out of his lodgings".*

Many a homeless person knew that getting arrested was a good way to get a bed in the police station for the night. Actually, up until 1953, prisoners at the St Helens cop-shop slept on planks – although I expect the incarcerated saw wood as an improvement on rope!

In 1934 when Byrne appeared in court for the 15th time, it was revealed that he had smashed a police station window in order to get out of the cold. Not only did he think that ex-soldiers had been let down by the authorities but he complained of being discriminated against because he was single. That was because in the Means Test system, single unemployed men only received the dole for a short period.

The St Helens Reporter described Byrne's subsequent court appearance on February 6th of that year:

Thomas Byrne, of 14, Salisbury-street, is 52 years of age and not married. He objects to the laws of England and the Means Test, and will not marry until he finds a woman who will take the place of his mother. His comments on these topics found a sympathetic hearing at the Borough Police Court, on Monday, when his action in throwing a brick through a pane of glass in the central police office door, Victoria-square, resulted in his appearing before the Bench.

He was charged with doing wilful damage to the extent of 24s. "I am sorry I have done it," he said, when asked to plead. P.C. Ball said he was sitting at his desk in the police office on Saturday night, when he heard a loud crash and saw splinters of glass flying from the police office door. He went to the door and Byrne walked in, saying "Here I am. It's me that done it." He agreed that he had smashed the window with a brick witness found on the floor. When charged, he said, "I did it because I want shelter." Byrne said he had a home in College-street, but he could not go into it because the application of the Means Test had turned him out. He was not married, but was that any reason why he had to be punished, punished because the laws of England said he had to be married?

"I will be married when I find a woman who will take the place of my mother," he added. Supt. Cust said defendant had appeared on fourteen previous occasions, once for a similar offence. He was then certified as a lunatic at large and went to Whiston for fourteen days. "They do not want me in some lodging-houses; I am too well-behaved," said Byrne. "They only want some poor old navvies who they can rob when they are drunk. I have a decent home and know what a decent bringing up is. If I make any mistakes, it is just like what any of you might do. It's simple. If I am not right in my mind, it's probably through the war. I am only one of the millions. Is anyone right who has been in it? I am sane enough to be among same people. Give me a chance as man to man, and I'll take on any of you."

A fine of 10s. was imposed and Byrne was ordered to pay the damage. "If you find me a job, I'll pay it," he said, as he turned from the defendants' rail.

The Irish Riot Of 1867

"A large crowd of the lowest rabble passed the time with an occasional fight and by making hideous noises"

Large-scale disturbances in Northern Ireland between Catholics and Protestants are something we still read about from time to time – and, perhaps, wonder why people of different religious denominations cannot get on with each other. But 150 years ago religious fights took place with some regularity in St Helens.

Catholics and Protestant supporters of the Orange Order were often in conflict – albeit usually in a minor way – after taunting had got out of hand. For example, in August 1869 a boy called John Halligan was charged in St Helens Petty Sessions with assaulting Ann Davies.

She told the court that he had called her an *"Orange bitch"* after seeing her carrying an orange handkerchief. Mrs Davies claimed that he and others had then given her *"vigorous abuse about the face"*. The defence was that the woman had provoked the assault after having shaken her handkerchief at a group of youths.

However, John Halligan denied playing any part in the assault to which Superintendent Ludlam interjected labelling him a *"complete outlaw"*. The man in charge of St Helens Police said the boy did as he liked and whenever the police attempted to arrest him, he fled to the house, got up the chimney, and once on the roof, would run along the eaves of a whole street of dwellings. *"The other day it took six policemen to capture him"*, Supt. Ludlam complained.

BATTLE OF THE BOYNE

But on Monday July 15th 1867 matters became far more serious when, for the first time in 29 years, a procession of Orangemen was held in St Helens to commemorate the Battle of the Boyne.

There had been much trouble on the previous occasion and so the local Catholic clergy had appealed to the town's magistrates to ban the parade. However, their pleas fell on deaf ears and at 8am on that day, members of the 219 Lodge of St Helens Orangemen assembled at their rooms in the town.

Then, led by the band of the 2nd L.R.V. rifle volunteers, the men processed down Bridge Street where they were joined at the Nelson Arms by the 123 Lodge. The enlarged procession then wended its way through Tontine Street to the railway station, where they awaited the arrival of more members of their brotherhood. These were coming to St Helens in large numbers from Liverpool, Manchester and Wigan.

ROMANIST RIOT AT ST. HELENS.
LOSS OF LIFE AND PERSONAL INJURY.
On Monday the Orangemen of the district of St. Helens and adjoining districts made a demonstration at St. Helens. The members of the 219 Lodge met at their lodge-rooms, in that town, at about eight o'clock in the morning, and, preceded by the band of the 2nd L.E.V., went in procession down Bridge-street, where they were joined by the lodge which assembles at the Nelson Arms. The procession then proceeded through Tontine - street to the railway-station, where they awaited the arrival of other members of the brotherhood from Liverpool, Manchester, and Wigan. Upon their arrival the procession was formed, led up by several bands, and the members wended their way by the route previously laid down. From the appearance of the large number of people who had assembled in the streets, it was quite evident that the Papists of the town were determined not to allow the demonstration to pass over without some manifestation of their feelings. The lower-class population of St. Helens is almost entirely Roman Catholic, and many of the large works were in consequence compelled to suspend business, while the streets were crammed with people. Upwards of 1,500 of the brotherhood of the Loyal Orange Institution of Great Britain are stated to have been present from Liverpool. The procession, amidst a heavy fall of rain, proceeded through Church-street, Bridge-street Liverpool

Manchester Courier July 17th 1867

The weather was appalling with the rain pouring down in torrents. But the soaking that they received did not in any way deter the Protestant paraders – or indeed their Catholic antagonists.

One female member of the latter was heard to say that the Virgin Mary in her wrath was emptying the contents of clouds upon the Orange marchers.

Under the headline *"Orange Demonstration At St. Helens – Desperate Riot – Personal Injury And Loss Of Life"*, the Ormskirk Advertiser on July 18th 1867 took up the story:

From the appearance of the large number of people who had assembled in the streets, it was quite evident that the demonstration would not be allowed to pass over without some manifestation of feeling. The lower-class population of

St. Helens is almost entirely Roman Catholic, and many of the large works were in consequence compelled to suspend business, whilst the streets were crammed with people. Upwards of 1,500 of the brotherhood of the Loyal Orange Institution of Great Britain are stated to have been present from Liverpool, and the bands played a succession of party tunes, which were received at every point on the road by a large party of Roman Catholics with hideous screeching and howling.

There were six bands and around 2,000 walkers wearing orange, black or purple scarfs. Each lodge was led by its own flag in either orange or purple and was followed by two members bearing their official warrant – with sword bearers on hand to guard the precious document. Beside these, many hundreds of other marchers wore the emblematic lily or the party neckerchief.

Marching through the predominantly Irish Catholic Greenbank area of St Helens was a highly provocative act. In Liverpool Road a man attempted to seize one of the marchers' banners but was arrested.

So was the assailant of Brother Thompson, one of the leaders of a St Helens lodge. The real trouble took place as the procession approached Lowe House Roman Catholic Church, as the Ormskirk Advertiser described:

A serious row took place whilst the procession was going down Cowley-hill. In the immediate neighbourhood of the Nunnery (Lowe House), a great number of the opposition party had assembled, and having supplied themselves with stones and other weapons, threw them into the ranks of the procession. The Orangemen then left the line of procession and attacked those who were hurling stones, and a scene of fighting occurred which defies description.

By the active efforts of the police, the line of march was again formed, not, however, without slight interruption from the Romanists, who made several efforts to wrest the banners from the Orangemen. Upon the procession arriving in Church-street, the first band struck up, "Croppies lie down," upon which a rush was made by the crowd to the tail end of the procession, and a fearful battle was fought in the square near to the Black Bull. Banners were wrested from the hands of the Orangemen, and a regular hand-to-hand contest was fought.

Swords and sticks were brandished, and made serious havoc with many heads. Severe cuts were made on the face, hands, and other parts of the body. In Raven-street fight succeeded fight, and the scenes enacted were of the most awful description. The ranks of the Orangemen having been broken up, owing to the incessant rain which poured down, bodies of two or three Orangemen were assailed and most severely beaten, thrown on the ground, and kicked without mercy. One poor fellow was carried away who appeared to have his skull kicked open.

The fighting continued for three hours with many battles fought in the neighbourhood of the railway station until the time arrived for the Orange brotherhood from the Liverpool lodges to depart.

What was described as a *"vast assemblage of people"* had gathered at the station to see the visitors off – but not to wish them *bon voyage.*

But once the huge party of Orangemen was safely ensconced in their carriages and the train set in motion, they were able to jeer at their Catholic opponents with some impunity – although an occasional shot from a pistol was heard.

FIREARMS

The Wigan Observer stated that several arrests were made for possessing firearms with the superintendent of police personally apprehending one man near the railway station in the act of loading a pistol.

Both sides possessed guns and as the Orange Order's train to Liverpool reached Newton-le-Willows, there was a delay while some carriages were being shunted. The passengers cheered and waved their insignia at those on the station platform and in retaliation one woman burnt an orange handkerchief. That led to a gun being fired from the train and the woman receiving a bullet wound in her shoulder.

Back in St Helens, the departure of most of the Protestant processionists did not mean all the fighting had ended. However, the town's streets were paraded by a body of constables and during the evening about thirty arrests were made.

On the following morning the rioters (all Roman Catholic except one) were placed before a magistrate and charged with breaching the peace. Most were bound over and the others were discharged.

The Ormskirk Advertiser reported that a *"large crowd of the lowest rabble of the town"* had gathered in front of the Town Hall in New Market Place where the court hearings were held. They added that these individuals had passed the time with an occasional fight and by making the *"most hideous noises"*.

The Wigan Observer in their account stated that the crowd was immense and as each prisoner was released from custody they were received with cheers and shouts from the mob. Later, a more serious incident took place, as described by the Advertiser:

Towards four o'clock an event occurred which gave renewed zest to the already inflamed passions of the Irish party. Amidst the crowd standing in Naylor-street, a man named

Casey was stabbed. Two men, named Thomas McKracken and James Mullen, both shoemakers, were charged with committing the offence, before Mr. Whitley, on Tuesday evening, and remanded until Friday. Casey was severely stabbed in the breast; and the evidences of the witnesses is to the effect that Mullen committed the act with a shoemaker's knife, and was shielded by McKracken.

However, both men would later be acquitted of the charges made against them.

The Corrupt General Election Of 1868

"Not only is bribery by drink carried on to a great extent, but personation and false representation are practised"

On September 3rd 1864 after a local election for improvement commissioners had taken place, the St Helens Newspaper wrote:

> Purity in elections is not one of the virtues for which St. Helens is famous; on the contrary, the town – but more especially the Hardshaw and Parr Ward – has become notorious for its drunkenness, its rowdyism and its total disregard of all decency, fair play and honesty in its elections. To such an extent is this system carried, that honest, respectable and intelligent men stand but a poor chance of being returned, whilst any dolt who will give away beer by gallons – give a posse of publicans a carte blanche and provide cabs and omnibuses to convey such 'fine and independent electors' as had already been made half drunk, to the polling places – is pretty certain of being returned at the head of the poll. Not only is bribery by drink carried on to a great extent, but personation and false representation are practised to a degree unknown in any other town and a great disgrace to this.

James Sexton was the Labour Member of Parliament for St Helens between 1918 and 1931. In his autobiography published in 1936, Sexton described how his father had been involved in fixing the 1868 general election from his Tontine Street home in favour of the two Conservative candidates.

St Helens was then part of the electoral constituency of South West Lancashire and there was no secret ballot. The resulting openness – with all votes being a public record – resulted in such corrupt practices as the Newspaper had described.

William Gladstone (left) and Sir James Sexton

WHOLESALE BRIBERY

General elections in the 1860s were very different to today, with voting throughout the country spread over a three-week period. Each constituency was allocated a different polling day with the date for the district of St Helens (which included Widnes) being November 24th 1868.

Only 2,210 men were enfranchised *(less than 10% of the town's male and female adult population)* and so every vote mattered – as Sir James Sexton described in his book:

Open voting and wholesale bribery were then the chief features of any Parliamentary election. St Helens was then the most important part of a county constituency returning two members on a limited but wholly corrupt franchise. One of the candidates was Mr. Gladstone, a whole-hearted supporter of the suggested Ballot Act. He was being opposed by a Mr. Cross. My father espoused the democratic side, at the same time taking full advantage of all that the existing system had to offer. There was in our backyard a fairly large shed, used sometimes as a washhouse, sometimes as a stable.

My father took charge of the shed on polling day. My job was to watch the return of the voting, which was posted up every hour at the grocer's shop, which was the polling booth, and carry the information to my father, whose task was to hunt up voters and 'persuade' them that it was worth their while to vote as he thought they should. If the figures showed any shrinking on our side, father assembled his forces and marched them into the shed, to be supplied with beer, tobacco, cards and bribes, and to remain there in readiness for any emergency.

The grim irony of the procedure is still with me. On the walls of the passage, as on those all over the town – even on the shed itself – huge posters depicted the honest blacksmith at his anvil, leaning on his sledge-hammer, and most indignantly spurning an offer of five pounds for his vote! I have since wondered whether his indignation was based on principle or price.

Eight days before the date set for the election in St Helens, William Gladstone had arrived in the town and received a rock star reception from its citizens.

The Liberal party leader planned to deliver a speech in the Volunteer Hall and thousands of excited townsfolk mobbed him from the moment he set foot on St Helens' soil.

The St Helens Newspaper wrote:

The principal streets were literally alive with human beings as if all the houses had disgorged their residents, and poured them out upon the thoroughfares. Around the railway station the crowding was tremendous, and the most eager anticipation was depleted in every face. When the expected train arrived, the cheers that went up from thousands of throats were deafening and incessant.

Crowds of excited persons thronged, pushing, struggling and wrestling towards the platform, until it was difficult for the object of the demonstration to make his way to the carriages. As soon as it was known that he was accompanied by Mrs. Gladstone, cheers arose for the highly respected lady, and blessings were showered upon her from all sides.

DENSE MASSES

The first task of the man who many believe was the greatest statesman of the 19th century was to safely navigate his passage through the *"dense masses"* occupying Church Street.

Not everyone was glad to see Gladstone and a stone was thrown and crackers were set off as his 20-strong convoy of horse-drawn carriages traversed Hardshaw Street.

According to the Liberal-supporting St Helens Newspaper, these acts *"in an evil direction"* had nearly caused a catastrophe through the frightening of horses in a crowded street.

The paper then described the scene as the procession wended its way towards the Volunteer Hall:

The route lay through Church-street, Baldwin-street, Duke-street, and Mill-street, and the feeling of a great proportion of the residents was evinced in brilliant illuminations. Flags hung at intervals bearing mottoes, which were lighted by handsome paper balloons, of fancy patterns. As the carriages rolled past the Fleece Inn, the Liberal committee rooms, the cheering was tremendous, and in the opener space near the Sefton Arms, impulsive multitudes pressed forward, in the vain hope that the "People's Premier" could grasp all the honest hands stretched out to him. Many did succeed in their wishes, and they fell back gratified.

Long before Gladstone was due to arrive at the Volunteer Hall in Mill Street, large crowds had besieged the building waiting patiently for admission. Once the doors were opened what was described as a tremendous rush occurred and every part of the hall was rapidly filled.

The walls inside were covered in slogans such as "Gladstone, The People's Premier", "God Speed The Right", "Peace and Prosperity", "Free Trade and Cheap Food", "Justice To Ireland" and the slightly odd, "Keep Moving".

Gladstone's speech mainly focused on Ireland – but he did mention how Prescot's many watch movement-makers were suffering through a depression in the United States caused by their civil war.

POLLING BOOTHS

When the election took place eight days later, five polling booths were erected on waste ground in Ormskirk Street, with each booth dedicated to voters from a different part of the district. Voting began at 8am and the St Helens Newspaper said it was conducted in a business-like manner.

The election agents had organised as many horse-drawn vehicles as they could muster in order to ferry electors to the booths. The Newspaper labelled them as *"motley a collection as could well be imagined."* The Wigan Observer went even further in their description of the variety of vehicles employed, particularly by the Liberals – which included large, horse-drawn buses:

> Every possible machine of every conceivable shape was dragged into the service of Messrs. Gladstone and Grenfell. To their use were devoted shandries, gigs, dog-carts, jaunting cars, waggonetts, phaetons, broughams, cars, handsoms, four-wheelers, carriages, coaches, and last, though in a useful sense, assuredly not least, those modest conveyances which are distinguished by the name of traps. In omnibuses of every size and conformation the Liberals in the St. Helens district most decidedly excelled. They brought in their voters from Widnes, Eccleston, Rainford, Rainhill, and the other townships of the district by means of these cumbrous vehicles, which were respectively drawn by two, three, or four horses, according as the necessities of the locality might require.

There were between forty to fifty policemen on duty around the polling booths armed with cutlasses in case of trouble. The Observer described a few hand-to-hand fights and wrote that some young men carrying sticks had marched *"to and fro in the streets, evidently courting a row"*.

However, little notice was taken of them and the day passed without serious trouble – although some gentlemen in making their way through the crowds were relieved of their gold watches.

UNWASHED AMAZONS

Women were not, of course, permitted to vote but some wished to participate just the same. The Liberal party committee was based in a nearby house and 200 young females stood outside. But their gathering did not impress the St Helens Newspaper:

These amazons, most of whom were of the type denonnuation 'unwashed', and we may add, unkempt, gave evidence that they were not only endowed with strong political, and in some cases, polemical prejudices, but also with rare strength and elasticity of windpipe, to enable them to make the public acquainted with the fact.

As James Sexton stated, hourly updates of the votes cast were posted for all to see – which meant candidates did not have to rely on exit polls or wait for a late night count to learn how well they had fared. That was a feature of the open ballot that fuelled corruption.

But despite Gladstone's tremendous popularity in St Helens, the small electorate with the aid of corrupt practices preferred the Conservative candidates – although only by 94 votes and the Tories also took the overall constituency of SW Lancs.

James Sexton provided first-hand testimony of the corrupt activities in aid of the Conservative party. However, what we don't know is how clean a fight the Liberal candidates' election team had fought.

How the Illustrated Police News of October 17th 1868 depicted a riot

After the St Helens' results were declared, the victorious Conservatives celebrated at the Raven Inn and cannons were fired for over an hour. The day had gone fairly smoothly – which couldn't be taken for granted like today.

Election riots took place in some places (such as Blackburn) and in Warrington three men were severely beaten with sticks and stones for voting for the "wrong" candidate.

In fact, when the results at Warrington were declared the winning candidate accused the loser of *"bribery, treating and intimidation"* and the loser's agent said the election result was illegal and steps would be taken to have it set aside.

It wasn't until 1872 that elections became secret and most of the issues of corruption and violence that dogged many a poll went away, although not immediately.

Despite Gladstone losing the election he was undaunted, as he had a backstop position. Candidates were then allowed to stand in two constituencies and the Liberal leader was more successful when standing for Parliament in Greenwich.

Three weeks after giving his speech in St Helens, William Ewart Gladstone began the first of his four terms as prime minister as part of a remarkable political career that lasted for over sixty years.

The Frogs That Fell From The Thatto Heath Sky

*"The road between Thatto Heath Library and
the reservoir was black with frogs"*

Thatto Heath Library, near where frogs supposedly rained down

Frog catching (and eating) used to be very popular in parts of St Helens. The Liverpool Daily Post reported in 1858 that great quantities of frogs were consumed in the town and that boys were kept busy catching them. A Daily Post correspondent came across a number of lads aged around nine or ten up to their knees in a pond in Sutton Heath fishing for frogs.

The reporter described seeing several pounds of the hind parts of skinned frogs stacked on one side of the pond, with their redundant foreparts and skins stored nearby. Upon questioning the lads as to what they would be doing with the hind bits, they replied: *"We putten them i'th' frying pan, and then i'th' hoon, and then they are gradely good."*

However, the good folks of Thatto Heath did not have to bother fishing for frogs – as the amphibians simply rained down on them from the sky! Or so it was claimed. And the event in 1894 was not a one-off affair, as it was reported to have happened twice in less than forty-eight hours.

These extraordinary downpours were supposed to have taken place close to the library in Thatto Heath Road, which later became a police station and then served as council offices.

SHOWER OF FROGS

On July 16th 1894 under the headline *"Shower of Frogs at Thatto Heath – Remarkable Phenomenon"*, the Liverpool Mercury described the first occurrence:

> Residents of Thatto Heath, St. Helens, are to-day concerned over what is apparently a shower of frogs or toads. Shortly before one o'clock a sharp shower passed over the district and lasted several minutes. Nothing was noticed before the shower, but when it ceased the road between Thatto Heath Library and the reservoir was literally black with frogs. The creatures were all of the same size, the body being about half an inch long. They were alive and quickly made their way into the adjoining fields.

On the day after the supposed shower of frogs and toads had occurred, the St Helens Examiner sent a reporter to Thatto Heath. However, he said that in spite of the minutest search, little evidence of such creatures could be seen on the streets and in the fields. This was explained by the claim that within hours of the amphibians' descent from the sky, many visitors had flocked to

Thatto Heath and collected them. The frogs and toads were then taken in their *"fifties and hundreds"* into St Helens – presumably to sell to townsfolk as foodstuff.

The Examiner reporter had chosen the wrong day to carry out his inspection, as on the following morning the frogs reprised their performance. Or so it was said.

But the newspaper was now convinced of the genuineness of the claims and published this account on July 21st:

> **A SHOWER OF FROGS AT THATTO HEATH.**
>
> **REMARKABLE PHENOMENON.**
>
> Residents of Thatto Heath, St. Helens, were on Monday concerned over what was apparently a shower of frogs or toads. Shortly before one o'clock a sharp shower passed over the district and lasted several minutes. Nothing was noticed before the shower, but when it ceased, the road between Thatto Heath, Library and the reservoir was literally black with frogs. The creatures were all of the same size, the body being half an inch long. They were alive and quickly made their way into the adjoining fields.
>
> **ANOTHER SHOWER.**
>
> The greatest excitement was manifest in Thatto Heath, St. Helens on Wednesday, there having been another shower of frogs or toads. Rain had fallen heavily in the district during the early hours of the morning, and workmen passing along the road to their work at half past five o'clock were surprised to see the toads (for such they have turned out to be) in greater numbers even than on Monday. In fact, they could scarcely walk along without treading on the small creatures. They had come down with the rain there is no doubt whatever expressed. The shoals that made their

St Helens Examiner July 21st 1894

The greatest excitement was manifest in Thatto Heath, St. Helens on Wednesday, there having been another shower of frogs or toads. Rain had fallen heavily in the district during the early hours of the morning, and workmen passing along the road to their work at half-past five o'clock were surprised to see the toads (for such they have turned out to be) in greater numbers even than on Monday. In fact, they could scarcely walk along without treading on the small creatures.

They had come down with the rain there is no doubt whatever expressed....and the fields which are known as the "Spout" fields, near Springfield-row, are full of the creatures. People who at first were not inclined to believe the report that they had come down in the rain can now find no other supposition, and the whole of the residents of Thatto Heath are discussing the phenomenon. Large numbers on Wednesday visited the place, the toads being on the road all morning.

Of course there is always some cynic that wants to ruin a good yarn! This is what the South Wales Echo had to say about the events in Thatto Heath:

Nature is bountiful – perhaps too bountiful – to the inhabitants of Thatto Heath, St. Helen's. If their land has not, like that of Pharaoh of old, brought forth frogs, their skies have rained toads upon them, and that twice within three days. There was a shower of toads on Monday, and another yesterday morning, and, naturally enough, we read that "no doubt whatever is expressed" as to the toads having "come down with the rain." Far be it from us to attempt, by a misplaced scepticism, to deprive the population of Thatto Heath of any legitimate satisfaction they may have derived from this remarkable phenomenon. Showers are frequent enough this summer, and now that we are approaching the latter end of July one may expect their component atoms to assume various and highly interesting forms. We shall no doubt before long hear of showers of big gooseberries, showers of sea serpents, and showers of "new women." Why not, then, showers of toads?

The "new women" reference concerned a feminist movement of independent career women that was gaining some support in Britain and America.

Another aerial phenomenon was said to have taken place in St Helens in September 1860 when it was reported that millions of gnats had visited the town. The strange event began at noon when the sky turned dark and a thunderstorm looked to be on the cards.

But instead of rain, millions of flying insects manifested themselves over St Helens. A particular focus of their activities was the middle of the market place and the gnats continued flying about until evening. The Manchester Courier called it a *"phenomenon never before known in the town"*.

Pilkington's Elephant Glass

"Daisy said no, and all the loaves of bread, persuasion, pushing, and shouting would not make her change her mind"

Elephants are thought to be the strongest animals alive. And so being large and highly visual are ideal participants for publicity stunts when a demonstration of brute strength is needed. Well, in theory, perhaps… But Pilkington's learnt in 1932 that theory and practice don't always go hand in hand – especially when dealing with a living creature with a mind of its own!

The St Helens firm had developed what they were calling "armour-plate glass" and began manufacturing it at their Cowley Hill plant. Ordinary polished plate-glass was subjected to a toughening process that involved a sudden cooling which was said to give the glass considerable strength and flexibility.

However, they needed a gimmick to show its strength off to the world and boost orders. After all, such protective glass that cost much more than ordinary glass would have a limited number of uses. There were only so many jeweller's shops whose windows could be replaced.

DAISY THE ELEPHANT

So, in order to spread the word an elephant called Daisy was hired to visit Pilkington's London warehouse. The beast belonging to Chapman's Circus weighed over three tons and it was intended that Daisy would be suspended from the one-inch thick glass as a test of its strength.

Today, we would consider the experiment cruel. But that was not how it was perceived then and the drop – if anything went wrong – was only small, limiting the risk of harm to Daisy. Under their headline *"Test For Armour Plate Glass – Will It Swing An*

Elephant?", the St Helens Reporter on December 2nd 1932 described what was intended to happen:

> It [the elephant] will be hoisted up by a steam crane and suspended in mid-air by means of a giant leather strap, from a piece of glass one inch thick. If the glass bears this test it will be a novel proof of all the claims that have been made for it, and the novelty of the test will provide admirable publicity for the firm.

Pilkington's boffins were confident that their new product would be able to take the strain and the glass giant would consequently get loads of free publicity. The Press were all invited to attend the event but elephants are exceptionally smart creatures and Daisy had not agreed to the stunt – it was her owners who had done that.

So she sensibly turned her nose (or, should I say, trunk!) up at the whole affair. Daisy refused to cooperate, despite much coaxing by her handlers. The Guardian explained exactly what had occurred:

> The less imaginative spectators crowded to the edge of the floor and for two long hours watched Daisy, the circus elephant, thwart the attempts of her owner, her keeper, and other intrepid assistants, to connect a noose on her harness with the hook that dangled beneath the piece of glass. This hung from a crane fixed on a lorry. As the crane could not swing round to follow Daisy, Daisy had to be brought underneath it. She nearly broke the hearts of her commanders, for each time they manoeuvred her into position, she decided to go somewhere else. Finally, a door rolled open and Daisy, followed by hosts of children who had been watching her through chinks in or under the doors, marched away majestically down Shepherdess Walk, leaving behind her evidence of her enormous strength in the crumpled section of a huge steel shutter against which she had flung herself.

However, Pilkingtons had a back-up plan. Or perhaps they expected that the elephant demonstration would be accomplished so quickly that they needed a secondary test for their new product.

And so the strength of the armour-plate glass was tested against the weight of a lorry loaded with a dozen people and it successfully held the strain.

Although the elephant stunt had failed, Pilks still received lots of free publicity. In their report the Edinburgh Evening News wrote:

Daisy said no, and all the loaves of bread, persuasion, pushing, and shouting would not make her change her mind. SHE – Resolutely declined to be suspended; Shook her head so violently that she unseated the keeper from her neck; Leaned against a steel revolving door and made a three-foot bulge in it; Tugged along a motor crane weighing tons with little apparent effort; Sat down and trumpeted. So Daisy was led away and a four-ton motor lorry was substituted. The piece of glass from which it was suspended was 45in. by 24in. and was an inch thick. With the weight of the lorry it sagged visibly. Man after man climbed on to the suspended lorry until the glass smashed with the 13th man.

Undeterred by the glass giant's failed experience with elephants in London, Pilks decided to have a second bash with the beasts at their base in St Helens. Three elephants from Chapman's Circus happened to be appearing at the Theatre Royal that week – and so the trio was taken to Cowley Hill and persuaded to perform.

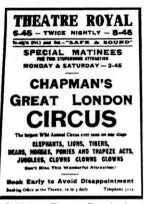

St Helens Theatre Royal advert

The total weight of the elephants – including the platform and their trainers – came to 5 tons, beating the weight of the lorry in London by a ton. Unlike Daisy in the capital, the prospect of safety in numbers appears to have calmed any unwillingness by the threesome to take part in the stunt.

Three young elephants and three men suspended at St. Helen's, Lancs, from a piece of armourplate glass, one inch thick. The total weight supported, including the suspending tackle, was over five tons. The glass is of British manufacture.

Photograph and caption published in the Daily Mirror on December 12th 1932

This report was published in the Liverpool Echo:

The elephants readily took their places on the stand, and the electric crane began its gradual lift until the wooden blocks at the corners of the frame could be removed. Elephants and structure were suspended with the sheet of glass above them for over two minutes. Then the elephants backed to one corner. This caused the platform to tilt and begin to swing. The balance being disturbed the glass broke, but if the animals could have been better controlled the test would have lasted longer.

Although St Helens' main industries were coal mining and glass making, in many British people's minds the town was synonymous with just one product – pill making. That was because of the fortune spent on advertising by Beecham's.

The Westfield Street pharmaceutical firm did not miss a trick when it came to promoting their products, spending hundreds of thousands of pounds a year by the end of the 19th century.

When on two occasions in November 1889 an elephant belonging to Sangers circus got loose and raided food stores in Accrington and Chorley, the Pall Mall Gazette published this jokey article:

There is a burglarious elephant about just now which will put any of Mr. Barnum's elephants to the blush. On Monday he broke into some stores in Accrington, and stole some jam and onions, which he found highly delectable. Not content with this feat, he broke out again yesterday in Chorley, another Lancashire town, selecting groceries for his prey.

He devoured a whole cheese, two boxes of biscuits, and other goods. When the show reaches St. Helen's, which is in the Lancashire circuit, the elephant will, no doubt, drop into Mr. Beecham's establishment and help himself to a few hundred boxes of pills to counteract the ill effects of his Chorley and Accrington feasts, which were rather a rich mixture.

Beecham's imaginative advertising department was unleashed by the prospect of the *"burglarious elephant"* restoring its tummy with their pills and published the advertisement shown below. Sadly there are no reports of food shops being raided in St Helens!

A GIGANTIC CURE.

Curious Coffin And Graveyard Stories

"They Don't Bury 'Em Like They Used To"

JOHN GEORGE ACKARY,
COFFIN MAKER,
AND GENERAL UNDERTAKER.
Chancery Lane, Parr Stocks,
AND AT 24, COLLEGE STREET,
ST. HELENS.

J. G. A. begs to inform his friends and the public generally that he intends to give his particular attention to this branch of his business (Joiner and Builder), having had considerable experience therein. He has made arrangements which will enable him to execute all orders whether from the town or country, at the shortest notice.

Parties leaving their address at either of the above places of business will be waited upon immediately and their orders promptly attended to.

COFFINS made and mounted in any style, to suit the various tastes and circumstances of the relatives and every article warranted perfect. Infants' and Children's coffins always on hand, ready for immediate use, at prices ranging from 2s. 6d. each and upwards.

This large advert from undertaker and coffin maker John Ackary was printed prominently on the front page of the St Helens Newspaper in 1869. It must have been a cheery sight every Saturday morning to pick up your weekly paper and see pictures of coffins staring back at you! That said people were then hugely pragmatic about death with so much of it about.

On January 1st 1870 the Newspaper published this editorial on the coming of the New Year:

Joy bells ring, and humanity makes merry, at the advent of the mysterious stranger [1870], forgetful for the moment, perhaps, that we have all just completed another step towards the grave to which we are hastening.

Yes, a very joyous thought! Note John Ackary's reference in his advert to *"children's coffins always on hand at prices ranging from*

2s 6d upwards". And with child mortality being extremely high in the 19th century, there was likely to have been a big stock needed.

Many undertakers like Ackary were skilled carpenters who crafted their own coffins. A hundred years later on August 14th 1970 – under the headline *"They Don't Bury 'Em Like They Used To"* – the St Helens Reporter published this article lamenting how standards had declined:

> Silver haired undertaker Bertie Woodward, 76, warns us that we're in the middle of a "funeral revolution". "Burials," he said sadly, "just aren't the same anymore. They don't bury 'em the same nowadays." Bertie, of Broad Oak Road, Parr, has been in the burial business most of his life. He retired last year. "I've noticed a tremendous change in my life-time," he said. "I've been burying Parr people for 50 years or more and making their coffins. In the old days people used to want a fine, hand-made oak coffin. Now they're content with a cheap elm one. I remember the hours and hours I've spent in my father's workshop making the coffins. It was a real art then.
>
> But now people seem to only want the cheapest. But they always want big cars and lots of flowers. But then the price of things has gone up a tremendous lot. New graves for instance used to cost £2 10s but now they're £9. And once you could get a beautiful coffin for £10. They vary in price now. But the cheapest is about £18. Then lots of people want cremations instead of burials. No," he said, "It's not the same at all. There's a real revolution going on. In a way I'm glad I'm out of it all."

COFFINS IN THE STREET

I expect Bertie would not liked to have found one of his carefully crafted coffins left lying about in the street. However, on July 12th

1904 the Daily Mirror described how PC Featherstone had made such an early morning discovery in Cotham Street:

A St. Helens policeman was startled to find, in the early hours of the morning, a coffin, with a brass plate bearing the name and age of an old man, lying in one of the main streets. It was empty, and he conveyed it to the Town Hall. It was subsequently discovered that two local undertakers, among whom there is great competition, had each made a coffin for the dead man. The undertaker who delivered the second coffin took the body out of the first, which he sent to the premises it came from. But these were closed when it arrived, and the singular course was adopted of leaving it in the street.

Seven decades later under the headline *"Mystery Coffin Awaits Owner"*, the St Helens Reporter of March 17th 1972 described how the police had received an anonymous telephone call alerting them to a coffin that had been abandoned in a hedge at Peasley Cross.

The casket had previously been seen being carried along Marshalls Cross Road by a group of teenagers. A police spokesman with a dry sense of humour told the paper:

"With something like this, when it seems unlikely that it will be claimed, we always put it in the dead section."

The poor people from the predominantly Irish district of Greenbank witnessed many deaths and these generated some curious coffin-related stories. Often these were related to wakes that had got out of hand. This article published in the St Helens Examiner of November 26th 1887 was a particularly sad one:

On Wednesday night Police-constable Henebery, was on duty near the Lingholme Hotel, [when] he saw two women, each carrying a coffin under her arm, going towards the cemetery. The women were from Greenbank, one of the lowest parts of the town, and were taking to the cemetery the bodies of twin stillborn infants of a relative. One woman was in such a tipsy condition that she fell to the ground several times, the box falling from her hold. She at the same time used such disgraceful language that the officer was compelled to take her to the Town Hall [police station], where she was placed in the cells.

The other woman, who had been allowed to proceed with the two boxes or coffins, one under each arm, was also in drink, and allowed one of the boxes to fall. She, however, with assistance, again started on her way, and when Henebery returned from the police station, he found the woman inside an inn at Denton's Green, with the boxes reared outside. On proceeding to the cemetery the woman was refused admittance, and the interment could not take place until a certificate and the necessary fees obtained.

COFFIN MADE BY CONTRACT

A large number of people within the St Helens district were members of so-called friendly societies during the 19th century. The insurance money that they paid meant their funerals were taken care of when they died.

Although I expect few folk went so far in planning the arrangements for their own demise as an unnamed Methodist minister from Crank did.

The Liverpool Mercury told his story on March 1st 1859:

Midway between St. Helen's and Rainford is a place called Crank-brow, where a few scattered cottages and farm houses are situate. At one of the latter lives a very eccentric old gentleman, belonging to a religious body of Methodists there prevailing, and prayer meetings are occasionally held in this house. A few nights ago, whilst he and a number of his brethren were engaged in solemn devotion, they were suddenly stopped and somewhat startled by a loud knocking at the door, followed by the entrance of an undertaker and his assistants, carrying a large coffin, which, being deposited in their midst, the old gentleman at once commenced examining inside and out, and finding all satisfactory and the flannel lining nice and complete, he dismissed the living intruders.

The congregation, hitherto gazing on in mute astonishment, now naturally sought an explanation, when the eccentric individual calmly informed them that some time ago when he buried his wife at Liverpool, he was sadly imposed upon by the undertaker there, and he had resolved to get his own coffin made by contract; and chuckled at the idea of having obtained one quite as substantial and far more comfortable for £1 cheaper. He has since got the plate affixed, inscribed with blank dates, and now rejoices in his speculation.

ANCIENT BONES

Workmen in St Helens have made the unpleasant discovery of decaying coffins containing ancient bones on several occasions.

In the late 1950s, the excavation of the inner ring road on Tontine Street unearthed an old Wesleyan Methodist burial ground.

The church had been built in 1815 but was demolished seventy-five years later after a grand new building had been constructed in Corporation Street – but the old graves connected with the church had seemingly been forgotten about.

Birthplace of the Late Rt. Hon. R. J. Seddon, St. Helens.

This beautiful cottage at Eccleston Park is the birthplace of Richard Seddon, who, between 1893 and 1906, served as the Prime Minister of New Zealand. The photograph became a popular picture postcard that many people mailed to friends and family.

However, in April 1922, workers widening Prescot Road dug into the ground adjacent to the cottage and disturbed a collection of broken bones. None were complete in skeleton form and no whole skull was recovered. The workmen also found an old stone cross in a good state of preservation, which had existed when Richard Seddon resided in the cottage.

The St Helens Reporter on April 28th 1922 wrote:

> When he was last in St. Helens, the late Mr. Seddon passed the remark that in his day there was a cross in that plot of ground but he missed it on his last visit.

It was, at first, thought that the discovery had been part of an old burial ground. However, a later edition of the Reporter stated that it was now believed that there had not been a graveyard at that particular location after all.

Many years earlier, when the road from Toll Bar to Portico was being made, the labourers had cut through a portion of an old graveyard on Eccleston Hill. A new home had to be found for the bones and skulls that the road building had disturbed and they were re-interred in the field by the Seddon cottage.

That accounts for the fact that the skulls and skeletons were not complete when dug up in 1922. Being hundreds of years old and very fragile, the bones had been badly damaged during their transfer.

Two old graveyards on the south side of Church Street in St Helens have been the source of unwanted discoveries of the dead. Old cemeteries tend to be the hidden repositories of what can be thousands of unmarked graves. And so if burials take place outside of the known limits of the churchyard, surprises can be in store when excavations take place.

Only two sets of remains were discovered in 1953 when GPO workmen were digging at what had been the burial ground of the Independent Chapel. This had been in Ormskirk Street and had by then become the site of the Congregational Church (later NatWest Bank).

A licence had to obtained from the Home Office to reinter the old bones in St Helens Cemetery and strangely – if not appropriately – the operation had to be carried out at the dead of night. On September 22nd 1953 the St Helens Reporter described the ghoulish task:

The human remains and pieces of coffin which workmen found recently near Ormskirk Street Congregational Church while carrying out excavations for the laying of a new G.P.O. line were re-interred in the early hours of Saturday morning in the borough cemetery. The coffins and bones lay in what is believed to have been part of the old churchyard which was incorporated in the highway when road-widening operations took place about 1927.

All coffins under headstones were removed and re-interred and a list made at that time but apparently the two found recently had been missed. Digging operations began about midnight on Saturday and the remains were re-interred in the Nonconformist portion of the cemetery about 6 a.m. under the memorial erected when the first coffins were placed there in 1927. The re-interment was carried out by the staff of the Parks and Cemeteries department under the direction of the superintendent, Mr. E. Thornton.

QUEER CASE OF TWO JOHN DOLANS

This is a photograph of Samuel Brighouse, the longstanding coroner for SW Lancashire, who in June 1933 had what the Daily Mirror dubbed the *"Queer Case of Two John Dolans"* to sort out.

The coroner had held an inquest on an 85-year-old inmate of Whiston Poor Law Institution called John Dolan who had died after a fall. The man's wife identified the body as that of her husband from whom she'd been separated for some years and the inquest jury returned a verdict of misadventure.

But later his stepdaughters visited the Institution *(that had formerly been known as Whiston Workhouse)* to pay their respects and upon viewing the body immediately declared that a mistake had been made. The dead man had a good head of hair – but their stepfather had been bald and also did not have contracted fingers on his right hand. The Daily Mirror described what happened next:

The West Lancashire coroner yesterday informed Mr. John Dolan, of Whiston, that he had not held an inquest on him. He went on to express the hope that he never would hold an inquest on him. The coroner was investigating the identities of two John Dolans. The living John Dolan was handed a photograph of his namesake in his coffin. After a glance at it he exclaimed: "Oh, no, I'm not having that." He refused to accept the coroner's view that they were as much alike as two peas.

The coroner said that on June 21 a verdict of Death by misadventure was recorded on a man identified by Mrs. Harriet Dolan, of Albert-street, St. Helens [off North Road], as her husband, from whom she was separated. "We had the body photographed and the finger-prints taken," said the coroner, "not only of the John Dolan who was dead, but of another John Dolan who is now here. I have no power to reopen the inquest. All that was put on the certificate is correct. The only mistake was that Harriet Dolan said that John Dolan lying dead was her husband, and he was not."

BODY DISAPPEARED

It is, of course, human nature to make mistakes – but when it comes to burials such errors are not merely an inconvenience but can severely exacerbate the distress of grieving families.

On January 11th 1920 Bessie Pimblett passed away in the St Helens Sanatorium in Peasley Cross. The little girl from Broad Oak Road died of diphtheria and her body was removed to the hospital mortuary. Two days later her parents decided to pay their final visit to Bessie prior to the child's funeral and found her body had disappeared.

Earlier that day the funeral of Herbert Hudson of Lyon Street had taken place at St Helens Cemetery and Bessie had been buried instead.

The families considered the mistake inexplicable as the children looked quite different, were of the opposite sex and had their names pinned to their bodies. But it was a far from simple matter to exhume Bessie's body from the grave and bury her again in a cemetery in Parr, as had been planned.

Dr Joseph Cates, the town's Medical Officer, had to despatch an assistant to London to obtain permission from the Home Office. Also, the Lord Bishop of Liverpool had to be visited and a permit obtained. However, these formalities were quickly undertaken and Bessie's funeral took place two days later than planned.

GRISLY FIND

A lack of care when burying the body of a child led to the next distressing example. On April 5th 1918, Cpl. Robert Bryant from Hamer Street was visiting his wife's grave at St Thomas' cemetery, off Knowsley Road.

While walking down the main path with his sister-in-law, he noticed a sack with a small hand protruding from it. At first he thought it was the remains of a dog but upon seeing the feet of a child, reported his grisly find to the police.

After an examination, Dr Eric Reid reported that the child had only been dead for a week and it was his considered opinion that the baby had not been stillborn.

The little boy bore a deep wound across the middle of his body and had seemingly been murdered. But there was another mystery, as

144

well as the identity of the killer, as was explained at the child's inquest.

Dr Reid told the coroner that his post-mortem examination had shown that a sharp instrument had made the wound. This had cut through the liver causing death, although curiously some gauze had been placed into the wound. This had been *"fairly neatly"* stitched up using the same type of thick catgut that surgeons used.

The coroner Frederick Jones said: *"It is quite clear that this child has been done to death by some person"* and the inquest jury returned a verdict of *"wilful murder by some person unknown"*.

Inquests were always held rapidly after death – and sometimes took place far too soon before all the facts could be known.

After a police investigation it was revealed that much of what was stated by the medical expert had been wrong. The baby boy had, in fact, been stillborn at St Helens Corporation's Old Whint Maternity Home in Haydock on March 19th.

A surgeon had decided to examine the child's organs to check for signs of a "hereditary taint". The wound was then sown up and the body handed over for burial.

The interment took place in St Thomas's cemetery but they didn't do a very good job, as it was believed that children had found the remains and been dragging them around in a sack.

This was then found by Corporal Robert Bryant when walking down a path to visit the grave of his wife – who he had only buried two days earlier. How distressing for all concerned – especially the mother of the baby.

Let's hope the child was given a proper re-burial and not deposited in an unmarked grave. As stated, all St Helens' cemeteries contain thousands of unmarked graves, with most holding six basic coffins vertically stacked.

A door would often separate the simple coffins with soil placed on top and the plot usually remained open until it had been filled. This might well have been how the St Thomas' baby came to be missing from its grave.

CURIOUS INSCRIPTIONS

There are some unusual inscriptions on St Helens' gravestones. Within St Helens Cemetery there is one that reads:

"I was not, I was; I did some work and now am not."

Mr L. Fletcher of Hillside Close in Billinge described this memorial in a letter to the St Helens Reporter in January 1985, explaining:

"This is a shortened biography of the dead person. I think this verse aptly sums up most of our brief existence on this earth."

The newspaper article also reported on a tombstone in Billinge Parish Churchyard that bears a crest featuring an adder.

This forms a circle with its tail in its mouth and encloses a pair of bat's wings and a human skull. The Reporter's editor wrote:

> The story behind this, I am told, is that one day in 1720 it was too hot for harvesting so a young farm labourer, George Smith, decided to have a nap on Billinge Hill. While he was asleep an adder bit him and he died. George's wife, Kitty, ordered a coffin-shaped stone tombstone and later, on her own death, was buried with her husband beneath it.

MYSTERY SKULL ON GRAVESTONE

Human skulls could also appear on memorials in gloomy graveyards in other ways. On June 5th 1965, under the headline

"Mystery Skull On Gravestone", this image was published in the St Helens Reporter:

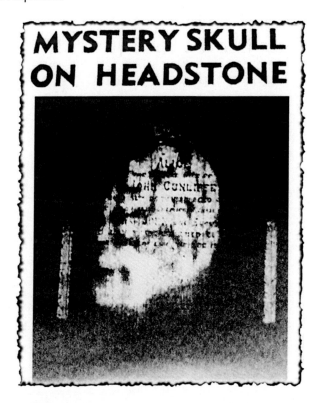

The accompanying text described how people were pouring into the churchyard at St James in Haydock in order to see what was claimed as a supernatural manifestation.

However, the local vicar, the Rev. Spencer Wilson, thought that the sudden appearance of the profile of a human skull on a memorial to a deceased parishioner had a more rational explanation – as the paper described:

Some people living in the vicinity believe the skull has appeared to signify something, and are convinced it is the work of the supernatural. But yesterday the vicar (Rev. S. W.

147

Wilson) told the Reporter: "There is nothing like that. This impression has been caused by wind and rain." The eerie outline, said to have appeared during Wednesday night or on Thursday morning, was spotted by children leaving the parish school nearby. It was not apparent when they walked through the graveyard earlier on Thursday.

The tiny churchyard has suddenly become a hive of activity, and scores of people flocked to see the skull on Thursday evening when the news spread. The grave is situated a few yards away from a communal grave where more than 100 miners were interred following a disaster at Wood Pit which overlooks the churchyard.

GHOST LIGHT

Twenty-eight years earlier there had been another strange graveyard phenomenon that was explained away as a natural event. The St Helens Cemetery *"ghost light"* or *"ghostly glow"* or *"gleam"* could be discerned soon after dark from points on Rainford Road where there was little street lighting.

The story was covered by a number of newspapers, including the Sheffield Independent, who placed it on its front page under the headline *"Ghostly Gleam In Cemetery"*.

The paper described how a party of investigators had kept a night watch on the cemetery in an attempt to *"lay the ghost"*. The only suggestion they could offer was that a glass or chromium fitting

GHOSTLY GLEAM IN CEMETERY

THE appearance of a ghost light in St. Helens Cemetery has caused a remarkable amount of interest in the district.

Shortly after dark a ghostly glow can sometimes be seen from the East Lancashire road and from Rainford road.

The absence of street lighting at this point makes the "light" plainly discernible from the roadway.

Recently a party of investigators went and kept a night watch in an attempt to lay the ghost. The only suggestion they could afterwards offer was that a glass or chromium fitting on a gravestone or wreath was reflecting the head-lights of a passing car.

CONSTANT BRIGHTNESS

Mr. Austin Watkinson, who lives near-by, discounts the car headlights suggestion. He said yesterday, "I have known of the light for over a year. I and a friend have often seen it at night.

Sheffield Independent May 3rd 1937

148

on a gravestone was reflecting the headlights of passing cars.

On May 7th 1937 the St Helens Reporter described how their reporters had made lengthy investigations into the phenomenon and come to the conclusion that it was an entirely natural occurrence. The paper published their explanation under the headline:

"The Truth About The Cemetery "Ghost" – Mystery Glow Among Gravestones – A Trick Of Reflection":

The "REPORTER" is able to state authoritatively that, far from being attributable to any supernatural cause, the "ghost light" is a mere trick of reflection, albeit a rather remarkable one. The source is the high-power standard lamps illuminating the traffic island at Windle Smithies and the reflecting surface would appear to be either a highly polished grave headstone, or a convex glass shade covering artificial flowers upon a grave.

That the light can only be seen from two positions in Rainford-road suggests that at other places, some other object or objects intervenes in the line of vision. It would also appear to prove that the object of reflection is only small.

SHOCKING SUICIDE

Three years earlier, the Hard Lane cemetery had seen a shocking suicide by one of its long-standing employees. On March 21st 1934, Henry Bibby of Abbey Road was found by his cousin hanging from a plank in a newly dug grave.

The 58-year-old had worked at the St Helens Cemetery for 30 years and at his inquest his wife Margaret stated that for the past few weeks Henry appeared very troubled about his work. The coroner was again the wise Samuel Brighouse who said:

The man had evidently been depressed for some reason that no one would ever know. People thought and imagined things that other folk knew nothing about. They would be astonished if they knew the troubles that other people were worrying about. Bibby had left notes which clearly showed that he thought the better way would be to leave this life so as to dispose of his real or imaginary troubles.

Our Giddy Youth!
Child Steeplejacks In St Helens

"They are all trained from infancy, and yesterday the baby, William Akiens, struggled up several rungs of the ladder"

DISCLAIMER! For those (like myself) who don't care too much for heights, just reading this next story may make you feel dizzy! It is the daredevil tale of the offspring of a Leicester steeplejack who in 1907 undertook repairs at a St Helens' brickworks.

It was then common for boys to follow in their father's footsteps and undertake the same employment – but John Akiens took that tradition literally and wanted his sons taking after him up high chimneys.

And his daughters too – and from a very early age, as well. In fact the 41-year-old admitted training his ten kids to climb from the moment they could walk.

The steeplejack was clearly proud of his children and liked to show off their climbing skills. However, it was that desire that got him into trouble with the police – and even led to questions being asked by the Home Office in London.

Akiens was particularly proud of his 15-year-old daughter, Lydia, and reckoned that she could match any other female climber. In August 1907 a number of newspapers stated that Lydia had been declared as not only the youngest but also the champion female steeplejack of the world.

That was after a challenge had been issued for other girl steeplejacks to compete against her – but none had come forward.

That was a common – if dubious – tactic for those involved in certain types of unusual activities or extreme sports. Issue a newspaper challenge and if there were no takers, call yourself the world champion by default.

The newspaper reports also revealed that Lydia planned to tackle a 400 ft. chimney shaft in the Liverpool area and have *"animated picture apparatus"* record her movements.

There were several other juvenile steeplejacks around. On September 3rd 1907, 10-year-old Ida Partington and her 9-year-brother Jack, climbed a church tower in Accrington, as the Preston Herald described:

> Two tiny school-children of Accrington have just achieved a remarkable feat. The son and daughter of a steeplejack named Partington, these daring youngsters scaled the lofty tower and spire of Christ Church, Accrington, and, standing on the ladders, 150 ft. above the ground, cheerily waved their hands to an amazed and almost terror-stricken crowd.

That appeared to have motivated the acrobatic Akiens family to put on a show in St Helens. Seven days later Lydia and two of her siblings scaled a 110 ft. high chimney in Chester Lane.

The Leicester-based steeplejack had moved his family to Clock Face Road while undertaking jobs in the town. And with hundreds of chimneys in St Helens there would have been plenty of work to keep him busy.

The climb at Roughdale's brick and tileworks was a breeze for the teenage Lydia, who ascended to the platform from where repairs were being carried out in just 65 seconds.

Her five-year-old brother Baden then climbed up the ladders in his clogs. He was soon at the top of the chimney, waving down to the few watching spectators below.

Roughdale's brickworks of Chester Lane pictured in 1890

Baden Akiens was an old hand at being a steeplejack having scaled a 150ft. chimney at Roughdale's two years earlier – when only three! His seven-year-old sister Gertrude followed him up the ladder and then it was the turn of the trio's elder brother, as the Liverpool Echo described:

> Tom Akiens, aged 18, is amazingly nimble on the ladders, and he yesterday descended over 100 feet in 15 secs. The prowess of this wonderful family have attracted a great amount of attention in the locality, as well as in the neighbourhood of their home at Leicester. They are all trained from infancy, and yesterday the baby, William Akiens, aged just over a year, struggled up several rungs of the ladder in an endeavour to catch his brother.
>
> Mr. Akiens claimed that Gertrude and Baden Akiens are the youngest chimney climbers in the world, and that his daughter Lydia will beat any other lady climber. She is prepared to go any height.

Both the Partington and Akiens families ensured that the gentlemen of the Press were notified prior to their child climbers springing into action.

The Liverpool Echo's St Helens' representative had certainly been given advance notice of the Chester Lane climb and considered it more impressive than the one held in Accrington a week earlier:

A climb of this character on the sloping side of a church steeple, and starting from the top of the tower, probably two-thirds up, is not near so exacting as a straight climb up the side of a chimney of a similar height.

BABY STEEPLEJACKS.

110FT. CHIMNEY CLIMBED BY A BOY OF FIVE.

At St. Helens, yesterday, three of the younger members of the family of Mr. Akiens, the well-known Leicester steeplejack, ascended one of the chimneys at the Roughdale Brick and Tile Works.

Mr. Akiens has been anxious for some time to match his daughter Lydia, aged 15, against any other lady climber in the world. She has made several journeys to the top of chimneys over 150ft. high, and yesterday the girl mounted to the platform from which one of the Roughdale chimneys is being repaired, 110ft. from the ground, in 1min. 5secs. She was followed by her brother Baden Akiens, aged five years, who, as an extra test, was allowed to climb the ladders in his clogs. Two years ago, when he had only just turned three, he climbed to the top of the 150ft. chimney at Roughdale's. Yesterday he was soon on top, waving his hand to those below. After Baden came Gertrude, aged six, who also went up the ladders and remained for some time on the scaffolding at the top.

Tom Akiens, aged 18, is amazingly nimble on the

JUVENILE STEEPLEJACKS AT ST. HELENS.

REMARKABLE PERFORMANCES.

The question of who is the youngest steeple-jack in the kingdom was probably settled for some time to come yesterday afternoon at St. Helens, when three of the younger members of the family of Mr. Akiens, the well-known Leicester steeplejack, ascended one of the chimneys at the Roughdale Brick and Tile Works. The climbing took place in the presence of our St. Helens representative. Mr. Akiens has been anxious for some time to match his daughter Lydia, aged fifteen, against any other lady climber in the world. She has made several journeys to the top of chimneys over 150ft. high, and yesterday the girl mounted to the platform from which one of the Roughdale chimneys is being repaired, 110ft. from the ground, in 1min. 5secs. During the past few days attention has been drawn to the performances of the ten-year-old daughter and the nine-year-old son of Mr. John Partington, who climbed the spire of Christ Church, Accrington, which is 150ft. high. A climb of this character on the sloping side of a church steeple, and starting from the top of the tower, probably two-thirds up, is not near so exacting as a straight climb up the side of a chimney of a similar height. Mr. Akiens has five sons and five daughters, who can all climb. Yesterday afternoon, after Lydia had ascended, she was followed by her brother Baden Akiens, aged five years, who,

Lancashire Evening Post and Liverpool Echo September 11th 1907

However, the publicity generated by the child-climbing stunt attracted the interest of the Home Secretary, who wrote to the St Helens Chief Constable about the case. There was also a concern that the Roughdale ascent had simply been a rehearsal for Lydia's proposed climb of a 400 ft. chimney in front of movie cameras.

154

So Detective Roe went to Chester Lane and spoke to John Akiens, giving him the impression that he was a reporter. The steeplejack foolishly sent 5-year-old Baden up the chimney to demonstrate his prowess to the undercover policeman – although he insisted there were straps that would prevent a fall.

ENDANGERING LIVES

John Akiens was subsequently prosecuted and on September 16th 1907 appeared in St Helens Police Court charged with allowing three of his ten children to breach the Dangerous Performances of Children Act.

The Chief Constable of the town told the magistrates that what had occurred had been highly dangerous and he hoped the Bench would inflict a penalty sufficient to deter the defendant and others from *"endangering the lives of children of such tender years"*.

Thomas Stevens, manager of Roughdale's, admitted watching the exhibition but insisted that he had not given his permission for the climbs to take place. John Akiens explained to the court that it was the custom of his family to train their children to climb from infancy – and he had never been told that doing so was wrong.

The St Helens Reporter of September 20th 1907 described the dialogue in the courtroom:

> The Clerk: These children are so young. Defendant: It is our custom to train them from the cradle, or as soon as they begin to walk. The Chairman: Are you going to make the girls chimney-jacks? Defendant said he thought it did them good. They were all swimmers, and in case of fire or an accident in the water they would all be able to look after themselves better. It learned them to keep a cool head. The best steeplejack in the world had learned to climb in his infancy; right from the cradle. He did not send his children up, for as

soon as they saw the ladders they wanted to be off up them. When they wanted to go up he encouraged them.

The magistrates said they thought what had happened had been a *"most objectionable practice as well as being dangerous".*

However, they also accepted that Akiens might have been under a misapprehension when allowing his children to climb high chimneys. And so they decided to only bind him over upon payment of sureties and court costs.

The steeplejack was told not to let such climbs occur again and he asked the court at what age apprentices could legally ascend a chimney. The answer was 16 for a boy and 18 for a girl.

Newspapers from all over the country reported on this highly unusual court case with that of the Dundee Evening Telegraph bearing the headline *"Our Giddy Youth".*

Six St Helens Ghost Stories

There have been many claims of hauntings within the St Helens district over the years. Most are well known and their tales have often been told. This chapter is devoted to stories of lesser-known manifestations that I have uncovered in my newspaper research.

However, I begin with the "ghost" that unquestionably was a living, breathing person!

a) The Living Boundary Road "Ghost"!

"What was thought to be the apparition
of a dead man returned to life"

This is a photograph of Boundary Road in St Helens where on September 28th 1899 a dead man returned to life. At least it appeared that way to the Jones family at no. 296 when Edwin Jones strolled inside. That was because his brother William had buried the miner a month earlier! The Manchester Evening News reported the amazing story on October 4th 1899:

The family of Mr. William Jones, milkman, 296, Boundary Road, St. Helens, received a great shock last night when, seated in the house after tea, by what at first was thought to be the apparition of a dead man returned to life, but what proved to be Mr. Jones's brother, on whose supposed corpse an inquest was held at the Town Hail a month ago. On the 23rd of August last it was reported that the body of Edwin Jones, labourer, aged about 40 years, had been found in the canal near Quirk, Barton, and Co.'s leadworks. Deceased's brother identified the body, and an inquest was held by the county coroner, at which formal proof was given, and a verdict of "Found drowned" was returned.

The body was buried under the name of Edwin Jones and some of his family drew out the life insurance cash that was due. When the man subsequently re-appeared in Boundary Road his brother fainted away and it was a considerable time before he and the rest of the family could recover from the shock.

Edwin Jones told reporters that he saw the account of his own inquest in the newspapers when staying in Wales, and had enjoyed the joke immensely. He said he had been afraid that the police might have a warrant out for his arrest and thought it advisable to allow his relatives time to *"draw the club money"*.

Just why Edwin Jones did not write to his brother William to explain the mix-up in advance of turning up at his house, I cannot say – although it seems he was still enjoying the joke!

At the renewed inquest hearing on October 4th Jones changed his story a little, claiming that he had left home in search of work, and did not know of the supposed death until the previous Thursday, when he learnt of it at Bolton.

Relatives, police officers and journalists all commented at the inquest of the remarkable similarity between the dead body and Jones, even to both individuals bearing scars on their faces.

b) The Beecham's Poltergeist

"But as soon as darkness sets in and the place is locked up, beings of an immortal shape take possession"

This is Beecham's warehouse in Lowe Street in St Helens pictured in 1925. Forty years earlier a ghost was supposed to inhabit the building – or perhaps *"poltergeist"* is a more accurate term?

That said some cynics thought that the being that liked to throw stones was very much a human one with impish qualities rather than spiritual ones.

The series of incidents began in August 1885 after the pill maker decided to rebuild its factory in Westfield Street. So all the firm's staff and machinery were temporarily moved into their Lowe Street building – which Beecham's appear to have only recently acquired and which had previously served as a sawmill.

My first report was published in the Manchester Courier on August 26th 1885 under the headline *"The Freaks Of A St. Helens Ghost":*

During the past few weeks the employés of Messrs. Beecham, manufacturers, at St. Helens, have been alarmed by an extraordinary series of performances of what has been termed a "ghost." During the day the work goes on without anything extraordinary taking place, but as soon as darkness sets in and the place is locked up, "beings of an immortal shape" take possession.

The public assemble nightly in Lowe-street watching for the "supernatural," which, however, has not been seen. So far as our inquiries go, it seems that the "antics" of the ghost are confined to stone-throwing. An entrance has not been made into the works since Sunday night week, but it is stated that missiles can be heard flying about. This extraordinary occurrence has caused great excitement, and will continue to do so until the mystery is solved.

The Cheshire Observer for their part wrote how a *"sensation is just now raging in St Helens"*, claiming that what they called a *"stone-throwing séance"* had taken place on almost every night for nearly three months. That had been when Beecham's manager, a Mr Andrews, made his nightly inspection of the works.

The chucking of missiles with considerable force and some accuracy had become such a regular event that a door had been installed opposite the building's main entrance to provide protection. Many searches by workmen for the source of the projectiles had drawn a blank and even the police had conducted an unsuccessful stake out – as the Observer explained:

A detective backed by five men, good and true, entered the works determined not to leave the premises until they had captured the intruder. The gas had been left burning low. The instant the stone throwing commenced the lights were quickly turned up, and the searchers rushed in the direction from which the missiles came. The mysterious one, however, had disappeared into thin air, and the detective and his five men quitted the premises, baffled and disappointed. On this night about 30 missiles – copper slag, pieces of brick, scraps of stone, &c., in weight averaging from four or five ounces – were thrown.

It having been suggested that the mischief-maker might be a member of the monkey tribe, dogs were introduced, but although the stones darted about as usual no "Jacko" could be found. Meanwhile the public got wind of the occurrence. Imaginative women, peeping through crevices, saw inhabitants of the invisible world in every shape and form floating about the air; and gossip-mongers knew for a fact that skulls had been dug up, pointing to the conclusion that all kinds of foul murders had been committed.

The Observer added that during the previous week crowds of hundreds had thronged Lowe Street and fried fish sellers and hot potato vendors had driven a roaring trade.

Then on August 28th 1885 under the headline: *"The St. Helens Ghost – More Extraordinary Performances – Suggested Work Of Dynamitards"*, the Liverpool Echo described how hopes the ghost had departed Lowe Street had been dashed.

The report explained how after a couple of days of quiet, a large piece of copper slag weighing half a pound had, without warning, come *"whizzing through the air"* towards the Beecham's manager and his son. Neither of them was hurt – in fact there were never any reports of any injuries caused by the missile throwing, despite the large volume of incidents.

Mr Andrews, the manager, told the Echo that many were saying that "Beecham's Ghost" had been "got up" as a publicity stunt but he insisted that was untrue. The paper added that the police were examining a letter addressed to Thomas Beecham that suggested that violent revolutionaries (known as "dynamitards") might be responsible. The badly-written letter read:

Dear sir, In Reference to the ghost in Lowe St by Reports i See you cannott find anything, have you, sir, Examined the floor, it is my firm opinion that there are someone Carrying on an illegal business and that there are subterranean vaults of which you are not aware, it may be a subterranean Passage from Cowley Hill (C. M.) Perhaps dynamitards it is advisable to be very Cautious in the proceedings or the consequences might be fatal should you fall on them in their lair they would in all probability be desperate it is quite evident that there are someone there that have no business there, and you are a stumbling block in their way, and so they have formed a conspiracy to try to frighten you from the premises.

The envelope carried the Prescot postmark, and was addressed to "Mr Beecham, pill manufacturer, St. Helens (private)."

Upon describing the letter, the St Helens Newspaper of August 29th 1885 wrote:

The affair is now verging from the ludicrous to the absolutely ridiculous....Of course, ghosts and goblins have been seen all over the place, if we are to believe all the wild rumours...Unearthly beings are said by gossip-mongers and superstitious grandmothers to quit the purlieus [surrounds] of their six feet of earth and go forward to annoy the world, as they did before the cold icy hand of death gave them (and their surroundings) rest which most people believe continues until the Judgement Day.

The Newspaper thought that *"vile delinquents"* were more likely to be responsible for the stone chucking – but accepted it was all very mysterious. And that's where the story fizzles out – as ghost yarns tend to do. I can find no further reports and you can decide for yourself whether the manifestations were a publicity stunt, the actions of a poltergeist or an extremely clever prankster.

The work of (literally) underground revolutionaries attempting to scare people off seems far-fetched – but who knows?

c) The Spook Scare in Thatto Heath

"The ghostly knockings and weird movements"

The Liverpool Echo's lengthy headline from August 24th 1923 summed up the ghostly goings-on in Thatto Heath: *"A Spook Scare – St. Helens Contributes A Sensation – Knocks & Open Boxes – Spirit Of Dead Brother Seen By A Medium"*.

The haunted house that was the focus of their attention was at 17 Parliament Street and occupied by a couple called Roberts. The claim was that a Welsh child – presumably a relative – that had been staying with the Roberts's and sleeping with the couple in their bedroom, had been the unwilling conduit for activity of a supernatural nature.

The *"ghostly knockings and weird movements"* had begun with a continuous noise that sounded as if a reel of cotton was rolling across the floor – and then strange knocks were heard.

SATURDAY, AUGUST 25, 1923.

HAUNTED HOUSE.

"Spirit" that Walked at Night.

Amazing incidents, which are said to have been proved to be beyond the power of practical jokers, are reported from a house in Parliament Street, Thatto Heath, near St Helens, Lancashire, occupied by an elderly couple, Mr and Mrs Roberts, and several lodgers.

Interviewed by a Central News representative, Mrs Roberts told a story of weird happenings.

"We had just gone to bed on Sunday night," she said, "when we heard a continuous noise like a reel of cotton rolling about the floor. Then there came knockings in different parts of the room—three sharp, determined knocks at regular intervals.

"Immediately afterwards a box containing collars fell to the floor, and then all the clothes in a large box were scattered on the floor. We slept in another bed next

Aberdeen Press & Journal Aug. 25th 1923

The 13-year-old girl became so frightened that she crept into Mrs Roberts's bed – but noises sounding like the tipping of coal out of a large bucket, shakings and knocks on the bed then occurred. And then a box of collars was seen to jump up high into the air and fall back to the floor.

Nothing occurred on the following evening when the threesome slept in a back bedroom. But once they reverted to their front bedroom, they had what was described as an *"awful night"* with knockings and scratching going on until half-past three.

Some neighbours had been invited to spend the night with them and they all saw a jug that had been placed on the floor being lifted up from the ground and spinning on its own in the air.

It was subsequently decided that the girl should return to her home in Wales and as soon as she departed, peace and quiet was said to descend on Parliament Street.

However, before leaving the Thatto Heath house, the girl had found a note in the bedroom bearing in large handwriting the words: *"Take care of yourself."*

The Liverpool Echo takes up the rest of the story:

> Mrs. Roberts, who has never before been associated in any way with Spiritualism, called in a well-known local "medium," who visited the house, to the occupants of which she was quite a stranger. The "medium" declared that she saw a man in spirit form walk through the kitchen and lean heavily against the fireplace. She described the man, and Mrs. Roberts recognised the description as that of her brother, who was killed in an explosion eleven years ago. There was nothing to fear the "medium" assured Mrs. Roberts, as the brother was simply trying to get a message to her.

d) The Ghostly Footsteps At A Crank Cottage

"Oh, it is only old Mrs. Ellison looking for her money"

This is the cottage in Crank at the corner of Berrington's Lane and Crank Road, where, in the 1930s, a ghost was claimed to have been exorcised. The act was not performed by a priest – but instead undertaken by the digging up of a chicken patch and the removal of an old lady's hidden "hoard" of a golden guinea.

The "John Public" column in the St Helens Reporter re-told the strange story in 1961. Before by-lines in newspapers became commonplace, journalists were unaccredited or used pen-names.

So Thomas "T. A." Owen was known as "Recorder" in the Reporter when covering rugby league matters and Agnes Duffy was known as "Vox". She was one of the first women employed by the paper – although her witty comments had to be made under a pseudonym.

Just who "John Public" was I cannot say – but his gossip column in the Reporter lasted many years and on May 20th 1961, "Joe" recalled the spooky events in Crank from three decades earlier after James Casey had got in touch.

James explained that upon getting married, he and his wife Helena had lived with his wife's parents in their 18th century cottage on the corner of Crank Road and Berrington's Lane.

They wondered why the older folk always insisted on going to bed at an early hour but the newly-weds were happy to stay up late.

One Saturday night, Mr and Mrs Casey were preparing for bed after spending the evening in town. Suddenly they heard footsteps made by someone wearing light wooden shoes, slowly pacing the ancient cobbled yard outside. Thinking it was probably a tramp, Mr Casey decided to investigate.

As he opened the door the footsteps came nearer – but he could not see anyone and so called out. There was no reply but the sounds drew closer until they passed directly in front of him – eventually stopping in the middle of a chicken patch.

Although a little unnerved by the experience, Mr Casey said he thought there must have been a rational explanation for what he had heard. However, from that time onwards, the couple regularly heard the late night footsteps and so did their friends.

Upon questioning his mother-in-law about the matter, she said: *"Oh, it is only old Mrs. Ellison looking for her money."* She explained that the previous occupant of the cottage had been an elderly lady who had been the widow of a wealthy businessman.

The woman had been in the habit of paying her bills with gold sovereigns but after her death, no trace of her reputed wealth could be found.

At Mr Casey's suggestion, the chicken patch was dug up and to the astonishment of all the family, an old ironbound wooden chest was unearthed.

However, it only contained a single guinea coin, similar to ones that had been discovered in nearby fields in Crank.

Since the excavation had taken place, the footsteps were never heard again, which led to "John Public" asking rhetorically in his column:

"Is it possible the ghost was "laid" by the finding of the remains of the old lady's 'hoard'?"

e) The Haunted Billinge Doctor's Surgery

"Boy Tucked In By Granny Who Died Before He Was Born"

Billinge is quite a haunted house hotspot. What with "Albert the Cavalier" at the Stork Hotel and the Eagle and Child's "Woman in White", there have been numerous reports over the years of mysterious manifestations in the village.

Claremont pictured in 1961

One of the most remarkable has to be the thirteen-year haunting of Claremont in Billinge's Main Street.

The 18th century house has served many different uses over the years – but for older Billingers it will always be associated with the Mathers. They were the longstanding doctor family who treated generations of local people.

Under the headline *"Thirteen-Year Haunting Of Local Family – Boy Tucked In By Granny Who Died Before He Was Born"*, the St Helens Reporter of May 6th 1961 described how an exorcism service a year earlier had finally brought calm to Claremont.

So much so that Betty Mather – the wife of Dr Richard Mather – now felt able to describe the strange supernatural occurrences.

Although every member of her family had witnessed inexplicable events, Mrs Mather felt that she and her son Richard Jnr had been the main targets of the ghosts and poltergeists that had inhabited their old house.

Their experiences included hearing footsteps climbing invisibly up an endless staircase and a feeling of dread that if she looked around the room, something terrible would be seen.

Mrs Mather described one occasion in the dining room when she had been holding a china dinner service and having a conversation with her husband and son. Suddenly an invisible force pushed against her violently and the dishes flew out of her hands and shattered on a wall 12ft away.

A son also had a pendant pulled from his neck by an unseen force; a visitor to Claremont had passed a young boy on the stairs when no-one of his description was in the house and one night four people sat watching television in the lounge had seen a cup leave its saucer and rise a few inches before settling back down again.

One night Mrs. Mather was taking a drink up to her bedroom. As she reached the top of the stairs, the glass suddenly left her hand and fell to the floor. Thinking she had perhaps knocked her elbow, she took another glass up the stairs but at exactly the same place the identical experience occurred.

A cleaner also reported witnessing someone dressed in white gliding through upstairs rooms – and promptly refused to go up there ever again!

However, one of the most peculiar happenings took place to Betty's son, Richard Jnr, when he was very young. The boy came downstairs one morning and asked his mother who the lady had been who'd tucked him in bed during the previous evening.

Mrs Mather asked her son to describe the woman and was astonished when Richard gave an exact description of his grandmother who'd died before he was born.

APPARITION

Not wishing to alarm her son, Mrs Mather said that a neighbour had gone into his bedroom to see him. But the apparition soon became a frequent guest at the boy's bedside and Richard became very used to these nocturnal visits. However, a visitor staying in the house had no prior experience of spectres smoothing bedclothes and was shocked when it happened to him!

Mrs Mather also told the Reporter about a number of premonitions that had come true. Eventually, a medium visited Claremont and said he felt the lounge of the house and part of the garden had been the site of an ancient burial ground.

It had been in the lounge where Richard Jnr's grandmother – who made nocturnal visits to his bedside – had died and where many strange occurrences were recorded. The Reporter described what happened next:

A séance was held in the lounge shortly afterwards, to which the medium took a number of his friends. The doctor and his family thought they were all eccentrics, and so did not attend. They were able to hear unknown voices inside the room, none of which they recognised, when suddenly Richard cried out that he had heard the voice of the grandmother he had never met, and his astonished parents were able to confirm this.

Later an exorcism service was performed in the lounge. That was a full year before the story was published in the Reporter and during that 12-month period the ghosts and poltergeists had deserted the 18th century house.

The newspaper summed up its lengthy article with this unusual statement supporting the credibility of the claims:

The exorcism would seem to be conclusive proof that there had been spirits inhabiting Claremont, but, as in other circumstances they disappeared after the Power of God was brought to bear upon them. That these incidents related are true is beyond question and it would be difficult to find a family with more integrity than the Mathers. All is now normal in the Mather's household. The encounters of the past, however, do not fade. They were too real for that.

f) Medium Lily Picton – The Billinge Ghost Writer

"The words came to me as pictures and
thoughts, which a voice was saying to me"

Many would-be authors receive rejections from book publishers because their work is not considered good enough. But Lily Picton claimed in 1971 that her manuscript had been turned down for a different reason – because a ghost had written it!

This is another Billinge story of the supernatural – but with a difference. 55-year-old Lily from Gorsey Brow claimed her body had been taken over by the spirit of a deceased rabbi and she'd automatically written down his 50,000-word tome. Philip Swift told Lily's story in the St Helens Reporter of June 4th 1971:

Lily Picton and some of her drawings

Housewife Lily Picton revealed her secret story of life with "another man" this week. She told of her dates with a tall German stranger – and the book of amazing events that have changed her life. For Lily is a medium, and through her psychic power she has written a 50,000-word biography of a young Hamburg rabbi who she never met and who died 26 years ago. Her fantastic story of Ali Arhmed Bastron, his family, and his death in a Nazi labour camp, is a

170

supernatural phenomenon known as automatic writing. There is no explanation for the leather-bound volumes. Yet 55-year-old Mrs. Picton, of Gorsey Brow, Billinge, who has little formal education, has written a detailed life-study which she claims is the work of another person's mind.

Lily's book told the life story of Rabbi Bastron who was born into a Jewish family in Hamburg in 1899. His mother Rachel died in childbirth and his father Isaac instructed him in the Hebrew faith.

Bastron married, however, his wife Hildegard went off with a doctor to Africa, leaving him to look after their daughter, Leah. The Gestapo imprisoned them both and the rabbi was shot in 1942.

Mrs Picton explained the process of writing the book to Philip Swift:

The words came to me as pictures and thoughts, which a voice was saying to me. When it was time to write I would feel a terrific hold come over my mind and I would sit with a pen and paper. There was terrific mental pressure ... then a feeling of peace. And episodes from the rabbi's life were being vividly described in my mind. I began to write fast and furiously without thinking what I was doing. I had no control over the words. I was merely copying down the things I was being told by a mild and cultured voice.

Mrs Picton said she had never visited Germany. Yet, when she borrowed a guidebook from St Helens Library, there were descriptions and paintings that matched what she'd written.

Lily also described how through the process of automatic writing, she had drawn sketches of the rabbi and his family:

I was told by his spirit to sit down and draw and he would show me his face. A strange feeling came over me and my hand began to quiver. Suddenly it was scribbling in wild, heavy movements. This went on for half-an-hour and at the time I did not know what I was doing. But when it was over I found I had drawn a face with close-cropped hair and a bushy beard and immediately I knew it was the rabbi.

Lily Picton had already approached two London literary agents in a bid to get her story published – but they had both turned her down. The Billinge ghostwriter felt they'd been frightened of handling such a work and seemed suspicious of the circumstances.

"I'd like the book published," she added, *"because I think they are good stories which would give a lot of pleasure to others."*

However, I can find no evidence of Lily's manuscript ever seeing the light of day in a published form.

The Sex Scandal At Whiston Workhouse

"The Master, who had been fast losing his temper, now broke out into the most abusive language"

In 1843 the small workhouses at Sutton, Bold, Windle, Prescot, Whiston and Speke were closed and their inmates transferred to the new, modern workhouse at Whiston. Run by the Prescot Union, the institution took in paupers from a large part of SW Lancashire and 28 elected Guardians oversaw its operations.

Three of their members represented the Windle township of St Helens and three others covered Sutton. There were two members each for Parr, Eccleston, Widnes and Prescot and one each representing Whiston, Bold, Huyton, Knowsley, Rainford, Rainhill, Ditton, Cronton, Hale, Halewood, Speke, Much Woolton, Little Woolton and Tarbock.

The workhouse is shown on the previous page during the 1880s, with the institution's Master and Matron, Arthur and Jane Hale, pictured standing outside. The couple seemingly gave the Prescot Union's Board of Guardians no trouble.

Not even Arthur Hale's hobby of pig breeding appears to have upset them! But the same cannot be said for Thomas Holmes.

He became Master of the workhouse in the late 1860s, soon after an adjacent hospital had been built to care for sick paupers. This had opened in 1866 and its head nurse was Elisabeth Evans.

On March 11th 1869 a letter from Miss Evans was read out at a Board of Guardians meeting in which the nurse criticised the behaviour of the Master – who was also known as the governor:

> Sir. I hope you will excuse me for troubling you with a complaint about the governor's conduct. I am constrained, however, to do so by the great tyranny he exercises over me in the discharge of my duties, and I trust to receive that protection from you as will enable me in future to perform them in comfort. Whenever he gives me an order about my duties, he does it in such an insulting manner that I feel grieved for hours after. He comes into the hospital in an excited state, and on two occasions he was intoxicated.

The letter was read out in front of reporters but the Guardians decided to discuss the complaint privately – which meant that the journalists present could not report on the outcome.

It doesn't appear that the Guardians did much, if anything, as at their next meeting a fortnight later, it was revealed that the head nurse and her assistant had both decided to quit.

The Guardians sent for the two women to ask why they had chosen to leave. Elisabeth Evans said she had never been comfortable in her job, having been treated more like a child than the head nurse of a hospital.

COURSE TREATMENT

At the Guardians next meeting held at the workhouse on April 8th, it was the turn of the institution's medical officer of health to make serious accusations against the Master. The St Helens Newspaper stated that Dr Rayner's *"grave charges"* against Thomas Holmes amounted to *"nothing short of manslaughter"*.

Among the long list of offences, Holmes was alleged to have prevented a nurse from dispatching an order for medicines and had also refused to allow a messenger to collect medicine from the doctor's surgery.

The most serious charge was a peculiar one. The doctor had ordered that two patients should be given brandy and beef tea as treatment for typhus fever. A nurse had requested these on three occasions but the Master would not allow them to be given. Subsequently one of the patients had died – hence the manslaughter claim in the Newspaper.

The Liverpool Mercury wrote that the Guardians upon hearing these charges being read: *"…were almost continually giving vent to feelings of surprise and indignation."*

The St Helens Newspaper added that the medical officer had warned the Guardians that the Master's conduct if not checked would lead to a cycle of resignations. Dr Rayner said that if the two nurses felt compelled to leave…

…others who may succeed them will, in their turn, have to be sacrificed, and so the thing will go on until the end of the chapter. For I am convinced that no sensible woman, be she nurse or otherwise will elect to stay here if the same harsh treatment be allowed to be exercised, as has hitherto been tolerated in this workhouse.

It was decided that the Guardians would hold a special meeting to consider the charges against the Master. During the hearing the doctor claimed that the elderly nurse who had been originally employed at the hospital had also left through the Master's behaviour and now lived in poverty.

Dr Rayner accused Mr Holmes of *"course treatment and harsh expressions"* towards the nurses, who he had resented since their appointment had been made.

However, the workhouse Matron – who was married to the Master – claimed a conspiracy had been got up against the couple and that her husband had done nothing wrong. The Guardians did not agree and of the five specimen charges made against Thomas Holmes, all but one were found proved.

The Master was invited to resign but refused to do so and the Guardians did not have the power to sack him. Only the Poor Law Board could do that.

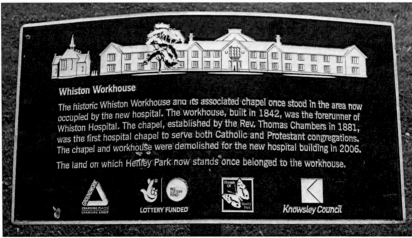

Plaque in Henley Park opposite Whiston Hospital

GRAVE CHARGE

The case was in limbo but at a Guardians meeting on May 6th the most serious complaint of the lot was revealed. A letter from Rev. Moore was read in which the workhouse chaplain described a sensational claim from a pauper. He said the woman called Mary Sixsmith had initiated a *"grave charge"* against the Master.

As a result of the claim, a poor law inspector called Basil Cane held a 7-hour inquiry into Holmes's conduct. The hearing took place on May 18th 1869 and the main charge against the Master was one of gross immorality with a pauper. Mary Sixsmith had alleged that Holmes had got her pregnant – from which she'd miscarried – after having had sex with her on several occasions.

The 36-year-old was now a patient in the workhouse hospital and had been an inmate of the house, along with two of her three children, for almost four years. Mary alleged that in return for sex, the master had allowed her more freedom around the workhouse and supplied her with more food, beer and clothing than the other paupers. On one occasion, she said, he had given her money.

The woman was too ill to attend the inquiry but had made a statement on oath and also provided the names of several inmates and officials to corroborate her account. A number of witnesses gave evidence at the hearing and all spoke of rumours prior to the

Three pauper inmates of Whiston Workhouse

miscarriage that the Master had made the woman pregnant.

But they also stated that Mary Sixsmith was often in a drunken state. Although that evidence did not help her credibility, the inmates were only allowed small quantities of alcohol for what was considered medicinal purposes. So the question in the mind of the

Inspector would have been where had the woman been getting the drink from, if it had not been from the master?

Mary Sixsmith's credibility was also not helped by the testimony of Thomas Harrison. The 67-year-old inmate gave evidence that while lying in his hospital bed, Mary had approached him while drunk and thrown herself upon him – and then he claimed she did the same to another patient.

The Master was reported to have *"positively and solemnly repudiated the charges"* of the woman and denied that any intimacy had ever existed between them.

The Inspector said he would report on the proceedings to the Poor Law Board and await their decision. Should it be necessary to hold an inquiry into the many other charges that the doctor and nurses had made against the Master, he would inform the Guardians.

Before coming to Whiston, Thomas Holmes had enjoyed a good reputation after having been employed at similar institutions for eighteen years – including serving a term as the Master of Ormskirk Workhouse.

He continued to deny all accusations of wrongdoing but finally got his comeuppance on May 25th when the Clerk to the Prescot Guardians heard from the Poor Law Board. They wrote that they'd studied their inspector's report and deemed Thomas Holmes unfit to hold the office of master – and so he would be sacked.

Although it's unwise to pass judgement on someone after 150 years, the sheer volume of complaints made against Holmes was extraordinary and I expect many people at Whiston were glad to see the back of him – although he wasn't prepared to go quietly!

On June 5th the Board of Guardians summoned the Master to their meeting and ordered him to leave the workhouse at once. Holmes replied that he was appealing against the Board's decision to sack him and demanded a month's wages in lieu of notice – which was refused by the Chairman.

FOUL TEMPER

There had been numerous reports of the man's foul temper during his time as master. So Holmes' parting shot – as described by the Liverpool Mercury – was probably not a great surprise and underlined the bad mistake that had been made in appointing him to such a responsible position in the first place:

> The Master, who had been fast losing his temper, now broke out into the most abusive language, and, turning to the chairman, said – I can tell you, sir, that, although I shall be sorry to part with many faces I have met here, I shall be really glad to get away from yours. You have conspired to injure me ever since I first came to the house, and I consider you anything but a gentleman.

Holmes accused other Guardians of the same, saying they would be *"able to fit the cap to their own heads"*. But that is not the end of this story.

Three months later Holmes was back in the news after a chance meeting with Dr Rayner at St Helens Junction station. Since the workhouse's medical officer had levelled his first complaints, Holmes had developed a loathing for him and issued several threats.

On September 13th 1869 the two men's paths crossed while Dr Rayner was changing trains. Holmes approached the doctor's companion and Dr Rayner took the opportunity to offer the ex-workhouse master his hand. However, Holmes rejected the friendly gesture, telling him he would never shake hands with a rogue.

The doctor then walked away to enter his carriage and was followed by Holmes who, without any provocation, struck Dr Rayner hard in his face. The Wigan Observer wrote:

> The blow covered his face with blood, and caused him to stagger and fall on one knee, and for a short time he seemed completely stunned. After he got up he stood upon the defensive, and some blows were exchanged of lesser consequence, but the parties were separated and Dr. Rayner left for Rainhill.

On October 19th in the Prescot Petty Sessions, Thomas Holmes was charged with assaulting Dr Rayner at St Helens Junction station and giving him two black eyes.

The latter's travelling companion supported his account, as did a Mrs Green, who said she was sat in a carriage and witnessed Holmes go up to the doctor and give him a blow.

The magistrates in the crowded courtroom told Holmes he had been guilty of a *"most unpardonable and unprovoked assault"* and fined him £5 with the alternative sentence of two months in prison.

Thomas Holmes immediately replied: *"Thank you, sir; I will take the two months"*. The former workhouse master left the court in police custody but later had a change of heart and paid the fine.

The last time we hear of Holmes was at another Guardians meeting on May 19th 1870 when a letter from him was read out. He continued to blame others for his misfortunes, writing:

"If ever there was a persecuted man, I am that individual", and added that he was *"out of health with anxiety, and have been for some time"*.

He claimed to be still owed £17 back salary, which the Guardians agreed to pay, no doubt hoping that would get rid of him for good!

The Fairy Invasion Of St Helens

*"18 tons of scenery and props had been
brought to the Theatre Royal from London."*

The headline in the Liverpool Echo of January 29th 1912 of
"Fairies To Invade St. Helens" was probably not the most
frightening news that the townsfolk ever read! They weren't
seemingly very educated fairies either, as a fortnight later another
article was published in the paper bearing the headline *"School For
Fairies In St. Helens"*. What on earth was going on?

Well, St Helens pill proprietor Joseph Beecham
had in September 1911 taken out a lease on the
Aldwych Theatre in London. After refurbishment it
reopened with a Christmas show called *'The
Golden Land of Fairy Tales'*. The production was
a compilation of Grimm brothers' stories and
featured a cast of 40 children playing the fairies.

Sir Joseph Beecham

A fortnight into its successful run in the West End, Beecham was
awarded a knighthood in the New Year's Honours list of 1912 and
he was also serving a third term as Mayor of St Helens. In
gratitude for these honours, Beecham decided to bring the show,
lock, stock and barrel to St Helens for the town's children to enjoy.

On February 6th 1912 the St Helens Newspaper described the
forthcoming treat:

> The arrangements are rapidly being pushed forward for the
> visit of the remarkable fairy play, "The Golden Land of Fairy
> Tales," which, through the generosity of the Mayor (Sir
> Joseph Beecham), some 14,000 of the children from the
> elementary schools of the borough will have the opportunity
> of witnessing. The company include some of the most

talented child artistes of the present day, who have deemed it a high privilege to be in the Beecham company, and we have no doubt they will delight the young folks of St. Helens with their performance.

There would be five matinees presented at the Theatre Royal and the education authorities had made arrangements for schools to be granted a half-day holiday, so their pupils could attend the performances. Then on the 9th, the St Helens Newspaper wrote:

It is perfectly safe to say that never have the children of St. Helens looked forward to any treat with such pleasurable expectancy as they are looking forward to "The Golden Land of Fairy Tales" in which they will revel next week, thanks to the generosity of the Mayor (Sir Joseph Beecham), who is bringing down, at great expense, the entire production from the Aldwych Theatre, London, where it has charmed delighted audiences of young and old during the past month.

However, for very young kids to be allowed to appear on stage in theatres, the local magistrates needed to grant permission. So on February 12th 1912, the show's assistant manager applied in St Helens Police Court for forty girls (27 of them under twelve) to be allowed to perform in the town.

It was revealed that their schoolmistress had accompanied the troupe to St Helens and after the magistrates were promised the girls' schooling would continue, permission was granted.

Mind you with Joseph Beecham being mayor and chief magistrate, it was most unlikely to have been refused! On the following day the Echo reviewed the first day's performance:

The first of the five matinée performances for the school children of St. Helens of "The Golden Land of Fairy Tales" took place yesterday afternoon, when the Theatre Royal was filled with an enthusiastic and wildly-demonstrative audience. The six fairy tales, with the prologue and epilogue, were exquisitely staged, and the performance all through went beautifully. Many of the youthful artistes are the sons and daughters of medical and other professional men, and the proprietor of the Aldwych will in years to come no doubt be able to point to a number of successful entertainers who made their debut with the present company.

The local children followed the various fairy tales with rapt attention, anticipating and appreciating them point by point with a keenness and enthusiasm which warmed the hearts of the few grown-ups who were present. Mr. Archdeacon [production manager] said to our representative that the theatre presented the most wonderful sight he ever saw in his life. They had played to large audiences in London during the past eight weeks, but they had never seen so extraordinary a sight as that. It was worth all their trouble.

Aldwych poster and Liverpool Echo article January 29th 1912

EIGHTEEN TONS OF SCENERY

Eighteen tons of scenery and props – including fifty-seven cloths, eighty wings and thirty-three baskets of costumes – had been brought to the Theatre Royal from London.

The last show at the Aldwych Theatre only ended at 11pm on the previous Saturday night. However, a special train to St Helens had arrived in the town on Sunday lunchtime and workmen immediately began the task of reconstruction.

That was only completed minutes before the curtain went up for the Monday matinée performance.

The cost of bringing the production to St Helens was estimated at being nearly £2,000 – of which £1,500 *(around £200,000 in today's money)* was borne by Sir Joseph Beecham.

Three St Helens Breach Of Promise Cases

"Damages heavy damages!"
"A more contemptible action was never brought into a court of law."

This illustration is taken from an 1865 edition of the Penny Illustrated Paper in which two breach of promise court actions were contrasted. In one case a Mr Da Costa had been told to pay his jilted betrothed £2,500 damages and, in another court, a Mr Kendall had been ordered to cough up £70.

The weekly *"friend of the people"* could not understand how different juries considered Da Costa thirty-five times *"more depraved"* than Kendall – although £70 in the 1860s was still a very considerable amount.

In the past, when respectability and reputation were all-important, there was shame and embarrassment in being rejected that could be ameliorated by money. This, of course, was the pre-telephone era and amorous letters were regularly exchanged between lovers.

These would invariably be kept and often figured in breach of promise cases where they made excellent evidence. In one action in Bristol in 1874, a bundle of 250 letters that weighed three pounds was presented to the jury!

Newspapers loved such cases, as the salacious details – albeit tame by today's standards – were pored over by readers. It was a rarely viewed mirror of people's personal lives. That was especially so when love letters and poems were read out.

Breach of Promise Case 1 – Harrison Vs. Sherlock

"He also spoke in censorious terms of the disgustingly immoral relations that had existed between the parties"

As we know starting legal proceedings against someone can be a dangerous game, as the other side can make all sorts of embarrassing counter-claims. That was certainly the case on December 7th 1892 when Sarah Harrison sued Henry Sherlock at the Liverpool Assizes alleging breach of promise of marriage.

Sarah was 28 and had spent most of her working life in the pub trade. Her parents kept the Royal Arms in Traverse Street in St Helens and her brother was landlord of the Victoria Inn in Market Street – locally known as the "Victoria Tap".

Henry was a 30-year-old house painter from New Market Place and had first met Sarah four years earlier when employed at the Victoria. Although Sarah was able to provide the court with letters from Henry in which he had written to her in *"endearing terms"*, there were no clear-cut references to getting hitched.

However, there were descriptions of sexual activity, which horrified the judge, although I expect they were mild by today's standards. Judge Bruce refused to allow the letters to be read out in full in court and at one point ordered all women present to leave.

Henry's counsel also claimed that Sarah had been seeing other men during the couple's courtship, which she strenuously denied. The barrister, Henry Shee, also made much of the fact that neither of Sarah's parents was being called to give evidence on her behalf, implying that they had disowned her.

The Liverpool Echo quoted the counsel in this fashion:

He also spoke in censorious terms of the disgustingly immoral relations that had existed between the parties. It was an entire misuse of the courts of law to bring such a case before them. He put it to the jury that a man, when he intended to settle down in life, wanted to have some guarantee of respectability with his wife, and would not be likely to have one of the character which the plaintiff's letters disclosed.

The Liverpool Mercury's version of the lawyer's remarks extended poor Sarah's character assassination by saying:

It was a case in which a woman relying upon these filthy letters believed that a man would not face exposure, and had brought a false charge against him by alleging that he promised to marry her. The plaintiff was a woman who would not live with her parents, and she and the defendant seemed to have been sowing their wild oats.

He thought that under such circumstances, and when there were so many links wanting in the chain of evidence, the jury would not believe that the defendant ever promised to marry such a woman. He asked the jury whether, when a man wished to settle down in life, he would choose a woman with whom he had improper relations.

The judge in his summing up said the case's *"gross immorality"* had to be ignored by the jury. They needed to focus their deliberations solely on whether or not they considered Sarah Harrison had received a promise to marry from Henry Sherlock.

After retiring for half-an-hour, the jury concluded that a promise had in fact been made – but no doubt influenced by what they had heard, only awarded Sarah notional damages of a farthing.

Breach of Promise Case 2 – Critchley Vs. Greenough

"The defendant commenced paying his addresses and in a short time an engagement was arranged between them"

A more successful action had occurred eighteen years earlier after Joseph Greenough had made Margaret Critchley pregnant – but failed to marry her. So on May 14th 1874, Margaret's father, James, brought an action for seduction and breach of promise against him in Preston's Sheriff Court.

The hearing was told that James Critchley was the landlord of the Mechanics Arms in Ellamsbridge Road in Sutton. Joseph Greenough was employed at the huge Sutton Glass Works nearby and had been a regular customer in the beerhouse.

That was a couple of years earlier, when Margaret was only 15 and working in the Mechanics as a barmaid. According to court testimony, Greenough began *"paying his addresses"* and soon the couple became engaged with the approval of their parents.

In May 1873 Margaret discovered that she was pregnant, or *"enceinte"*, as it was more delicately put in court. As a result of Margaret's father, James, having what was described as *"a conversation"* with Greenough, the young man went to a Widnes church where the *"askings"* or banns of marriage were put up.

But Greenough got cold feet and just before the wedding bolted to Belfast leaving his intended in the lurch. Once Margaret's pregnant condition became known to her family, she was ordered to leave the house – but a friend interceded with the parents and she was allowed to return to the pub.

Some weeks later Greenough came back to Sutton, apologised for his actions and repeatedly assured the family that he would do the right thing and marry Margaret.

However, nothing came of Greenough's promises – although by this time Margaret's pregnancy was probably too advanced for a wedding ceremony to take place.

A child called Frederick was born and just before Christmas 1873, the glass works fitter was reported as having "seduced" Margaret again, getting her pregnant for a second time.

SLY COURTSHIP

Still Greenough promised marriage. But in January 1874 there were suggestions that he was carrying on a *"sly courtship"* with a woman called Elizabeth Thorpe, who was said to be worth £1,000. When the Critchleys challenged Greenough about the rumours, he vehemently denied any such affair – but then married the woman!

That was the final straw for James Critchley and his wife Jane, and so they began court action in Preston on behalf of their now 17-year-old daughter. Breach of promise cases were usually heard away from St Helens, in order to maximise the amount of damages that might be awarded.

Their solicitor claimed in court that Margaret no longer had any opportunity of marrying respectably and had been ruined for life. A substantial sum was consequently demanded in compensation.

However, Greenough only earned 34 shillings per week, although with overtime his earnings usually came to over £2. It was stated that the defendant did have a share in some property in St Helens – but the value of it was disputed.

The jury eventually awarded the Critchleys damages of £150 to compensate for Greenough's seduction and breach of promise. But Margaret had not been ruined for life, as had been claimed.

In 1878 she married George Code and the couple moved to Horwich, near Bolton. Sadly, it appears that her son Frederick died in 1881, aged only eight.

Breach of Promise Case 3 – Seed Vs. Caldwell

"It seemed to him to be about the most blackguardly thing that a man could write to any woman"

"HE WAS A PERFECT DUKE."

A WIDOW'S BREACH OF PROMISE CASE.

A breach of promise case, which proved to be very amusing, despite the fact that Mr. M'Keand, in opening it, said he feared was devoid of those little elements of romance which make our law courts a little cheerful at times, was tried before Mr. Justice Day at the Manchester Assizes, on Tuesday. The plaintiff was a widow of about 38 years of age, named Seed, and the defendant a widower, in the prime of life, named Josiah Caldwell, a general dealer, of St. Helens. The defendant was represented by Mr. Littler. The plaintiff was a nurse, and on August 13th last year went to the house of a St. Helens lady named Andrews, who happened to be the sister of Caldwell. Mrs. Seed was introduced to him. The acquaintance developed and rapidly ripened into a very strong affection on the man's part, for four or five days later he was found asking Mrs. Seed to be his wife. The defendant took Mrs. Seed to visit his friends, and she introduced him to hers. The friends of both actually BOUGHT THEM WEDDING PRESENTS, the children even clubbing together to buy them one. Caldwell gave her £5 to buy bedding and table linen, and also took her to Liverpool to buy some furniture, and they were each as merry as a marriage bell until October. Then Mrs. Seed received a most extraordinary letter from Caldwell's sister, Mrs. Andrews, which was followed up by a scandalous letter written by the defendant. The defendant had a son of about

The Blackburn Standard March 10th 1894

On March 10th 1894 the St Helens Examiner described how at the start of a recent breach of promise case that had been heard at the Manchester Assizes, the jury had been prepared for a dull hearing.

"This case is without any of those elements of romance which sometimes made courts of law a little more cheerful", declared the counsel for the plaintiff.

In other words, loads of titillating letters were not going to be read out. The parties involved were considered too old for all that business – although widow Mary Seed was only 38 and her former fiancé Josiah Caldwell was 42.

The jury was told that Mary was a nurse from Preston who had come to St Helens to care for Josiah's sister when she was unwell. After only a few days of acquaintance with the widower, she was surprised to receive a proposal of marriage from Caldwell.

The man from College Street in St Helens claimed to be the chief partner in a firm of general dealers in North Road and had money in the bank. Caldwell even boasted of possessing his own pony and trap and owning shares in a ship – and so seemed a good catch as a husband. Mary said she was rather startled by the offer of marriage – but soon decided to accept.

AS MERRY AS A MARRIAGE BELL

The Lancashire Evening Post wrote how Caldwell subsequently gave his fiancé £5 to buy bedding and table linen and had also taken the *"comely woman"* to Liverpool to purchase some furniture.

"They were each as merry as a marriage bell", the paper commented.

However, that state of bliss did not last long. Mary told the court that out of the blue she received an extraordinary letter from Harriet Andrews, Caldwell's sister, alleging *"carryings on"* with her fiancé's 21-year-old son, Willy.

A further letter was then received from Caldwell himself that read:

Mrs. Seed, After having heard of your bad behaviour with my son at my sister's, and your lying deceitful work, we do not wish to have anything more to do with you. Send what belongs to me at once, and I will send yours by return.

Mary insisted that there was absolutely no truth in the imputations contained in the letters. There was also seemingly no truth in the claim that her ex-suitor was a partner in the firm of Caldwell and Savage. His father David was the joint owner – but Josiah Caldwell simply worked for the firm, earning no more than 20 shillings a week. At least that is what the court was told.

The St Helens Examiner wrote how the defendant had appeared in front of the magistrates dressed in a *"rough jacket"* without collar and tie. He seemed to have decided to dress down in court to give the impression he had little money.

Jury awards in such cases were roughly commensurate with the defendant's earnings and status in life. So Caldwell had apparently decided that he didn't have a leg to stand on in terms of the breach of promise and so could only mitigate the award. That he would do by saying he earned very little – and by looking the part in court.

Mary's counsel ridiculed Caldwell for his blatant attempt at poverty and showed the jury a previously taken photograph of the man looking – as he put it – like a *"perfect duke"* and a *"bit of a swell"*.

More seriously the lawyer said his claim of misconduct against his ex-fiancé was the *"most blackguardly thing that a man could write any woman"*.

The suggestion was that Caldwell had simply changed his mind over his marriage proposal and had decided to fabricate a reason. The judge said it was a clear case of breach of promise, and that "the plaintiff had been dismissed with insult and contumely [insulting treatment]".

Those comments impressed the jury who awarded Mary Seed damages of £50.

Coming A Cropper On Croppers Hill

"We went like lightning down the hill"

This is the steep Croppers Hill on Prescot Road in St Helens in 1890. It was not a place where you would want to lose control of horses – or indeed steam engines. When the photograph was taken, the era of traction engines hauling other vehicles on the roads had begun.

Steam-driven trams were replacing horse-drawn versions in St Helens and the noisy engines were pulling a variety of other conveyances too. Under the headline *"A Travelling Show Wrecked At St. Helens"*, the St Helens Examiner on January 25th 1890 described how these vehicles could include hobby horses:

An extraordinary street accident occurred at St. Helens on Tuesday afternoon. A travelling showman, named Green, of

Preston, was entering the town from Liverpool, and his "cavalcade" consisted of six trucks of hobby-horses and other paraphernalia, drawn by a traction engine. As the engine was coming down the steep incline of Cropper's hill, Prescot-road, some portion of the machinery gave way and the engine swerved round against one of the dwelling houses on the side of the street. Happily no person sustained any injury, but the show and hobby-horses were seriously damaged. The cars were twisted and hurled about the road; a lamppost at the spot was nearly destroyed, and three of the vehicles and their contents were scattered in a heap in the middle of the road. The street was rendered impassable, and all vehicular and tram traffic was blocked for over an hour. Another traction engine was obtained, and ultimately the disabled trucks were dragged to the fairground in College-lane.

A TRAVELLING SHOW WRECKED AT ST. HELENS.
An extraordinary street accident occurred at St. Helens on Tuesday afternoon. A travelling showman, named Green, of Preston, was entering the town from Liverpool, and his "cavalcade" consisted of six trucks of hobby-horses and other paraphernalia, drawn by a traction engine. As the engine was coming down the steep incline of Cropper's hill, Prescot-road, some portion of the machinery gave way and the engine swerved round against one of the dwelling houses on the side of the street. Happily no person sustained any injury, but the show and hobby-horses were seriously damaged. The cars were twisted and hurled about the road; a lamppost at the spot was nearly destroyed, and three of the vehicles and their contents were scattered in a heap in the middle of the road. The street was rendered impassable, and all vehicular and tram traffic was blocked for over an hour. Ordinary vehicles were sent round by Eccleston-st. and Boundary-road, a distance of half a mile, while

The St Helens Examiner January 25th 1890

COMBSHOP BROW

Croppers Hill was also known as Combshop Brow, as it had been the main site in St Helens where ivory combs were made, linking the town with the slave trade. The Dagnalls, who owned the comb works, even signed a petition protesting against the abolition of slavery.

On September 7th 1867 an omnibus accident led to the deaths of four passengers as four, frightened, out of control horses sped down the hill at tremendous speed and failed to navigate the turn into Liverpool Road.

The inquest was held a few days later at the Prince of Wales Inn in Ormskirk Street in St Helens after two of the men had died – with the others yet to succumb to their injuries.

The deceased so far were 28-year-old fitter Charles Morris of Brook Street and 25-year-old William Makin of Peasley Cross. The coroner was told that the bus had been hired to take a party of about 28 workers from Varley's Brookfield Foundry in St Mary's Street to New Brighton.

Moulder Thomas Watts from Edward Street gave evidence that on the return journey the bus had stopped at Knotty Ash and then at Prescot. At the Eccleston tollbar, the horses started to gallop and although the driver had tried his best to slow them down, Mr Watts described how the nags were soon out of control:

> We went down Combshop-brow at an enormous rate. The driver stood up, and pulled as hard as he could. He made every effort to stop the horses, and kept the brake on. We went like lightning down the hill, and when we were turning into Liverpool-road the 'bus turned over on its side, and dragged a dozen yards. I was on the third step when the 'bus went over, and was very much frightened. I knew the driver by sight. He was sober and capable. I saw him at

Prescot, but did not see him drink anything. It was dark all the way home. There were lights at the tollbar, which we passed at eleven o'clock.

HURRAHING AND SHOUTING

A foundry clerk from Chapel Street called Henry Ashton next gave evidence at the inquest. He had been walking down the hill and first heard the noise of the bus as it passed the Bird i' th' Hand pub and said the galloping of the horses and the *"hurrahing and shouting"* did not cease until the bus passed him.

Samuel Greenhalgh was another witness to the tragedy, telling the inquest:

> On Saturday night last I was standing in Eccleston-street, near to the foot of Combshop-brow, when I heard a great noise like thunder. I looked up the hill and saw the 'bus coming down it at great speed. It was rocking from side to side. When it reached the foot of the hill I heard the crash of the wheel, and then saw the 'bus fall. I saw the deceased man Morris fall from the top. The driver was pulling with all his might and doing his best to stop the horses.

The inquest was adjourned and then resumed on September 17th at the Fleece Hotel in Church Street. By then Thomas Winstanley had become the third workman to die from his injuries.

These buses were smaller, horse-powered versions of the open–top double-decker motor buses that we are familiar with today and all the fatalities had been sat up on top.

William Varley, the acting manager of the works, had been injured in the crash and was carried into the Fleece to give evidence. Varley stated that the horses began galloping after the driver had sounded his bugle and the men on board had started singing and shouting. However, when questioned by the jury, he said he felt the lights of the cottages at Eccleston had also frightened the horses.

That was because most of their journey from Liverpool had been in complete darkness. The driver, William Povey, thought differently, telling the inquest that he thought the men's shouting had been responsible for upsetting the nags.

There was a suggestion of a faulty wheel on the bus but the jury felt no one was to blame and delivered the usual verdict of "accidental death".

Nine months later the driver Povey – who the Liverpool Mercury said had been made a *"hopeless cripple"* by the accident – died from his injuries at the age of thirty-five.

DRIVER ASLEEP

Many carters returning to St Helens after making deliveries would have a few pints before going home – sometimes with serious consequences. Late at night on October 12th 1859, a farmer from Newton-le-Willows called William Hunt was returning home from Liverpool in his horse and cart.

At St Helens the horse began running at full speed and continued galloping down Croppers Hill until it reached the corner of Liverpool Road and Westfield Street. The animal then crashed into William Johnson's grocer's shop, with the shafts of the cart driven right through a brick wall and knocking down shelves inside.

The horse was instantly killed, with its head reported as being completely driven into its body. The driver escaped with minor injuries for the simple reason that he had been asleep!

Horses often knew their way home as well as their masters and, after having had a few drinks on the road, Mr Hunt had made himself comfortable in the back of his cart and set his horse on its way. The man only woke up when thrown from the vehicle against the wall of the shop.

However, it was reported that the circumstances of the accident and the loss of his horse – which he had only a short time earlier bought for £50 – was preying on Hunt's mind so much that it was feared he would be driven mad.

WAGONETTE CRASH

Wagonettes were four-wheeled horse-drawn carriages that, like omnibuses, were often used for excursions. At eight o'clock on July 2nd 1893, a driver of a wagonette carrying about eight persons down Croppers Hill lost control of his horse and his vehicle plunged into an iron lamppost, shattering glass all over the road.

Some children who were playing near the gas lamp had a lucky escape – in part through the actions of magistrate Thomas Glover. He happened to be passing and realising the imminent danger that the kids were in, sprang into action and dragged a child away from the oncoming vehicle.

Several persons were thrown out of the wagonette, with a companion of Mr Glover managing to catch one young woman before she could hit the ground. One person was knocked unconscious but there were no reports of serious injuries. Thirteen years later Thomas Glover became St Helens' first Labour MP.

THREW ITS RIDER TO THE GROUND

On April 18th 1896 the Liverpool Mercury described how a carter had been killed on Croppers Hill by his own vehicle:

> Yesterday Mr. S. Brighouse, county coroner, held an inquest at St. Helens Town Hall on the body of Frederick Mills, a, carter, of 7, Pitt-street, who was killed by being run over by his runaway horse and lurry in Cropper's-hill, St. Helens, on

Wednesday night. A verdict of "Accidental death" was returned. Mr. James Cook, who appeared on behalf of the employers, expressed their intention of doing something for the widow and family.

William Kitchen was a well-known St Helens' estate agent who lived on Croppers Hill and was also killed by his own horse during that same year. The Bolton Evening News described this tragedy on February 17th 1896:

A sad accident, resulting in the death of Mr. W. Kitchen, house and estate agent, Cropper's-hill, St. Helens, occurred on Sunday. About a fortnight ago Mr. Kitchen purchased a spirited young colt, which had not been "broken in," and had taken it out several times attached to his trap. At noon on Sunday, however, Mr. Kitchen changed the exercise by mounting the saddle and driving the animal about on some vacant land behind his residence.

The colt suddenly became restive, and as Mr. Kitchen's foot slipped from a stirrup the animal dashed away into Maxwell-st., where it threw its rider to the ground. Mr. Kitchen's head came in contact with the kerbstone, and he was rendered unconscious. Mr. Kitchen received a large wound on the back of his head and a severe bruise on his temple, and, notwithstanding every attention, he never recovered consciousness, and expired four hours later. Deceased was 56 years of age, and leaves a widow and several children.

The Cruel And Callous Councillor Kirkham

"From his commencement in business down to this very time,
he has been guilty of oppression and cruelty."

This 1880 advert for William Kirkham's new premises in Tontine Street gives the impression that the auctioneer was a highly respectable St Helens businessman. What the newspaper ad does not reveal is that the 26-year-old had already served a month in prison for his part in the Greenough house demolition scandal of 1877.

KIRKHAM'S NEW SALE ROOMS

60, TONTINE-STREET, ST. HELENS.

ESTABLISHED 1872.

WILLIAM KIRKHAM,

AUCTIONEER AND VALUER,
RENT AND DEBT COLLECTOR.

LIFE AND FIRE INSURANCE AGENT.

W. Kirkham begs respectfully to announce to his friends and the public generally, that he has opened a large and commodious Sale Room, suitable for Furniture, Drapery, and other sales of any description.

OFFICES AND SALE ROOMS:
60, TONTINE STREET, ST. HELENS.

And at the same time as the ad was being published in local papers, Kirkham was embroiled in a court case in which he was accused of *"hard-heartedness and villainy"* through attempting to remove a cot from a house in which two babies were dying.

Born in Toxteth Park in 1854, William Joseph Kirkham moved to St Helens at an early age. In the 1871 census he is listed in Westfield Street as a 16-year-old apprentice joiner to his father Luke. However, Kirkham had bigger ideas than carpentry and in the following year – according to his advert – had set up his own estate and debt-collecting agency.

Kirkham's first brush with the law was in March 1875 when the Prescot Reporter described how the *"respectable dressed young man"* had made a huge deal out of a prosecution for not paying for a train ticket. Instead of admitting the offence and accepting the usual small fine, Kirkham asked the magistrates for an adjournment, obtained counsel to represent him, put up a complicated defence and summoned a doctor as a witness to help him prove his case – but was still fined ten shillings! He had also to pay all the associated costs, which probably did not leave him much change out of £10.

In September of that year Kirkham married Jane Rowland, something the young woman would come to regret. Within three years she had taken her husband to court and charged him with assault for which he was fined 20 shillings.

Then in 1877 Kirkham was with the party of men who accompanied Joseph Greenough to Parr Moss to help the councillor knock down the walls of a cottage – while the occupants were inside!

It was connected to a dispute over land ownership and Kirkham was given a month's hard labour in Kirkdale Gaol for his part in the crazy affair – and there would be more prison time to come.

I don't think Kirkham was an auctioneer in the same vein as J. B. Leach of Hardshaw Street, William Gerard of Bridge Street or Thomas Lyon of Baldwin Street. These respected individuals were often commissioned to auction large properties or estates – but Kirkham was little more than a rent or debt collector.

If he could not obtain the cash, then he would ask for a court order to seize goods in lieu of the amount owed. That was known as "distraint", and as most people then had few possessions, it usually meant confiscating their furniture, as well as bits and bobs. Those items Kirkham would then sell off at rock bottom prices in his Tontine Street saleroom.

OPPRESSION AND CRUELTY

Executing one distraint order in November 1880 against a man called Thomas Corless, led to Kirkham being sued for £50 damages. St Helens Corporation had hired the debt collector to chase up townsfolk who had not paid their water rates. Kirkham only received commission if he recouped any money, which motivated unscrupulous individuals like him to play the dirtiest of tricks on poor folk in debt.

Corless kept an unprofitable beerhouse in Brook Street called the Moss Rose Inn and owed the Corporation just over £2 in water rates. When confronted by Kirkham, Corless managed to pay 15 shillings off the debt.

The landlord promised to find the balance in a few days' time – but the debt collector refused to wait and despite the fact that two babies were dying in the house, confiscated all the furniture. Corless's solicitor, Thomas Swift, explained to the judge in St Helens County Court what had occurred:

> The things were put up for auction, and absolutely given away, and every stick of furniture was sold about the place. There were six or seven little children in the place who had to be taken in hand by charitable neighbours, and while two of them (twins) lay dying in a cradle, the defendant absolutely wanted to turn the dying children out and sell the cradle from underneath them, but the neighbours would not let him. The children had died since, and had been carried out of an empty house – a house stripped by the hard-heartedness and villainy of the defendant....From his commencement in business down to this very time he [Kirkham] has been guilty of oppression and cruelty.

More goods were seized from the Moss Rose Inn than were needed to pay off the debt. And despite the furniture being described as being in a *"shipwrecked"* condition, the jury awarded Thomas Corless £22 13s 11d damages for what had been needlessly and illegally removed from his home.

In April 1881 Kirkham entered a form of arranged bankruptcy and in August of that year was back in court, this time at Leigh. While seizing property at a farm at Astley under a court order, Kirkham had confiscated a cart that belonged to another farmer despite being repeatedly told it was not the debtor's property.

That matter appears to have been settled privately but in the following October, Kirkham brought an action in St Helens County Court against Joseph Dennett, claiming the Westfield Street publican owed him £3 10 shillings. However, after witness evidence proved that Kirkham in providing a service for Dennett had committed blatant fraud, the judge rejected his claim.

On January 11th 1884 a blacksmith named William Boardman brought a summons against Kirkham accusing the debt collector of attacking him in Boundary Road. Boardman gave evidence that Kirkham had followed him out of a shop, told him he had an old grudge against him and then knocked him down and kicked him *"so savagely"* that one of his ribs was broken.

But after hearing the evidence of witnesses and Kirkham's complete denial of responsibility, the magistrates felt compelled to dismiss the summons.

In November 1884 Kirkham made his first attempt at becoming a councillor – but only received 263 votes. The St Helens Examiner described the declaration of the results and the candidates' speeches to a large crowd on the Town Hall steps:

> Mr. Kirkham, the rejected of East Sutton, was received with loud groans and slight cheering. The remarks he made did not reach the crowd, who persistently hissed.

However, Kirkham claimed that his unsuccessful campaign for election had saved St Helens' ratepayers £4,000. That was because he reckoned his fighting talk over profligacy had forced the councillors to reduce their proposed spending on improvements to the Town Hall. I expect the council had a different view on the matter!

Three years later Kirkham stood for election for the third time in East Sutton (having been beaten again in 1886) and as popular incumbent Amos Hanson had chosen to retire from politics, the debt-collecting auctioneer stood a far better chance of winning.

This he did by 70 votes, after making many promises to the electorate that he was unlikely to be in a position to keep. At his first council meeting, the new boy kicked up a fuss over the council committees that he had been allocated, saying:

> I find from the list which I have received that I have been fixed on three of the most unimportant committees that there are. I do not know why; whether it was that possibly the gentlemen who had the fixing of the committees might have thought I have no ability, or perhaps they might have thought I would turn out a little troublesome. But I must say that I should like to be put on the Paving and Highway Committee. I have to go before my constituents, and I have promised them that their roads should be put in better order, and I do not see how I am to fulfil the promise unless I get on that committee.

Kirkham was the only member who complained and was essentially told that new councillors had to learn the ropes first on more minor committees before progressing to weightier ones. That did not satisfy Cllr. Kirkham, who declared:

> I represent East Sutton Ward, one side of which is like a palace and the other like a pig-stye and you ought to have someone who would explain to the committee what state the roads were in.

Of course, the council knew the state of the roads in the borough and were improving them each year – but there was a limit to what could be done with the funds that were available. On the one hand Kirkham wanted the rates that paid for council spending to be kept low – but also demanded considerable expenditure within his East Sutton ward.

CONTEMPT OF COURT

Within a matter of weeks of the council election, an application was made to St Helens County Court for Councillor Kirkham to be committed to prison for contempt of court. That was because the 32-year-old was the official receiver of the Sutton Rolling Mills Industrial Co-operative Society. A complaint had been made that moneys paid to him in that capacity had not been deposited as required into Parr's Bank and the appropriate declarations made.

Kirkham had taken no notice of a court order concerning these failures and so the contempt charge was brought against him. His response was to claim that he had transferred the money into the bank – but at an adjourned hearing a week later he admitted that he hadn't. £21 13s 8d was now paid into court and he was ordered to pay the costs of the hearing, with the judge criticising the councillor for his negligence.

Many councillors would attend the various events that were held in St Helens and Kirkham certainly liked to put himself about. However, it was noticeable from the lists of attendees published in local newspapers that his wife never accompanied him.

The St Helens Examiner revealed the reason on June 16th 1888 – Jane Kirkham had left her husband and was seeking a divorce on the grounds of his cruelty and adultery. Being divorced had a

A ST. HELENS TOWN COUNCILLOR IN THE DIVORCE COURT.

The case of Kirkham v. Kirkham was called on for hearing in the Divorce Court on Friday afternoon. Mr. Justice Butt was on the bench. The petitioner's application was for a dissolution of marriage on the ground of several acts of cruelty and adultery on the part of the respondent, William Joseph Kirkham, an auctioneer, carrying on business in Tontine-st., St. Helens, and a member of the Town Council. The respondent filed a counter petition for judicial separation on the ground of the petititioner's cruelty and desertion. There were fourteen witnesses in the case, five for the petitioner, and nine for the respondent.—Mr. Middleton appeared for the petitioner, and Mr. Barnard for the respondent. The parties were married in September, 1875, the respondent being an auctioneer carrying on business at St. Helens. There were several children of the marriage, four of whom were still living. According to the petitioner's counsel the marriage from the first was an unhappy one, the wife being subject to numerous acts of violence on the part of her husband. He had repeatedly given her black eyes, had knocked her down, and had knocked her about the head with a poker, and had also burnt her clothes. In 1878 petitioner found a bundle of letters in her husband's desk, and these convinced her that he was carrying on an improper intimacy with a young woman of the name of Duffy. Subsequently it came to the knowledge of the wife that respondent had been unduly intimate with a char-woman whom she occasionally employed. In the month of March, 1886, the petitioner had occasion to think that her husband was locked in his

St Helens Examiner June 16th 1888

205

huge stigma attached to it and for a councillor in the public eye, divorce was far from helpful to his personal ambitions.

And so he filed a counter petition for judicial separation on the grounds of what he claimed to be his wife's cruelty and desertion of him. Of course, it is impossible to know the truth of exactly what goes on in any couple's marriage. However, with the man's track record *(and with events that I've yet to reveal)*, Kirkham as the victim of domestic violence from his wife seems laughable.

But the judge appears to have been taken in by the debt collector's claim because of one particular event. Women in Victorian times who did not act in a passive way to spousal abuse and who drank to make their lives that bit easier could make matters far worse.

If court proceedings took place, then their cruel husbands would exaggerate their wives' behaviour and use it against them – and in the bargain make themselves out as the innocent party within a troubled marriage.

Divorces in the 19th century were rare and only for the well-heeled. And so the few divorce proceedings that did take place were given huge publicity by the newspapers – with all the juicy claims and counter-claims pored over by the public.

The fact that one party in the Kirkhams' case was a local councillor, added extra spice to the St Helens Examiner's coverage of the mud throwing – which bore the headline *"A St. Helens Town Councillor In The Divorce Court"*:

> The case of Kirkham v. Kirkham was called on for hearing in the Divorce Court on Friday afternoon. Mr. Justice Butt was on the bench. The petitioner's application was for a dissolution of marriage on the ground of several acts of cruelty and adultery on the part of the respondent, William Joseph Kirkham, an auctioneer, carrying on business in Tontine-st., St. Helens, and a member of the Town Council.

The respondent filed a counter petition for judicial separation on the ground of the petititioner's cruelty and desertion. There were fourteen witnesses in the case, five for the petitioner, and nine for the respondent. Mr. Middleton appeared for the petitioner, and Mr. Barnard for the respondent.

The parties were married in September, 1875, the respondent being an auctioneer carrying on business at St. Helens. There were several children of the marriage, four of whom were still living, According to the petitioner's counsel the marriage from the first was an unhappy one, the wife being subject to numerous acts of violence on the part of her husband. He had repeatedly given her black eyes, had knocked her down, and had knocked her about the head with a poker, and had also burnt her clothes.

In 1878 petitioner found a bundle of letters in her husband's desk, and these convinced her that he was carrying on an improper intimacy with a young woman of the name of Duffy. Subsequently it came to the knowledge of the wife that respondent had been unduly intimate with a char-woman whom she occasionally employed.

In the month of March, 1886, the petitioner had occasion to think that her husband was locked in his bedroom with this woman, whose name was Dickson, and she broke the door open with a hatchet. She, however, found he was alone. Upon that she returned to her bedroom, and about half an hour afterwards the respondent came in, violently assaulted her, and turned her out of the house in her nightdress.

After that she never returned to her husband, but lived with her mother. It was further alleged that since then an improper intimacy had existed between the respondent and another woman, who was ostensibly living with him as his housekeeper.

The cross-examination that Jane Kirkham received from her husband's counsel was severe – with a long list of allegations thrown at her. She denied a claim that she had struck her spouse with a slipper; had threatened to cut her husband's throat or drank too much. Mrs Kirkham admitted using the axe to break into her husband's bedroom – but denied that she had struck him with it.

In the witness box William Kirkham gave an emphatic denial to the charges of misconduct alleged against him. Instead he accused his wife of being a very violent woman who had frequently assaulted him. He admitted giving her a black eye but claimed it had been accidentally caused during a struggle for a poker.

Kirkham declared his wife to be a very jealous woman and that, he said, had been the key to all their quarrels – and he insisted that Miss Adamson was simply his housekeeper. The Examiner wrote: *"He denied in the most positive manner that he had ever misconducted herself with her."*

When the judge gave his decision, he said he considered the evidence of the alleged adultery with the girl Duffy to be unsatisfactory – but he had no doubt that Mrs Kirkham was a violent woman.

Justice Butt added that as a result he accepted the wife's evidence with considerable hesitation. He did not think, therefore, that the charge of adultery had been proved.

A VIOLENT WOMAN

As to the cruelty, while he had no doubt of the wife being a violent woman, he said he considered her husband's conduct not always justifiable. As a result he held that cruelty had been proved sufficiently to allow Mrs Kirkham a decree of judicial separation.

Much was made of the axe "attack". I think if I had been the judge I would have enquired why Kirkham had not immediately opened his bedroom door when his wife was loudly banging on it, well before the axe was brought into play. Was the time used to hide his girlfriend somewhere in the bedroom?

Thirty minutes later Kirkham chucked his wife out of the house. Why did it take him so long? Was he ensuring that his lady friend had got out of the house first? Somewhat forgotten in this debacle was the couple's four children – although the judge felt they should remain with their father, at least for the time being.

However, the people that William Kirkham did not forget were his constituents – or to put it another way, the councillor was concerned as to how his appearance in the divorce court might affect his electoral standing.

The debt-collecting auctioneer had given a good account of himself in court – seemingly through telling many lies – and although the judge had some criticisms of his behaviour, His Honour had been much more critical of his wife.

The councillor's majority at the last election had only been 70 votes and with literacy levels improving all the time, more people than ever were reading newspapers. Access had been boosted in the previous year through the opening of a library in Sutton Road.

All the local newspapers were available in its newsroom, allowing Kirkham's constituents to pore over the details of his divorce case to their heart's content.

RIGHT AND JUSTICE

So he needed to take the bull by the horns and on June 19th Kirkham called an open-air meeting on land behind Sutton National School in Ellamsbridge Road. The handbills advertising the gathering said its purpose was to…

...take into consideration the question of the desirability of my resigning or retaining the position I now hold as your representative in the Town Council.

The St Helens Examiner described how 400 persons had attended the meeting with Kirkham telling the gathering that he wanted them to say *"boldly and plainly"* whether or not he was still worthy to represent them, and adding: *"So long as I have right and justice at my back I will fight on as I have done in the past."*

One elector called Ashley stepped forward and said he dared say there were worse men than Mr Kirkham on the council, and he did not see what family affairs had to do with the electors as long as they had a good representative. All present shared that opinion and so Kirkham received the ringing endorsement from his constituents that he sought.

But within weeks the man who believed in "right and justice" was reported as having left the country, taking with him his "housekeeper" Miss Adamson and his oldest daughter Eliza. Councillor Kirkham had been awarded custody of the children and his separated spouse Jane had subsequently moved in with her mother at Southport.

Once the news broke that her husband was believed to have sailed to the United States leaving their three young boys behind, Jane returned to St Helens to care for them. However, she had no legal right to do so and no money.

DISGRACEFUL, SHAMEFUL THING

So at a Prescot Board of Guardians meeting on October 25th 1888, it was revealed that Mrs Kirkham had applied for outdoor relief. Also called parish relief, this was a meagre amount of money that was usually given in the form of food to the poorest of folk.

The Board of Guardians was also in charge of Whiston Workhouse and as a last resort Jane and her children could have been placed in the institution. But it was far cheaper to provide the poor with relief within their own home than in the workhouse and the Guardians decided to grant the Kirkham children 3s 9d per week.

One guardian, James Burchall, called it a *"disgraceful, shameful thing"* that the councillor should have deserted his children. Such an act was a crime, if no provision for the man's dependents had been made. So the Guardians' Clerk was told to take out a warrant for Kirkham's arrest.

On April 3rd 1889 the first meeting of St Helens Town Council was held since the town had become a county borough. One item on the agenda was to declare William Kirkham's seat in East Sutton vacant, as six months had elapsed since he'd sailed to America. That was the minimum amount of time needed to kick absent members off the council and a by-election could now be held.

Throughout the rest of that year nothing further was heard of ex-Councillor Kirkham. The man had seemingly sailed off to the New World with his charlady / housekeeper, the woman who he had sworn in court that he was not in a relationship with.

But that was one of his many lies – including letting it be known that he was departing for a holiday in America at the time of his leaving St Helens. In actual fact Kirkham and Miss Adamson (and daughter Eliza) had only relocated to Sunderland, where they were calling themselves Mr and Mrs Dalton and running an oyster shop.

A St Helens man living in Sunderland had recognised the disgraced ex-councillor and during the evening of July 9th 1890, KIrkham was arrested by police and returned to Lancashire.

Upon appearing before the magistrates in Prescot, Kirkham, through his solicitor, blamed his estranged wife Jane for his situation. He insisted that upon leaving St Helens, sufficient money and clothing had been left with friends in order to keep the children. The case – it was argued – was simply the result of vindictive action by Mrs Kirkham because of her failure in the divorce proceedings.

WEEPING BITTERLY

However, the days of blaming his wife and getting away with the telling of outrageous lies were at an end. Later that month Kirkham appeared at the Woolton Petty Sessions and was sentenced to a month's hard labour – the same term that he had served in 1877 when mixed up in the Greenough house destruction scandal.

The St Helens Examiner described his reaction during the hearing:

> Kirkham was weeping bitterly while the case was proceeding, and he was so deeply affected that he turned his back on the court, and stood facing the wall with his handkerchief to his eyes.

Although the ex-town councillor now clearly felt very sorry for himself, I expect few others in St Helens did. But why did he flee the town in the first place?

Presumably, it was for financial reasons. Kirkham had been involved in a court case shortly before his departure as the victim of a £50 fraud.

Ironically, that was the same amount that the Prescot Guardians spent in feeding his boys during the 21 months he was living in Sunderland with his housekeeper.

WIFE DESERTION BY A ST. HELENS EX-COUNCILLOR.

A MONTH IN GAOL.

On Friday, at the Woolton Petty Sessions, before Mr. J. Bingham (chairman), and Major Gaskell. the charge preferred by the Prescot Board of Guardians against William Kirkham, an ex-town councillor of St. Helens, came up for hearing, the prisoner being charged, on remand from Prescot, with having deserted his wife and family, thereby leaving them chargeable to the common fund of the Prescot Union Workhouse. The case for the prosecution was conducted by Mr. J. O. Swift, the prisoner being defended by Mr. H. L. Riley. Mr. J. P. Mearns watched the case on behalf of Mrs. Kirkham.— The prisoner on being charged said, "I am advised to plead guilty."—The Clerk: We don't know anything about your advice. Are you guilty or not guilty?— Prisoner: I plead guilty.—Mr. Swift, in stating the case for the prosecution, said that he was instructed by the guardians to prosecute the prisoner under the vagrancy act, which provided that any person running away and leaving his wife and family should be punishable as a rogue and a vagabond, the penalty prescribed being imprisonment for a term not exceeding three months with or without hard labour. Up to September, 1888, the prisoner had lived in St. Helens, where he had carried on business as an auctioneer. As a result of divorce proceedings, he and his wife had separated. He had then in his house a lady who was considered to be the housekeeper, and there also lived with him his eldest daughter, a girl of 14 or 15, and

St Helens Examiner July 26th 1890

212

I expect that he had taken his oldest child Eliza along with him because she would have been an asset – able to work for him and provide a wage. That's unlike his three young boys who would have been a burden. That does appear to have been how he perceived his younger children.

Although Kirkham was discharged from prison in mid-August of 1890, the boys were reported to be languishing in Whiston Workhouse in early December. How long the lads had been placed in the workhouse, I have not been able to learn. But on December 4th at a meeting of the Prescot Guardians, it was decided to take legal action against Kirkham once again.

The intention of the summons was to force him to remove his children from the workhouse and for him to pay for their keep while they were being cared for at Whiston. After that report, Kirkham disappears from the newspapers and I have been unable to trace him in any of the censuses.

I think there is every chance that the disgraced ex-councillor changed his name again and left St Helens to try and seek his fortune elsewhere.

The Day Two Princes Dropped In On Rainford

"Farmhands in corduroys doffed their hats
and the prince raised his bowler in reply"

I wonder how many farmers can claims that two princes once "dropped in" on them by air? Perhaps a few might have experienced Royal visits by helicopter but not many, I expect, by aeroplane – and piloted by the two princes themselves in separate aircraft! But Mossborough Hall Farm in Rainford can boast that rare honour, which occurred on one day in 1932.

Mossborough Hall in Rainford which received two Royal visits in 1932

Royal protocol prevents heirs to the throne from flying in the same aircraft and so on March 18th of that year, the Prince of Wales *(the future Edward VIII)* and his brother Prince George *(the future Duke of Kent)* flew to Mossborough in separate planes. Both had a pilot's licence, as in fact did their brother, the future King George VI.

It wasn't the farm that interested the pair but the adjacent field. It was considered an ideal place to land their aircraft and then drive to Aintree via Coach Road to watch the Grand National.

One might have thought that Speke Aerodrome would have been a more suitable venue for landing. Although the future John Lennon Airport had not yet been officially opened, scheduled flights from London were already taking place.

However, it was at least a 12-mile drive from Speke to Aintree and the Royal siblings appeared to have preferred a shorter trip from Rainford – in spite of a possible bumpy landing in a farmer's field!

MOSSBOROUGH HALL

On the morning of March 18th the Manchester Guardian stated that the Prince of Wales and Prince George would be watching the Grand National at Aintree from a special stand that had been erected near to Valentine's Brook.

The two Royal pilots would be leaving London later that day in their own private aeroplanes with their destination being a *"specially arranged landing place"* at Mossborough Hall, on the estate of Lord Derby.

PRINCES FLY TO AINTREE

The Prince of Wales and Prince George flew to Aintree to-day to see the Grand National.

The Royal brothers left Smith's Lawn, the Prince of Wales's private flying ground in Windsor Great Park, just after 11 o'clock. They had motored over from his country home, Fort Belvedere, at Sunningdale, and took off in their private aeroplanes.

The Princes landed at Rainford at one o'clock. They were met by Lord Sefton and motored to Aintree.

Dundee Evening Telegraph March 18th 1932

The report added that the princes were expected to arrive at Rainford between 12:30 and 1 o'clock in the afternoon. They would be met by Lord Sefton and would motor directly to the racecourse and fly back to London after the race.

Later that day the Liverpool Echo described the events that had occurred at Mossborough:

> The Prince of Wales and Prince George had an early glimpse of the Grand National course, to-day, from the air. Their planes, like two spots of red and silver, hovered for a moment or two away to the right of the course, and then they made direct for the rolling parklands near Mossborough Hall Farm, Rainford. They started from the Princes' private air ground at Windsor Great Park about eleven and landed just before one o'clock. Near the Hall Farm, two farmhands steadily fed bonfires with hay to act as guiding pylons to the planes. Farmhands and dairymaids had come straight from their jobs to be present, together with school children, and they chatted excitedly along the hedgerows, round the cottages of Bunkers Hill waiting to see the Princes.
>
> The distant hum of the planes was heard over the trees and soon the two Royal planes with a pilot plane were clearly silhouetted overhead against the dappled blue and white sky. They glistened in the sunshine. The pilot 'plane circled round, and then the Prince of Wales' 'plane came gracefully down in the field next to that in which the bonfires were blazing. A second or two later Prince George's plane had landed. Meanwhile, the waiting group were cut off from the landing spot, but they did not miss the Princes.
>
> Together with the Chief Constable of Lancashire (Mr. W. Trubshaw), they had to tramp nearly a quarter-of-a-mile over pasture land to the gate in the field near Bunker's Hill Cottages, where two cars were waiting. There were cheers as the Princes came nearer and nearer to the group across

the field, and an impromptu guard of honour was formed midway in the field near Bunker's Hill Cottages by farmhands in corduroys. This little group all doffed their hats, and the Prince raised his bowler in reply. The Prince looked very fit, and was dressed in a thick brown coat, fur-lined, and Prince George wore a dark grey overcoat, with astrakhan collar, and no hat. Both had binoculars slung over their shoulders, and they were accompanied by Mr. Ll. Thomas, the equerry, and Captain Field, pilot. A round of cheers rent the air as they neared the gate, and one old woman in a high-pitched falsetto voice, exclaimed: "God bless the Prince of Wales, and all the Royal Family." The Prince doffed his hat in salute, and Prince George smiled and bowed.

Strangely the St Helens newspapers failed to cover this unusual occurrence and so I cannot provide any more details of the children – although, I expect they were from Rainford Village School in Cross Pit Lane.

YON'S A GRADELY MON!

The Prince of Wales returned to the district eight months later when on November 24th 1932 he visited St Helens as part of a tour of Lancastrian industrial centres. However, this time Edward travelled by motor car.

Despite wet weather the Prince still received a rapturous reception. The St Helens Reporter described how so many umbrellas had been raised that the pavements resembled mushroom beds.

An old man was reported as doing brisk business selling paper batons in red, white and blue with streamer tops, shouting to prospective purchasers: *"Summat to wave to t' Prince!"*

And in the YMCA where the prince chatted to a number of the unemployed, an elderly man remarked: *"Yon's a gradely mon"!*

St Helens Poker Bashing Stories

"He flung a poker at his wife. The weapon struck her head, pierced the skull, and penetrated into the brain."

There is a surprising variety in the types of pokers that were employed during the 19th century. However, they were usually made of wrought iron and as such, quite substantial implements.

Illustrated Police News Jan. 9th 1892

With coal fires in virtually all homes, heavy pokers designed to stoke fires also served as handy weapons in passionate, spur-of-the-moment crimes and some serious damage to many a St Helens' resident's head and body was done with a poker.

In this chapter I have four newspaper accounts of such attacks. The first example might have the moral, "don't introduce a poker into a row unless you are prepared to use it"!

The St Helens Examiner published details of the case on May 17th 1884 in which a man was charged in court with committing a violent assault on a young woman:

> A rough-looking young fellow, named William McCormick, was charged with committing an aggravated assault upon Agnes McGill. The prisoner pleaded not guilty. The evidence showed that the prosecutrix is a domestic servant at the Travellers' Rest Inn, Eccleston, and on the previous afternoon (Sunday) she was standing at the corner of

Mount-street. A man named Griffin came up and hit her on the mouth. Her brother then went to her assistance, but Griffin and others knocked him down and severely kicked him. She thereupon ran in the house and brought out a poker, and said the next man who struck her brother would be hit with the poker.

A man named Priestly took it from her, however, and the prisoner took it from Priestly. Other men stuck her, and the prisoner violently hit her on the left arm with the poker, breaking it in three places. He also kicked her about the body and head. Superintendent Johnson gave the prisoner a very bad character, remarking that he had been previously convicted of a similar offence. The prisoner was sentenced to two months' hard labour, the Bench remarking that but for the prosecutrix having fetched the poker into the street the sentence would have been a heavier one.

IRRITATING TONGUE

Plenty of St Helens males have used pokers on their wives during arguments – such as Thomas Shaw of Burtonhead Road. The young man was convicted of manslaughter after flinging a poker at his wife during a drunken row. Shaw's father told the court that his daughter-in-law, Elizabeth, had an *"irritating tongue"*.

The Liverpool Echo on March 14th 1895 described the sentencing hearing:

Thomas Shaw (23), engine-tenter, who was convicted the previous day for the manslaughter of his wife at St. Helens, on the 25th November last, now came up for sentence. Evidence of prisoner's previously good character having been given, his Lordship said the jury in effect had recommended prisoner to mercy upon the ground that he acted under great provocation. But he acted like a brute. He flung a poker at his wife. The weapon struck her head, pierced the skull, and penetrated an inch and a half into the brain substance. It must have been a blow of enormous violence. Were it not for the previous good character prisoner had received he (his lordship) would make a singular example him. As it was his punishment must be serious – twelve months hard labour.

Mothers-in-law were often the victims of poker attacks. On March 23rd 1914, the Echo described this hearing that had taken place in St Helens Police Court:

Michael Mitchell, collier, of 16, Leicester-street, Thatto Heath, was charged with wounding his mother-in-law, Mrs. Alice Stanley, of 40, Sandon-street, by striking her a violent blow on the head with a poker. The Chief Constable said that Mitchell fell out with his wife and threatened her. She went to her mother's for protection. The man followed her, and challenged his brother-in-law out to fight. James Stanley went to the door and was pulled out by the prisoner and beaten. Mrs. Stanley went to rescue her son, when she was struck on the head with a poker that Mitchell had brought from his house. Prisoner denied the poker belonged to him.

A witness spoke to seeing Mitchell beating the door with the poker, and striking Mrs. Stanley. She immediately dropped and had to be carried into the house and attended by a doctor, who found a wound which necessitated four stitches. The doctor said it would be three weeks at least before Mrs. Stanley was recovered. The bench decided that it would be unwise to deal with the case summarily, and committed Mitchell for trial at the sessions.

Mitchell would later be given two months hard labour for his attack. Pokers were also handy implements to bash impatient debt collectors with – and the Liverpool Mercury of December 17th 1855, described such a case that had been heard at the Lancashire Winter Assizes:

Edward Gaskell was charged with assaulting James Berry, with intent to do him grievous bodily harm, at Sutton, near St. Helen's, on the 29th November last. Mr. Laresche prosecuted, and Mr. Simon defended. It appeared that on the day in question the prosecutor went to the house of the prisoner to execute a distress warrant. The prisoner told his wife to go to St. Helen's for the money. The prosecutor said the cart to carry away the goods would be there in ten minutes.

The prisoner said, "Do you think I can go to St. Helen's and back in ten minutes?" and, taking up the poker, ordered the bailiff to leave the house. The prosecutor replied that he dared not, whereupon the prisoner struck him a blow on the head, which rendered him insensible. The jury found the prisoner guilty of unlawfully wounding, and he was sentenced to six months' imprisonment with hard labour.

Three Thatto Heath Runaway Romances

*"The Chief Constable described Bevan as a proper scamp,
and deserved all their worships could give him"*

SEQUEL TO AN ELOPEMENT - PARR ST HELENS.

Nothing got tongues wagging more than rumours of affairs – and especially when couples ran off together. This illustration was on the front cover of the newspaper known as the Illustrated Police News on August 26th 1882.

It depicts the wave of moral outrage that swept through Parr after a married woman who had gone to Scotland with her lodger came back home to St Helens. The return had been by agreement with the husband who had brought his wife home.

It was a private matter but that did not stop a mini-riot occurring in Higher Parr Street with a large crowd beating tin kettles, pots and pans to show their disapproval of what the mother of six had done.

Elopements came in different forms with the first of my three examples from Thatto Heath concerning a 15-year-old girl who had run off to Liverpool with her older lover to get married.

The St Helens Examiner on October 18th 1879 described the pragmatic – but curious – way the authorities dealt with the case:

> A few weeks ago a young girl named Mary Case, aged 15, daughter of Margaret Anders, who resides at Brown-edge, Thatto Heath, suddenly disappeared from her grandfather's house, for whom she was keeping house at Portico. The fact threw the inhabitants of that district into an unusual state of excitement, and first one and then another advanced an opinion as to the whereabouts or fate of the lost girl. The fact that a young man Samuel Rowley, a convict on license, was also missing, led the parents and friends to believe that they had gone off together, or at all events that he was concerned in her departure from that neighbourhood.
>
> Consequently information was given to the police, and a warrant issued for the man's apprehension. He was apprehended on Wednesday in Dale-street, Liverpool, by a detective and this being made known to the St. Helens police, Sergt. Whittaker went over and brought the runaway couple back, and lodged them at the Town Hall [police station]. The man, attended by his spouse, was arraigned before the Magistrate on Thursday, and both for the present regarded their marriage as anything but one productive of "much joy and happiness."

A marriage certificate was produced in court that revealed that the couple had wed on October 6th at St Matthew's Church in Toxteth

Park. The 15-year-old girl's age was falsely stated on the certificate as being 18 and the age of the groom was shown as 24.

If such an occurrence had taken place today, I think the man would have been in serious trouble – on several counts. But instead of being sent to prison, the convict on licence was praised for what he had done.

The prosecuting solicitor told the magistrates that on account of the *"honourable way"* in which Rowley had acted by marrying the girl and promising to be kind to her, he would withdraw the charge that had been made against him.

It was also claimed that Rowley had sent a letter to the girl's mother a couple of weeks earlier explaining the marriage – but the mother said she had not received it.

The St Helens Examiner's report ended with this sentence:

> The prisoner, his young wife, and the mother then went away, apparently well pleased, the couple appearing to be fond of each other and happy once more.

The article inferred that Samuel had made Mary pregnant and in the 1881 census – taken 18 months after the wedding – there is a one-year-old son listed in residence that confirms this.

The couple are shown still living in Thatto Heath, with Mary falsely claiming to be twenty and Samuel stating his occupation as an unemployed chemical labourer.

However, five months after the census was taken, Samuel was sentenced to seven years in prison for stealing a coat – having been given the same sentence for committing an identical crime in 1874. It was after being let out of prison on licence for committing that offence that he met Mary.

ELOPEMENT FROM ST. HELENS

The sympathy shown in Samuel and Mary's case did not extend to married individuals. This has already been exemplified in the Parr case alluded to at the start of this article.

Under the headline *"Elopement From St. Helens"*, the Liverpool Echo on March 5th 1894 described a similar decampment from the town by another couple:

> The neighbourhood of Thatto Heath, St. Helens, is considerably perturbed by the simultaneous disappearance of a single man and a married woman with several children. The blonde swain was a colliery labourer, and the brunette, unassisted by her husband, earned a living on the pit brow. The gay Lothario became enamoured of Bridget, and undisguisedly declared his affection and paid her attention, the sequel being that an early train on Saturday morning bore them away to parts unknown.

Whether Bridget ever returned home I couldn't say. But under the headline, *"A Blighted Romance – Punishment For A Scamp"*, the Liverpool Daily Post of October 9th 1909 described how a 20-year-old Thatto Heath girl had eloped with an older, married man – and taken some of her father's possessions along with her:

> Ivy Lancaster, a young woman who had formerly lived with her father in Emily-street, Thatto Heath, was charged at St. Helens yesterday, along with a man with whom she had run away, with stealing two silver watches, a chain, and travelling bag. The evidence was that for eight years past the girl had been housekeeper for her father. For some time a man named William Bevan, who, it was alleged, was a married man, had been lodging at 16, Emily-street. By some means the two had become acquainted. A week ago the father went to work, and when he returned at night his

thirteen-year-old boy gave him a note in which Ivy said she had left the house and taken what belonged to her. The father then found that the two "had been carrying on," and that they had gone, taking the watches.

The police were contacted and discovered that Bevan had pawned one of the timepieces and sold the ticket. The couple had then left for Shropshire, where they were arrested at the man's grandmother's house while posing as man and wife.

In court the police said Bevan had two convictions for theft and was legally separated from his wife, after walking out on her. The Chief Constable described Bevan as a *"proper scamp, and deserved all their worships could give him"*.

That did not appear to be Ivy's opinion as she told the Bench that she did not want to go back to her father, because she had not been comfortable living there. The Daily Post wrote: *"The father tearfully said he wanted her to come back and be a good girl"*.

The magistrates placed Ivy on probation and sent Bevan to gaol for six months' hard labour. She clearly did go home, as the 1911 census shows Ivy living with her widower father Michael and her brother Ernest – although the family had relocated to Nutgrove.

The Criminal Career Of Catherine Flynn

"He saw the prisoner, with a shawl over her head, leaning towards the boots. He saw her snatch the boots from the rail and run down the street."

This is the prison photograph of Catherine Flynn of Union Street in Cowley Hill in St Helens. The widespread process of digitisation is making many more court and prison records available to researchers.

This is allowing more insights to be provided into the characters of criminals than just bland newspaper accounts of their court cases. Not that motivation for crimes can be established with any degree of certainty – whether it had been greed, poverty or inducement by others – but a more rounded picture is certainly provided.

During the Victorian era theft was often taken much more seriously than violence. Of course, a serious life-changing and violent assault would likely still result in a custodial sentence – but giving a policeman a good kicking would probably only merit a fine.

However, a recidivist thief like Catherine Flynn, who repeatedly stole relatively cheap items, could expect to be imprisoned for a lengthy period of time. And so in 1880 at the age of 24, Catherine was sentenced to five years in gaol for stealing a pair of boots worth only half a crown.

On May 8th of that year the St Helens Examiner published this report on her initial court appearance:

> Catherine Flynn, Windle, a young woman, was charged with stealing a pair of boots, value 2s. 6d., the property of Charles Munsey. Thomas Reece, shopman for Mr. Munsey, 5, Naylor-street North, said that about twenty-five minutes past ten o'clock on Saturday night he was inside the shop, and the boots were hanging inside near the door. He saw the prisoner, with a shawl over her head, leaning towards the boots. He saw her snatch the boots from the rail and run down the street. He followed her, and saw her drop one of the boots in East-street. He picked it up. He continued the chase, and overtook her in Naylor-street South. On capturing her, she said she was a poor woman, and asked him to let her go.
>
> Two policemen then came up, and he gave her in charge. After he had given her in charge the other boot was handed to him by a man, who said that he saw prisoner throw it away. The boots were the property of Mr. Munsey, and were worth 2s. 6d. P.C. Marriott, stationed at St. Helens, said he received the prisoner into custody from the last witness. She was under the influence of drink. He charged her with stealing the boots produced from a shop in Naylor-street, when she replied "Did you find them on me? I did not take them." Prisoner denied stealing the boots, and she was committed to take her trial at the sessions.

You might wonder about Munsey's boot shop being open so late. That was then very common in St Helens, especially on Saturdays.

That was payday for most workers and some shops would not shut their doors until midnight, as they wanted to take full advantage of the cash burning a hole in people's pockets.

and costs, and the glasses were ordered to be destroyed.

THEFT OF A PAIR OF BOOTS.—Catherine Flynn, Windle, a young woman, was charged with stealing a pair of boots, value 2s. 6d., the property of Charles Munsey.—Thomas Reece, shopman for Mr. Munsey, 5, Naylor-street North, said that about twenty-five minutes past ten o'clock on Saturday night he was inside the shop, and the boots were hanging inside near the door. He saw the prisoner, with a shawl over her head, leaning towards the boots. He saw her snatch the boots from the rail and run down the street. He followed her, and saw her drop one of the boots in East-street. He picked it up. He continued the chase, and over-took her in Naylor-street South. On capturing her, she said she was a poor woman, and asked him to let her go. Two policemen then came up, and he gave her in charge. After he had given her in charge the other boot was handed to him by a man, who said that he saw prisoner throw it away. The boots were the property of Mr. Munsey, and were worth 2s. 6d.—P.C. Marriott, stationed at St. Helens, said he received the prisoner into custody from the said

St Helens Examiner report from May 8th 1880

Naylor Street was in the district of the market place and said to have been quite well lit by gas lamp – although Catherine Flynn presumably thought there would be sufficient darkness to enable her "hit and run" theft to be successful. But she was wrong and at her trial in Liverpool on July 13th, a 5-year sentence was imposed.

Justice was often swiftly despatched at the quarter sessions or assizes with twenty or more trials commonly held on a single day. Cases could be dealt with in 15 minutes with no reports from probation officers or psychologists to be considered prior to sentencing. It was straight to gaol and don't pass go!

Five years seems grossly excessive for stealing goods worth just half-a-crown. But Catherine Flynn had a lengthy criminal record – albeit for relatively petty, non-violent offences – and that made all the difference.

In January 1874 she had been given six weeks in prison for stealing two coats and then in July of that year a sentence of four months was imposed for stealing what were described as prints.

229

Then in January 1876 the theft of more clothing led to a custodial sentence of eight months – followed by eighteen more months of prison in July 1877 after Catherine had stolen another coat.

Her final incarceration – prior to the boots theft from Munsey's shop – had been a further year inside, which was handed to her in April 1879 after she was caught stealing some beef.

So almost every year since 1874, the short young woman with dark brown hair and grey eyes had been before the courts and the sentences imposed on her had got longer – leading to five years for her latest boot stealing offence.

If criminals did not mend their ways then the judge's punishment became more and more severe. It was almost as if they took offence that the offender had not yet learned their lesson.

But were Catherine's non-violent crimes because she desired new boots or fancy clothes? Or was it simply poverty, as she claimed, that drove her to crime – and then to the nearest pawnshop to convert her theft into badly needed cash?

The latter seems more likely but it is, of course, impossible to be certain. Some clues might be gained by studying newspaper accounts of her previous convictions.

IMPUDENT ROBBERY

On November 27th 1875 the Liverpool Daily Post wrote of what they described as an impudent robbery by the young woman:

> At the St. Helens Petty Sessions, yesterday, Catherine Flynn was charged with stealing a black dress coat from the dwelling-house of Mr. McNicoll, surgeon, St. Helens. On Thursday week the prosecutor saw the woman upstairs, but not suspecting robbery, more especially as nothing was apparently missing, he let her go. He afterwards found a

number of articles of wearing apparel removed from one room to another ready for carrying away, and on Sunday morning he missed the coat, value £5, named in the present charge. On Monday night the woman was apprehended on another charge, and identified as the same who had been found in Mr. McNicoll's house. The coat was subsequently found pledged at Bardsley's pawnshop, in Liverpool-road. She was committed for trial at the next Kirkdale Sessions.

That and another offence led to the eight months' sentence previously mentioned being imposed on Catherine. Then on July 4th 1877, the Warrington Examiner wrote:

At the St. Helens Petty Sessions yesterday, a woman named Catherine Flynn was charged, on remand, with stealing an overcoat, value £2, from the dwelling-house of George Binkhill, Brook-street, on Sunday, the 24th ult. It was not missed until Friday, when information was given to the police, who already had the prisoner in custody on suspicion of having stolen the coat in question, she having been detained and handed over to the police when offering the coat in pledge. As she had been several times previously committed for felony, she was committed for trial at the sessions.

So the pattern of her criminal career appeared to be stealing in order to obtain small amounts of money at the pawnshop. Of course, an overcoat might be valued at £2 by the victim – but certainly not by the pawnbroker!

Like most medium to long-term prisoners, Catherine was moved from prison to prison during her five-year sentence for boot stealing. Most of her term was served in the south, mainly at Mill Bank gaol in London and at Woking prison.

It's unlikely that her husband Michael would have visited her much if she'd remained at Kirkdale Gaol in Liverpool, where she began her incarceration. However, as soon as Catherine was removed to prisons in the south of England, visits from home became virtually impossible.

Michael was also not a big letter writer with only one recorded missive sent by him to his imprisoned wife. Complete dislocation from family was extremely common and appears to have been a deliberate part of the punishment for offenders. That could easily mean the missing of crucial family events.

DANGEROUSLY ILL

Prison records show that one of the few letters that Catherine did receive informed her that her child was dangerously ill – and then a fortnight later another told her that it had died. And, of course, compassionate leave to attend the child's funeral was out of the question.

Despite the hardships, the records show that Catherine's behaviour in prison was quite good – but not perfect. Her disciplinary record lists her getting into trouble for such offences as singing in her cell and quarrelling with other prisoners.

At one time she threw her cocoa over a fellow inmate! However, most punishments for such infractions of the rules simply involved a day or two in solitary confinement.

In November 1883, Catherine was released on licence from her 5-year term and I can find no further accounts of her activities. Maybe she learned her lesson, as the authorities hoped, and realised that in the long run it was better to suffer the privations of poverty at home than in some prison many miles away.

The Sufferings Of The Salvation Army

"The parents were ordered to give their lads a good flogging"

Members of the "Sally Army" were not initially made very welcome in St Helens. Historian Frank Sheen has written:

"When they arrived in the 1880s they were confronted by a howling mob who gave them verbal abuse, kicked them and threw stones and rotten eggs at them."

St Helens members of the Salvation Army

Frank added that their members even carried first-aid kits round with them in case of assault. Mind you there were very few places that did welcome the Salvation Army with open arms. People were suspicious of their "religious fanaticism", noisy parading and pseudo-military set up that gave their members army ranks.

Even their HQ within Beecham's building in Lowe Street was called a barracks – although simply being different appeared to have been their main "crime". However, some of their members' behaviour was damaging to the church's reputation.

Under the headline *"Salvation Army Scandal At St. Helens"*, the Liverpool Echo wrote on December 29th 1884:

In St. Helens Police Court, to-day, before Messrs. W. Blinkhorn and T. Pilkington, a young man named James Preston, glasscutter, living in Morley-street, St. Helens, appeared in answer to a summons to show cause why he should not contribute to the support of the illegitimate child of Annie Lee, single woman, who resided with her parents at Windle City. Mr. John O. Swift appeared for Miss Lee, and stated that she made the acquaintance of defendant a little before Christmas, 1883.

He was [a] member of the St. Helens contingent of the Salvation Army, and took her frequently to the meetings. He was accepted by her as her lover, walked her out, and was generally considered to be her accepted suitor. When found what her condition was, he said he could not afford to pay for it, and he should pray it might die.

He afterwards promised to make amends and marry her, but he had not done so, and, unfortunately for him, the child had lived. The magistrates decided to make an order for defendant to pay 3s 6d per week and the usual expenses. Defendant: "No fear."

REFORMED CRIMINALS

One problem was that some members of the Salvation Army were reformed criminals – and occasionally these would relapse into their old ways. Even when they themselves were the victims of crime, much was made of their past.

On December 22nd 1884 five small boys were charged in St Helens Police Court with breaking into the Salvation Army barracks in Lowe Street and stealing various items

THE SALVATION ARMY BARRACKS ROBBED.
At the St. Helens Town Hall, on Saturday, before Mr. A. Sinclair, five lads, named William Mercer, Samuel Thompson, Hugh Penketh, James Topping, and Robert Mercer, whose ages varied from 10 to 13 years, were charged with stealing a number of hymn books, tea party tickets, "shields" or brooches, and 2s 1½d in money from the Salvation Army Barracks, Lowe-street, St. Helens. Formal evidence to justify a remand having been given, they were remanded.—The lads were again brought up on Monday before Mr. Sinclair and Alderman McBryde. Mr. H. L. Riley, solicitor, defended the two Mercers and Penketh.—James Kease, residing at 20, Bank-street, St. Helens, deposed that he was the "captain" of the St. Helens Salvation Army. At 9-30 on the previous Wednesday night he saw the barracks door locked. From something he was afterwards told he went on the Friday and examined the storeroom. He missed a lot of hymn books and periodicals, altogether of the value of 8s; eight "shields" or brooches, value 4s; and 2s 1½d in money. He also missed ten tea party tickets. The articles and money were the property of "General" William Booth. In reply to Mr. Riley, witness said there were three members of the Army who had a key to the storeroom.—Mr. Riley: These boys are what are known as "little soldiers?"—Witness: Not that I am aware of.—Mr.

St. Helens Examiner December 27th 1884

234

– including brooches and 2 shillings in cash. It was needlessly stated in court that James Keats – the captain of the St Helens branch of the Army – had a criminal record. Solicitor Henry Lindon Riley asked him:

"Have you ever described breaking into a house when one of your companions got seven years, and you yourself got three months".

The implication was that such behaviour was being encouraged – rather than being used as an example of a criminal reformed through God. Children in the Salvation Army were, by the way, referred to as *"little soldiers"*, and those in court were discharged, with the St Helens Examiner writing:

"The parents were ordered to give their lads a good flogging".

Although members of the Salvation Army were at times poorly treated in St Helens, it was nothing compared to the persecution they endured in other places.

The authorities in some towns prosecuted the organisation for simply parading through the streets and holding religious services in the open air.

Such behaviour, they said, was causing obstructions and unlawfully prevented the free passage of the streets. It was even claimed that they incited disorder.

At a St Helens Town Council meeting held on June 4th 1884 it was revealed that Hastings Council had sent them a letter. They were requesting support in their campaign to get the Government to bring in new powers to control the activities of the Salvation Army on the streets.

The Town Clerk told the meeting that the organisation had caused no problems in St Helens and so the council wisely decided to have nothing to do with the petition.

GREAT HAND-TO-MOUTH CONFLICT

On September 15th 1884 the Liverpool Echo described how mysterious posters were appearing on walls in St Helens designed to attract new recruits to meetings:

> The latest addition to the mural literature of the St. Helens contingent of the Salvation Army is an announcement that on Saturday next there will be a "Great hand-to-mouth conflict with ham and tongue!" At 3 p.m. the major will "Review troops and try guns on the barracks;" at 6.30 there will be a "Great attack on the enemy – great slaughter anticipated;" and at 7.45 there will be "Great rejoicing over battles fought and victories won." What next?

On August 1st 1885, General William Booth, the leader of the Salvation Army, came to St Helens and addressed a large audience in the Volunteer Hall in Mill Street. Five years later he returned to the town and was given lunch in the Town Hall with a number of dignitaries in attendance.

Although locals soon got used to the activities of the Salvation Army, they were still victims of the occasional assault.

On March 28th 1891 the St Helens Examiner wrote:

> John Carney, of St. Helens, will have occasion to remember his visit to Warrington on Saturday. He assaulted an old man, who was walking in the ranks of the Salvation Army, in what was described by the magistrates, after hearing evidence, on Monday, as an unprovoked and cowardly manner. The idea seems to have got into the heads of certain roughs that the Salvationists are fair subjects for the exercise of their brutality. Carney has been sent to gaol for a month to "cleanse his bosom of this perilous stuff."

Then on October 10th of that year the St Helens Examiner described how the Army in Earlestown now had a band – but had yet to learn how to play their instruments:

> Verily, the Salvation Army is moving apace in Earlestown; if not in membership, they are advancing musically. They now have a band, with brass instruments and a big drum, and the comments I have heard respecting that band are certainly not the most courteous or encouraging to the players. Music, they say, hath charms, but the sounds emanating from the Salvation Army band cannot be said to fall under that category. Last week was a week of self-denial, and I fancy we could do with a self-denial week every week, and deny ourselves the pleasure of the "Army" band.

The Salvation Army was attacked in many ways but my final example of prejudice against the movement came from a drunken farmer. This piece was published in the Liverpool Echo on November 23rd 1897:

> John Burrows, farmer, of Knowsley-road, was charged at the St Helens Police Court to-day with being drunk in charge of a horse and cart. Constable Chorlton said that [on] the previous evening the defendant was in charge of a horse and trap, and behaved in a most extraordinary manner. He drove up the main street, and dashed through the Salvation Army, when they were holding a meeting. When he had got through the crowd he turned round and charged the Army again. He took him into custody, and found he was very drunk. Inspector Hunter and Sergeant Small corroborated. Defendant was fined 10s and costs or fourteen days.

The Deadly Firing Of Cannons In St Helens

*"Cannons were fired, rockets were sent up and
until dinner time pandemonium reigned."*

This photograph taken in the 1920s shows a young lady posing
with the cannon that used to be situated in Taylor Park in St
Helens. The big gun was removed for scrap, along with the park
gates, at the start of World War 2.

During the 19th century the firing of cannons was a common
means of celebrating events in Lancashire. These included Guy
Fawkes Night and on November 8th 1862 an angry letter writer in
the Preston Chronicle said:

> Every night this week cannons have been fired and crackers
> let off, to the great annoyance of quiet neighbourhoods, and
> to the danger of persons riding or driving.

Many towns – including St Helens – let off cannons on the morning of Queen Victoria's coronation in 1838. But firing the rusty old things would make modern-day health and safety managers turn white!

There are no reports of injuries in St Helens while marking the coronation. However, while practising in Liverpool on the day before, a man had both his hands blown off and subsequently died.

And in Warrington on Coronation Day itself, a cannon burst and killed the firer, who – according to the Liverpool Mercury – *"left a wife and many children to deplore his loss"*.

It was common for workers to celebrate their boss's marriage with cannon fire. The Mercury in 1846 wrote that a 15-year-old boy in Runcorn had his head *"nearly severed from his body"* when firing a cannon to mark his employer's wedding.

When Edward Sullivan – one of the bosses of the Ravenhead Glass Works in St Helens – got wed in September 1859, cannons were set off all day long. However, it cost one worker an arm, as the Liverpool Mercury described:

> On Thursday evening, Thomas Shelley, a glassman employed at the Ravenhead Plate Glassworks, had his right arm shattered so severely that amputation was deemed necessary, by the bursting of a cannon which he was firing at Ravenhead in celebration of the marriage of Mr. Sullivan, the manager at the works.

LEFT EYE ALMOST CUT OUT

On March 12th 1863, the Liverpool Mercury wrote about an accident with a cannon at the Sutton engine sheds:

> Whilst celebrating the wedding day of his Royal Highness the Prince of Wales and the Princess Alexandra, at the

Sutton Sheds, near St. Helen's, some youths were severely wounded. In discharging some cannons, one, a 56-pound weight, which had been bored, was burst, and pieces of the iron struck several of the persons present. One, William Burrows, had his left eye almost cut out; Thomas Holmes was severely wounded in the thigh, and William Hill was hurt in the face.

ACCIDENT THROUGH THE BURSTING OF A CANNON.

On Monday, while the workmen at the Waterloo Foundry, St. Helens, were busily engaged firing cannon in celebration of the coming of age of Mr. James Varley's eldest son, an accident occurred by which six of them were more or less injured. One young man, named Joseph Howe, had his face fearfully scorched, and for the present, at least, he is blinded. The accident occurred through the charge being rammed home too tightly.

Manchester Evening News March 30th 1870

In March 1870 some of the workmen at Varley's Waterloo Foundry in Waterloo Street in St Helens celebrated the 21st birthday of their boss's son. They fired off several rounds from what the Prescot Reporter called a *"rough sort of cannon"*.

Appreciating the danger James Varley ordered them to cease. This they did until their employer went to dinner and then the workmen decided to let off another shot. It didn't go off and a boy called Joseph Howe stooped over the fuse to see what had happened.

The cannon suddenly exploded, severely scorching his hands and face. Three men also received burns and it was thought likely that the boy had been blinded.

Sacred Heart Church School in St Helens kept a diary describing events in its school life. Its entry for October 26th 1877 reads:

The master warned the boys about having matches and [gun] powder in school. However, nine boys used some powder in the letting off [of] a cannon, causing one of the boys to get a severe cut on the cheek – the cannon having burst.

Cannons were not only let off as weapons of war in South Africa during the 2nd Boer War – they were also fired at times of celebration back in England.

On March 2nd 1900 the St Helens Examiner wrote of the joy expressed in the Newton-le-Willows district when news filtered through that the siege of the British garrison at Ladysmith had been broken:

> The long expected news of the relief of Ladysmith was received at Earlestown and Newton about 10 o'clock on Thursday morning and at once the town gave itself up to the wildest enthusiasm of a kind never before witnessed. Immediately, all the buzzers in the place were set going, cannons were fired, rockets were sent up and until dinner time pandemonium reigned.

There were no reports of the cannon firing causing any injuries. However, things did not go so smoothly in St Helens, as the Liverpool Mercury explained on March 3rd:

> Thursday's rejoicings at St. Helens over the relief of Ladysmith were in several instances turned to sorrow. Three men, named W. T. Swift, of 1, Manor-street; Edward Roughley, of Peter-street; and William Cartwright, of Albert-street, were loading a small cannon at Messrs. Cannington and Shaw's bottle works, when it exploded. Swift was shockingly injured about the legs, arms, and face. Roughley had one eye totally destroyed through two inches of metal bursting it, and Cartwright was also injured. They were treated by Dr. Gray at the St. Helens Hospital, and are going

on favourably. John Gavin, of 43, Roughley-square, Thatto Heath, was the victim of a similar accident. A toy cannon was improvised out of some copper tubing. It exploded prematurely, and the sight of one of Gavin's eyes was entirely lost.

TOY CANNONS

So-called "toy cannons" could be just as dangerous as the real thing. On November 5th 1893 a boy called William Hall loaded what was described as a toy cannon with gunpowder – but it failed to fire. So the 15-year-old from Golborne Road in Newton decided to place his toy cannon in the fire – but still no bang.

William removed the cannon and started ramming its barrel, when it suddenly burst. As a result his left hand had to be amputated and it was feared he would also lose an eye.

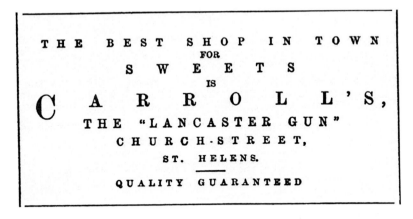

THE BEST SHOP IN TOWN
FOR
SWEETS
IS
CARROLL'S,
THE "LANCASTER GUN"
CHURCH-STREET,
ST. HELENS.

QUALITY GUARANTEED

As well as the cannon that was on show in Taylor Park, the large-calibre weapons used to be on display outside two shops in St Helens. A sweet shop in Church Street – called at various times Carroll's and Mrs Webb's – had a cannon mounted over its window that was known as the Lancaster gun, and the shop used that name in its adverts (as shown above in the St Helens Examiner). Another cannon was fixed above a shop in Peter Street.

The Shooting Of A Sweetheart in North Road

"A sensational tragedy resulting in the death of one person shocked the residents of the Cowley-hill district."

Guns used to be very easy to obtain in St Helens – if you had the cash. It wasn't until the passing of the Firearms Act of 1920 that such weapons began to be properly regulated in Britain. Before then virtually anyone could possess a pistol.

All they needed was a licence from the post office, as they would for their dog. Even some churchmen kept firearms and during the 1880s, a revolver was a prize in a fundraising raffle in aid of St Anne's Church in Sutton.

The only concern that police usually had over someone caught in possession of a gun was whether they were licensed. If not, the case was passed onto the Inland Revenue (who had responsibility for gun licensing) and it was they who would prosecute the offender.

For example, on December 29th 1890, Robert Holt from Bewsey Street in Thatto Heath appeared in St Helens Police Court charged with carrying a firearm without a licence. An Inland Revenue supervisor called Mr Heald told the magistrates that the defendant had been creating a disturbance on-board a St Helens' tramcar.

CONCEALED WEAPON

Constable Patterson was called to put him out of the tram and upon searching the man found him to be in possession of a revolver with two of its barrels loaded. Holt claimed that the gun had been given to him and he was taking it to be cleaned. He told the magistrates that he never intended using it and since committing the offence three weeks earlier, had obtained a licence for the weapon.

The Bench characterised the case as a bad one but only imposed a fine of £1 and costs. There was no prosecution for carrying a concealed weapon and no suggestion that the gun had not been immediately returned to Holt by the police.

Then under the headline *"An Unlicensed Gun"*, the St Helens Examiner three weeks later described another similar case:

> On Monday, at the Town Hall, Thomas Jones, a resident of Boundary-road, was summoned by Mr. Heald, supervisor of Inland Revenue, for carrying a gun without a license. The defendant pleaded that he was only taking the gun to be repaired, and that he had not "handled" it for six months. Constable Fillingham, however, gave evidence that he met defendant carrying the gun, which was loaded, and the defendant had a flask containing powder and some shot in his possession. A fine of 20s. and costs was imposed.

Just where another Boundary Road resident named Joseph Pickavance had acquired his weapon was unexplained in newspaper accounts – but he used it to deadly effect in North Road four years later. The headlines in the St Helens Examiner from March 24th 1894 summed up the dramatic events as *"Shocking Tragedy At St. Helens – Shooting A Sweetheart – Suicide Of The Assailant"*. Their account began:

> A sensational tragedy resulting in the death of one person and serious injury to another shocked the residents of the Cowley-hill district, St. Helens, last night. It appears that about half-past nine o'clock, Mr. Charles Sharples, one of the borough magistrates, was sitting reading in the parlour of his house in North-road, near St. Mark's Church, when he heard a couple of shots fired, followed by screams of

murder, from the direction of the waste land between the back premises of his house and the top of Oldfield-street. Mr. Sharples at once made his way to the Town Hall, where he gave information to the police authorities.

Sergeants Strong and Sisson immediately proceeded to the spot, and on making a search with their lanterns they came across the lifeless body of a young man, who afterwards proved to be Joseph Pickavance, of 33, Boundary-road, St. Helens. He was bleeding from a wound in the right temple, and grasped in his hand, a six-chambered revolver, two of the barrels of which had been discharged.

While Sergeant Sisson had the body of the unfortunate young man removed to the public mortuary, in Foundry-street, Sergeant Strong prosecuted inquiries in other directions, and soon ascertained that the death of Pickavance had come about by his own hand after a desperate attempt to take the life of his sweetheart, a girl named Elizabeth Johnson.

DREADFUL TRAGEDY AT ST. HELENS.

ALLEGED ATTEMPTED MURDER OF A SWEET-HEART
SUICIDE OF THE LOVER.

Shortly after nine o'clock on Tuesday night, the neighbourhood of Cowley Hill, one of the residential districts of St. Helens, was alarmed by hearing several shots from a revolver indicating to even the most uninitiated ears that something of an extraordinary nature had occurred. Several persons at once sought for the police, and Mr. C. Sharples, J.P. personally conveyed the information to the Town Hall. Police Sergeant Sisson immediately proceeded to the place, and there found a young unmarried man named Joseph Pickavance, an apprentice glass maker, at Messrs. Pilkington Brothers sheet glass works, lying on the ground bleeding from a terrible wound in the right temple. In his right hand he was tightly grasping a revolver. An examination showed that death had been instantaneous, and the body was removed by Police-sergeants Sisson and Moffat, and Police-constable Platt to the public mortuary. The body then presented a terrible sight, the bullet having entered the temple, and apparently lodged near the right eye. It was stated, though at the time of writing the rumour had not been confirmed, that the young man had quarrelled with a young woman with whom he had been keeping company

St Mark's Church in North Road and Widnes Examiner March 24th 1894

The two sergeants did not discover young Elizabeth at the scene of the tragedy as two glassblowers named William Langley and Patrick Riley had arrived before them. The small firm of Langley's claimed to have been blowing glass in St Helens as far back as the 17th century and kept premises near St Mark's Church.

The two men heard the shots being fired and walked across some wasteland to investigate. They found the young woman lying on the ground with her child in her arms bleeding from wounds to her neck and hand. However, Elizabeth was sufficiently conscious to be able to give the pair the address of her residence in Frederick Street, opposite Birchley Street.

It was then the usual practice for injured people to be taken to their homes and a doctor summoned – rather than for the patient to be taken to hospital. So the two men had removed the girl and her baby to the house where Elizabeth was staying before the police had arrived on the scene.

The St Helens Examiner continued their description of events:

> Inquiries late last night elicited that the terrible affair was the outcome of a quarrel between the young couple who had been keeping company for about eighteen months past. The deceased man, Joseph Pickavance, was 19 years of age, working as a glass gatherer at Pilkington's glassworks, and resided with his widowed mother at 33, Boundary-road. His sweetheart was Elizabeth Johnson, 17 years of age, who resided with her father in Johnson-street, Parr. Up to about six weeks ago he lived with his mother in Frederick-street, but his father died there two months ago, and the family then removed to Boundary-road.
>
> Pickavance and Johnson were considered a loving couple, but the girl found herself in an unhappy condition, and it is said she was asked to stay with a married sister, a Mrs.

Chorley, at 127, Frederick-street. This removal was effected six or seven weeks ago, just about the time when the Pickavances were removing from Frederick-street to Boundary-road. The girl Johnson gave birth to a child five weeks ago, and since that period the couple seemed to have occasional quarrels. It was freely stated last night that Pickavance had several times, threatened to take the life of the girl Johnson, and then do for himself. It was this double tragedy that he attempted to carry into execution last night.

Elizabeth and Joseph Pickavance had arranged to meet in North Road but upon reaching St Mark's Church, the young mother had said that she wished to return home.

An annoyed Pickavance then drew a revolver from his pocket, pointed it at his sweetheart and pulled the trigger. The gun initially misfired, giving Elizabeth time to raise her arm to protect herself.

A BULLET WAS FIRED

Pickavance pulled the trigger of his revolver again and this time a bullet was fired. It caught Elizabeth's hand and neck and she dropped to the ground with the couple's child still resting in her arms. However, she had not been seriously wounded.

But Pickavance did not know that and thinking he had killed his lover, placed the revolver to his temple and fired again. The bullet entered his skull and he was instantly killed.

It took almost a month before Elizabeth was fit to attend the inquest into Joseph's death. She told the coroner that the father of her child had been depressed and had suggested a suicide pact.

The impact of the death of the boy's father on his mental state just before the birth of his child can only be guessed at. The couple's young ages were clarified at the inquest – Elizabeth had only been eighteen and Joseph seventeen.

The Thatto Heath Women
With Water Cans On Their Heads

*"There are a very large number of families in Thatto Heath,
the female members of which have to carry on their heads,
each night, large cans of water."*

On May 25th 1872 the St Helens Newspaper published this brief letter from someone concerned about the water crisis:

> Sir, – I beg to ask you to allow me a few lines in your paper, on the scarcity of water. There has been no water in Elephant lane, for two days, where the small pox is raging fearfully, and the sick are crying for water, and the public are running from one house to another. – **A Ratepayer**, Thatto Heath

These days if we want water, we turn on a tap. And don't we get annoyed if occasionally the liquid is discoloured, or if there's low pressure, perhaps, through a leak in a pipe somewhere?

Water is still not taken for granted in many parts of the developing world – and it certainly wasn't in St Helens 150 years ago. The problem was particularly grave in some poorer parts of the town, such as Thatto Heath.

During 1869 and 1870 the St Helens Newspaper campaigned for improvements to *"the heath"*. They claimed the district had the poorest provision for water – which they called an essential for domestic life, health and cleanliness – than elsewhere in the town.

Thatto Heath was then part of the Sutton Township and, along with Parr, was being incorporated into the newly created St Helens borough. On July 10th 1869 the Newspaper published an editorial called *"Water For Thatto Heath"* which illustrated the difficulties that many housewives faced in sourcing clean water for their families:

> Now that the St. Helens Town Council have got their Bill safe through Parliament, we hope that no time will be lost in supplying a very important portion of their newly acquired territory – Thatto-heath, with water for domestic purposes. There are a very large number of families in that district, some hundreds we understand, the female members of which have to carry on their heads, each night, large cans of water a distance of nearly half a mile, to supply their families' domestic consumption on the following day. On a fine evening there may not be much hardship in even a female carrying a large can of water on her head for a considerable distance, but everybody must feel that in wet and wintry weather such an occupation is one quite unsuited for females. Now that Thatto-heath has been brought within the corporate boundary, the people there have a right to equal consideration, with those in the town, in respect to water, and we believe there is not a cottager in the heath who would object to pay his twopence per week to save his wife or daughter from the indignity and slavery of water carrying.

The women collected the precious H20 for their families' use from wells or springs – as did many others in other parts of the town.

The twopence a week reference in the article concerned the water rates that each householder with their own supply was expected to pay. And the water was for their family's exclusive use and not to be shared with others.

STANDPIPE

Three months earlier in the St Helens Petty Sessions, a little girl called Eliza Young was charged with taking water from a standpipe while not being the person paying the water rate. Patrick Dooley was also charged with permitting the offence.

This was a curious case in which a man called Alexander Athwell – who appeared to have been hired by St Helens Corporation – had been hiding in an empty house to spy on residents. He told the court he had been informed that it was a common practice in the unnamed street for water to be illegally shared.

Athwell saw little Eliza draw water from her neighbour's house *(with Patrick Dooley's permission)* and take it to her mother. The woman was not paying the Corporation any water rates and so committing an offence – but it was her child who was prosecuted.

However, the family's solicitor successfully argued legal technicalities concerning the summons, including the fact that the Corporation was not the actual water provider. The principle of the prosecution was not questioned but the case was dismissed and the unnamed little girl's court ordeal was at an end.

VERY OFFENSIVE SMELLS

Communal wells could be super-spreaders of disease. Some wells were shallow and contaminated by organic matter from peat soil and – in many cases – from the contents of neighbouring cesspools and ashpit middens. The ashpits were the dumps containing human waste, which were mixed with ashes to reduce the stench and deter pests.

Rural areas like Rainford relied much on wells, as well as the Randle Brook. In 1870 up to 30 cases of typhoid were reported in the village and in one block of houses by the Bridge Inn, 15 out of 35 residents were struck down.

Each of those homes had a backyard that extended to the brook and often *"very offensive smells"* had been reported. The heavily used wells in Rainford were also infested by sewage from midden dumps and from dung heaps close to the brook.

Communal wells also brought warring neighbours into conflict. When St Helens Petty Sessions was held on August 23rd 1869, Martha McDonald from Sutton was charged with assaulting Mary Johnson by throwing a bucket of water over her!

Several houses in Peckers Hill opened into a yard that contained a well that a number of families used for their domestic supply. Mrs Johnson told the court that on one day during the previous week, she had gone to use the well and Mrs McDonald had approached her carrying a *"vessel of water"* and then she proceeded to throw it over her.

Her assailant also warned her not to use the well anymore *"under the pain of receiving a bath each visit"* – as the St Helens Newspaper put it. There were, of course, two sides to every tale told in court. The defence claimed the squabble had been caused by Mrs Johnson having used *"very impudent and abusive language"* – and so the case was dismissed.

At a St Helens Town Council meeting held on July 6th 1870, it was revealed that the town's water supply was turned off at night to save on supply. Councillor Johnson argued that it should be left on all night, saying there were many complaints that townsfolk could not get any water before eight in the morning.

Also much water was wasted as householders turned on their taps during the night, only to find there was no supply. Some then left their taps in an open position and so water was needlessly run off when the supply resumed in the morning.

The council surveyor explained that in the past the waterworks at Eccleston had run dry and until their new works at Whiston was operational there was little that could be done.

The St Helens Newspaper reported how Cllr. William Hibbert then complained of a scarcity of water in parts of Parr:

Councillor Hibbert said the people at Parr had no water to drink. He believed the people there, and some of the firms, would take the water [i.e. pay rates for it] if they could get it. The people of Parr were carrying water for domestic use every day during the summer, and they would be content with a portion of the water which was supplied elsewhere. He thought the matter should be brought before the committee strenuously. The people were taking water from any place where they could get it, and many were seriously ill through a scarcity of wholesome water. The Mayor said the Council had decided to send the water into Parr. Councillor Hibbert said not to that portion of Parr going up to Ashton-green. The Surveyor said he had visited the place a few weeks ago, and the people there were really very badly off for water.

A motion was passed that pipes be laid in Fleet Lane as long as the owners of cottages and works paid the cost. That was not always straightforward as some property owners simply refused to pay for the cost of water pipes being laid for the benefit of their tenants.

THE YIELD OF THE WELL.

Alderman Radley now moved the adoption of the minutes, and he said he could not pass without congratulating the Council and the town upon having obtained a providential, opportune, and plentiful supply of water at Whiston. (Hear, hear). He did not think he required to say anything further. According to the pumping into St. Helens for the last fortnight the yield of the well was 720,000 gallons per day, and the pumping had been continued with but one slight stoppage. There was still something like 26 yards of water in the well, and the supply being drawn did not appear to lower it any farther. It was quite fair to assume that if the springs were relieved of the column of water in the well, the yield would be much greater. He believed the water was good, and would prove a great blessing to the town.

Mr. Hibbert seconded the motion.

Mr. Johnson—What is the yield of the Eccleston well?

Alderman Radley—About 620,000 per day.

Mr. Johnson—Have you any opinion as to the probable increase at Whiston?

Alderman Radley—I believe you have a million gallons there now. The tunnel has only penetrated a few feet into the new strata. I am of opinion that the present

St Helens Newspaper June 8th 1872

The new waterworks at Whiston was seen as the solution to the supply problem. On April 5th 1871 councillors attending the monthly St Helens Town Council meeting heard that it was finally in operation and pumping 275,000 gallons per day. That was not a massive amount but it was considered a very good start.

However, problems soon set in and boring of the intended 100-yard well had to be suspended upon reaching 37 yards. A second well had to be sunk and it took another year before the councillors were able to congratulate themselves on their new scheme. This occurred at another council meeting, which was described by the St Helens Newspaper on June 8th 1872:

> Alderman Radley now moved the adoption of the minutes, and he said he could not pass without congratulating the Council and the town upon having obtained a providential, opportune, and plentiful supply of water at Whiston. (Hear, hear). According to the pumping into St. Helens for the last fortnight, the yield of the well was 720,000 gallons per day. He believed the water was good, and would prove a great blessing to the town. Alderman Radley went on to say that the quantity was indefinite, but very great.

However, much of the water was required by industry for cooling and other purposes and getting a supply into every resident's home within the St Helens district would prove a long-term project.

A Collection Of Curious Police Stories

"The horse dashed into the shop window of Edwin Hulme, boot dealer, carrying the policeman with it."

HARBOURING A POLICEMAN AT RAINHILL – We are all familiar with the charge of harbouring a fugitive. However, in Prescot Petty Sessions on February 1st 1870, David Slater was charged with harbouring a policeman! The landlord of an unidentified Rainhill pub had let PC Ashton sup beer at 3am when he should have been on his beat.

It appeared not to have been an unusual event, as Superintendent Fowler told the court that he had warned licensees against harbouring police constables on duty. The man in charge of Prescot Police also called for a substantial penalty against Slater for committing the offence.

As a result, the landlord was fined the hefty amount of £5 with twelve shillings costs or if in default of payment he had to serve two months in prison.

A PECULIAR MANIA – The St Helens' bobbies were used to being beaten up. Friday and Saturday nights were particularly risky times for them to walk their prisoners to their station at the Town Hall. The officers regularly passed a gauntlet of drunks – with the detainees encouraging the inebriates to intervene on their behalf.

For example, on October 3rd 1887, Edward Pickavance of Parr Street was fined 20 shillings and costs after assaulting Sergeant Hunter. The officer had been escorting a prisoner to the Town Hall, when Pickavance ran out of a crowd and struck him a violent blow in the eye and then kicked him on his leg.

However, on January 27th 1914 under the headline *"A Peculiar Mania – Always Wanted To Strike Policemen"*, the Liverpool Echo wrote how an old man from the Croppers Hill district of St Helens liked to give the police a thumping whenever he saw them:

Remarkable statements were made at St. Helens Police Court, to-day, when Joseph Poole, an elderly man, of 4, Duncan-street, was charged with assaulting two constables. Constable Connors said that at ten minutes past five that morning he was in Westfield-street on duty in plain clothes. He met prisoner, who cursed him, and immediately he passed him Poole struck him with an open pocket knife. He jumped away and caught Poole by the arm, upon which he began to kick and fight like a madman. Another officer assisted, and was also assaulted.

The clerk said prisoner appeared to have a mania for assaulting policemen as he went to his work in the morning. Police-constable Prickett said that he assisted in the arrest, and was badly kicked. He had met prisoner several mornings, and he always cursed him. Constable Patterson said that policemen who knew prisoner's mania kept out of his reach when they met him. He did not seem to interfere with ordinary pedestrians, but he nearly always struck at a policeman when he met him.

It was decided that a doctor should medically examine Mr Poole to see if he was sane.

THE PAINFUL SPECTACLE OF ST HELENS PRISONERS – In the city of New York they have their *"perp walks"* in which the police frogmarch accused persons in handcuffs within public view. The practice apparently arose out of the need to transport defendants from police stations to court hearings.

Well, St Helens used to have its own version of the walk. Prisoners remanded in custody or jailed were removed from the court at the Town Hall to the railway station for despatch to prison in Liverpool. There were no cameras recording the walk as in New York – but it must still have been a humiliating experience.

On September 27th 1879 the St Helens Examiner called for the walk to end:

> The painful spectacle witnessed twice or thrice a week of prisoners being marched from the Town Hall to the railway station, handcuffed, and closely guarded by police constables, who are followed by a crowd of idlers, ought to be brought to an end as speedily as possible. Many a poor person is committed for trial and of course, unless bail be forthcoming, must pass the interim between his preliminary trial and the trial at Quarter Sessions, or the assizes, where he perhaps proves his innocence, in gaol.
>
> Others are summarily committed and yet both are conveyed to the county gaol together. After every session there is a batch of prisoners, men and women, handcuffed without any discrimination and marched through the public streets to the railway station, thus adding the double punishment of having

to face the gaze of all they meet on the way. Would not a van remedy this? It would be a very good thing and do away with much of the vulgar curiosity exhibited by the public.

Just when this pedestrian practice was brought to an end and vehicular transportation of prisoners to the railway station began, I cannot say, exactly – although it clearly had by 1909. On July 13th of that year, James Paget of Lyon Street was charged in St Helens Police Court with assaulting PC Adams.

The Examiner was right to say that a more humane system would do away with "much of the vulgar curiosity" – but not all of it. Those members of the public determined to take a peek at the prisoners could still do so by hanging around the railway station, as Constable Adams explained.

He told the magistrates that when detainees were transported to the station, a *"gang of young roughs"* went to watch them board the train to Walton Gaol. As a result of complaints from railway officials about the youths' behaviour, he had been sent to disperse them.

However, James Paget refused to leave the station and struck, kicked and head-butted the constable. The accused said the officer had brought the trouble upon himself, as he had only wanted to watch the prisoners. The good news for James Paget was that for the next three weeks he would be able to look at prisoners to his heart's content – as he was sent to prison for 25 days.

THE PARSIMONIOUS POLICE – In the days before the NHS, deciding who should pay the doctor's bill for medical treatment was not always straightforward. Was the patient the one responsible or the individual who had summoned the doctor? Usually it was the former – but patients would sometimes refuse to pay the medic, complaining that they had never called him.

Under the headline *"A Parsimonious Town"*, the Lancashire Evening Post of December 10th 1901 published this article on the policy of St Helens police not to summon a doctor in cases of emergency – as they wanted to protect themselves from any liability to pay their bill:

At an inquest at St. Helens on the body of Mary Pennington, who was found in a brook, and died shortly after she was removed from the water, Constable Morrison, who was called to the spot by Messrs. Woodcock and Telford, who were using artificial respiration, said they suggested sending for a doctor, and he told them they might do so on their own responsibility [i.e. agree to pay the doctor's bill]. The Coroner: I should have thought the police would have sent for a doctor on their own responsibility, and not leave it to private citizens. Surely the police in St. Helens are not so parsimonious as not to send for a doctor when a person's life might be saved? Inspector Steele informed the Coroner that those were the instructions the force had received. They were not to send for a doctor except on the responsibility of a private person who chose to pay for medical assistance.

HALF A TON OF POLICEMEN – Some drunks upon being taken to St Helens police station did not meekly accept their fate and prepare for a night's kip in a cell. They resisted wildly – but with many policemen on hand, it was always a futile gesture. On December 17th 1907, the Manchester Guardian wrote how it had taken half a ton of coppers to placate one such individual:

During a case at St. Helens yesterday, in which a young Irishman was charged with being drunk and assaulting two constables an officer stated that it took half-a-ton of policemen to hold the prisoner down. The Clerk: How many policemen go to make a ton? The Chief Constable: Seven.

THE BOBBIES THAT COULDN'T GET OUT OF BED – Of course, young policemen and women are no different to anyone else –

particularly, it seems, when having to rise for an early shift. On February 19th 1952, the Guardian also published this short piece:

The Chief Constable of St Helens (Mr W. G. Symmons), at a local police dinner last night, praised the younger members of his force, but said he had one complaint. "They can't get up in the morning." He advised an alarm clock, but they gave the old excuse that it did not go off. Older members were more punctual.

Long-serving members of the St Helens Borough force in 1912

THE DIRTY BEGGAR WITH FLOWING LOCKS – On April 12th 1941, William Lynch was sent to prison for 21 days for a *"thorough wash and brush up"*, as Ald. William Burrows, chairman of the St Helens Bench, put it. The Liverpool Echo wrote that when Lynch appeared in the dock, he gave the magistrates a *"bow that shook his long flowing locks and swept the dock rail with his beard"*.

Lynch had been arrested for begging a month earlier and taken to Sutton Police Station in Sutton Road. However, he was in such a dirty condition that they wouldn't have him in the station. Instead Lynch – who had fifty-one previous convictions – was released and then summoned to appear in court.

ROMANCE ON THE BEAT AT ST HELENS – That was the headline to this article in the Echo on February 19th 1954:

Years ago in St. Helens, police patrolled parts of the town in pairs. This idea could be revived now – to keep married couples together. To-morrow Policewoman Jean Parker and Constable George Frederick Arnold, of the Lancashire County Force, stationed at Huyton, are to marry at Nutgrove Methodist Church, St Helens. Another couple, Policewoman Betty Robinson, of Woodlands Road, St. Helens, and Constable William Eric Guest, a noted St. Helens cricketer, have also named the day. It is March 4 at St. Mark's Church, St. Helens. Mr. and Mrs. Dickson are both serving members of the St. Helens force. The first member of the St. Helens force to choose a policewoman for his wife was Constable Harry Potts, who, in 1948, married Policewoman Emma Anders. The Chief Constable, Mr. W. G. Symmons, says: "The Watch Committee and myself are pleased to see these happy marriages. It tends to show that the womenfolk have confidence in police work as a career for their husbands as well as themselves."

A TRAMP'S DODGE AT HAYDOCK – Just because some people had adopted a life of vagrancy did not mean they were stupid. On September 26th 1891, the St Helens Examiner described how one such individual had outwitted the police at Haydock:

The Haydock police arrested a tramp named John Renshaw for drunkenness, and when on Monday they started for Warrington to put him before the magistrates, he suddenly became helpless, and none of the efforts of the officers could induce him to move. Under these circumstances, the charge being only one of drunkenness, a magisterial discharge was obtained. As soon as John heard the good news he jumped to his feet, and, laughing at his successful ruse, made off as fast as be could go.

MIRROR   Friday, January 16, 1953

Their prisoners will now sleep 'a la Ritz'

A COUNCIL is to spend £47 on three foam rubber mattresses and pillows for cells in the town's police station, so that prisoners can have a luxury bed.
They replace the regulation gaol beds of two wooden planks, with a block of wood for a pillow, that have served for eighty-four years. In the last few

ST HELENS PRISONERS SLEEPING "A LA RITZ" – I doubt that many prisoners at St Helens police station slept well in their cells – at least not until the 1950s. That was because those who were assisting the police with their enquiries were expected to snooze on wooden planks and lay their heads down on wooden pillows. Blankets were not even provided until after WW2.

When the decision was taken to treat prisoners like human beings and provide them with proper bedding, it made a big story in the Daily Mirror who on January 16th 1953 wrote:

A Council is to spend £47 on three foam rubber mattresses and pillows for cells in the town's police station, so that prisoners can have a luxury bed. They replace the regulation gaol beds of two wooden planks, with a block of wood for a pillow, that have served for eighty-four years. In the last few years, however, three or four blankets have been added. The chairman of the St. Helens (Lancs) Watch Committee, Councillor G. Marsden, 65, told the Daily Mirror yesterday: "I think we are the first town to give prisoners luxurious beds. We just could not let them go on sleeping on planks. It seems so out-of-date – and so uncomfortable, too. We have not bought mattresses for each of the police station's cells – they are not always full up." The police officer in charge of the cells said: "We don't mind giving some prisoners a mattress, but others deserve a hard bed. They will be wanting breakfast, shaving water and the morning papers in bed next."

THE TWO BENT ST HELENS POLICEMEN

– November 1913 was a very bad month for the Chief Constable of St Helens. During a period of just four days, not one but two of Arthur Ellerington's officers were handed substantial prison terms after committing separate crimes. The first one in the dock was Ernest Grainger of Brynn Street who at Manchester Assizes on the 20th was charged with two counts of burglary.

The 26-year-old had been accused of breaking into Thomas Middlehurst's confectioner's shop in Higher Parr Street while on night duty and stealing a watch. It was also alleged that while a police constable *(he had now been sacked)*, Grainger had entered the premises of Thomas Charnock's outfitters in Duke Street and stolen articles to the value of 30 shillings.

Bobby in Peasley Cross

The court decided to try Grainger on the first charge only and the ex-bobby with 3½ years service in the force denied the break-in but admitted the theft, saying: "I found the premises insecure. I had to rouse the occupant to tell him of it. I saw the watch lying on the sideboard and yielded to sudden temptation."

On the following day after stealing the timepiece, Grainger went to a watch repairer's shop in Westfield Street and had a new glass fitted. That was his undoing and the young man – who had also spent three years in the Coldstream Guards – was found guilty of burglary and sentenced to a year in prison. The judge was scathing in his remarks:

> For a man in the uniform of a police officer, who has the opportunity every day and every night of being dishonest, to be putting the blame upon other people, is one of the most serious and dangerous offences that he could be guilty of. There is no doubt whatever that your whole scheme in this case was to put the blame on someone else, perhaps some poor individual of bad character.

Four days later in St Helens Police Court, William Weaver was sentenced to 6 months hard labour after attacking a senior officer. The assault on Inspector William Jackson – who was in charge of the Sutton district – had occurred around midnight on November 15th. This was after he'd instructed PC Weaver to return to the Sutton Road police station after finding him drunk on duty.

The 28-year-old denied he was drunk and as the pair walked past Weaver's house at 29 Mill Lane, the constable gave the 48-year-old Jackson a violent blow on the back of his head and kicked him on his thigh. The inspector described Weaver as behaving like a madman, with the constable yelling:

"You have got your time in, and you are going to break my home up. I will kill you." Then he took Inspector Jackson's walking stick off him and hit him hard in the face with it. That broke the bridge of

his nose and bloodied his face so much that Jackson thought he'd lost an eye.

After being sentenced to prison, Weaver was taken by Black Maria to St Helens Railway Station to catch a train to Preston. By the time of his arrival hundreds of people had congregated in Shaw Street. The St Helens Reporter wrote that upon seeing the handcuffed ex-policeman, there was a *"tremendous outburst of cheering, which he replied to by nodding his head."*

Hundreds of people were also standing on the platform, the Reporter saying: *"The automatic platform ticket machine having the busiest time of its life."* Further cheering and the singing of 'He's A Jolly Good Fellow' took place by those who hated the police and applauded Weaver's violent act on a fellow officer.

THE HORSE THAT DRAGGED A POLICEMAN THROUGH A SHOP WINDOW – Sefton Place, at the corner of Ormskirk Street and Baldwin Street in St Helens, became a busy part of the town once motorised vehicles joined the mix of transportation types. So a police officer was often placed on point duty at Sefton Place to direct the traffic. That included horse-drawn vehicles and in 1926 a runaway nag dragged the bobby on duty into a shop window.

The Manchester Guardian of December 21st of that year described what had occurred:

> A remarkable accident occurred in the centre of St. Helens this morning, when a horse dashed through a shop window, carrying with it a policeman, who made a vain attempt to stop it. It appears that William Jones, of St. Helens, was driving a horse and cart along Back Lane, Haresfinch, when the horse suddenly bolted. After going a few hundred yards the cart broke at the shafts, and the horse careered on with his harness and the shafts dragging behind. The horse with another cart, which was being driven by John Jones, was startled by the runaway horse, and it, too, bolted and dashed

into the main street. On reaching the Sefton Arms corner it tried to swerve into Westfield Street, and as it did so Police Constable Taylor, who was on point duty, caught hold of the reins. The horse, unable to turn and unable to stop, dashed into the shop window of Edwin Hulme, boot dealer, carrying the policeman with it. The window, which was set out for Christmas, was completely demolished, and glass flew in all directions, and the constable's thumb was badly cut. The horse was so severely injured that it had to be destroyed. The damage to the shop window was estimated at £40.

IS JAMES HARRISON IN COURT? – On May 21st 1895, the Liverpool Mercury reported on a remarkable coincidence involving St Helens police. PC James Harrison had served a summons on another James Harrison for assaulting James Harrison (his father). And which magistrate on the St Helens Bench had signed the summons? It was Alderman James Harrison, who the Mercury wrote *"now attends the court only on very rare occasions"*.

The St Helens Railway Embezzler

"The disgrace it has caused my dear wife and children, causes me deep and bitter pain and distracts my brain"

Many employees holding responsible positions in St Helens have succumbed to temptation and stolen their boss's cash. In some cases they were one-off moments of madness when greed got the better of them. On other occasions the thefts took place over a period of time and in the mind of the thief their firm intention was always to repay the "borrowed" cash.

The latter was the case with Fred James of Chapel Street, near North Road. What is unusual with his situation is that he described his actions and deep feelings of regret for what he had done in a long letter that was read out in court.

The 1891 census states the occupation of the then 34-year-old as simply "railway clerk" – but does not tell the full story. In fact Fred was the chief booking clerk at St Helens Station and as a result handled all the cash paid in at Shaw Street – and that amounted to a whopping £30,000 a year, around £4m in today's money.

I think chief cashier would have been a more appropriate job title for Fred but it was a responsible position that he'd held in St Helens for 11 years. For doing that job he was paid about £2 6 shillings per week, which was on the low side considering the important nature of his employment.

BORROWED CASH

Unfortunately, Fred developed a gambling habit and got into a mess betting on the races and so "borrowed" railway money with the firm intention of replacing it once his luck changed. But, of course, it never did and over a period of several months during 1893, Fred James helped himself to a total of £622.

That was a huge amount, which he used in a futile attempt to win back his gambling losses. It was a race against time, as Fred knew the railway auditor would soon undertake an inspection and realise the station books did not add up. Eventually time ran out for Fred and like so many folk in similar situations, he panicked and ran.

Some embezzlers would brazen it out until tracked down by the police some months or years later – if at all. But Fred had a conscience and missed his wife and six children back in St Helens.

Ten days after absconding to the Isle of Wight, he sent this despairing letter to railway superintendent James Shaw:

> Dear Sir, – For the wrong I have committed whilst in the employ of the railway company I am deeply pained and truly sorry, and I feel it my duty to inform you fully the true facts of my trouble, brought on by folly and created with a desire to improve my income, having by rash and foolish speculation lost the whole of my own money, amounting to upwards of £400, and in a moment of weakness appropriated the moneys of the company in the hope of retrieving my losses and replacing what I had so wrongfully used. Fate, however, was adverse to me, as every transaction I entered into proved a disastrous failure, and increased my liabilities, until finally I was compelled to adopt the course I have taken, as the money I expected to receive on the 2nd inst. to meet it was not forthcoming.
>
> The thought of having betrayed the confidence you reposed in me, and after receiving so many kindnesses in a variety of ways, together with the disgrace and distress it has caused my dear wife and children, causes me deep and bitter pain and distracts my brain. Why I should have acted thus I

cannot comprehend. The exact total of my deficit is £621 0s. 3d., and I shall be glad if you will inform my dear wife, whose address is 78, Chapel-street, St. Helens, that if the money be reimbursed to the company whether you would or could forego any proceedings that you may already have instituted against me.

I have no wish to be dishonest, and would like to make reparation for my errors if it can be arranged. Kindly write her early. If the proceedings cannot now be withdrawn I will return and undergo the punishment I deserve, relying upon you to consider my wrongs in as lenient a view as you can, and trusting you will not be too unduly severe in this the greatest trouble it is possible for anyone to undergo, I remain, dear sir, through circumstances which have proved adverse to me in all my dealings, a miserable, unfortunate, and ruined man. Therefore I pray you will consider my position favourably for the sake of my dear wife and six young children. Yours truly, **FREDERICK E. JAMES**.

Victorian justice centred on punishment and deterrence with far less concern for the welfare of the offender than today – and so not prosecuting Fred for what he had done was completely out of the question.

The disgraced booking clerk voluntarily returned to St Helens to face the music and although Fred admitted taking £621, he only faced a specimen charge of stealing £30 10s.

CHARGE OF FRAUD AGAINST A ST. HELENS BOOKING CLERK.

At St. Helens Police Court yesterday Frederick Edward James, who for eleven years prior to December 3 last occupied the responsible position of chief booking clerk in the passenger department at St. Helens station of the London and North-Western Railway, was placed in the dock charged with having embezzled £30. 10s. on the 1st December, 1892, the moneys of his employers. Prisoner absconded on the 2nd December, but surrendered to the St. Helens police on Monday. There were on the bench Alderman James M'Bryde and Mr. W. J. Thomson. Some delay occurred owing to the late appearance of Mr. Fenna, solicitor for the Railway Company, and upon his appearance in court James was was called up the steps into the dock. He looked very pale. He was represented by Mr. Swift, of St. Helens.

Mr. Fenna commenced his statement by saying the charge was a most serious one. It was that of embezzling £30. 10s., the moneys of the Company. James

Manchester Guardian January 4th 1893

268

The court hearing took place on January 11th 1893 with Fred's solicitor making an earnest appeal for leniency, saying:

The prisoner had already suffered very considerably in his own conscience, and by witnessing the sufferings of his wife and family. James had now lost his situation, his superannuation money from the company, and all chance of advancement in life, and for the last six months he had suffered a hell upon earth.

DEEP REGRET

The Mayor of St Helens, Arthur Sinclair, was the Chairman of the Bench and as a longstanding railway man had known Fred James for many years. Sinclair was reported to have been considerably affected when sentencing the defendant and said he felt deep regret that a career of many years' honour and credit should finish as it had. He felt pained to have to deal with the case but must give him six months' hard labour.

A fortnight later there was more trouble for the James family. A cruel conman visited Fred's wife Elizabeth at her Chapel Street home. The well-dressed man claimed to be a prison official and appropriated the sum of £2 from her. That, supposedly, would be used to provide her husband with better food whilst in prison – and an overcoat was also taken as part of the swindle.

In the 1901 census, the now 44-year-old Fred is listed as a tobacconist's assistant living with wife Elizabeth in Harris Street. Ten years later *"commercial traveller and tobacconist"* is his stated occupation in the 1911 census.

However, in the wartime census known as the 1939 Register, *"retired chartered accountant"* is the surprise employment given for Fred, who was still residing in Harris Street.

So the Mayor and Fred's solicitor were wrong when they said he had lost all chance of advancement in life. Fred did seemingly have a second chance to make something of himself and I doubt got into any form of trouble again.

Professor Slavin's Electric Shock Stall

"Joseph Slavin, who stands in the market with a galvanic battery, and known as Professor Slavin, was summoned for threatening to assault, beat, and ill-treat".

This image from the 1890s shows "Professor" Joseph Slavin's electric shock stall in St Helens market place. Yes, people actually paid good brass to receive an electric shock! I've arrowed the handles of the apparatus that those desirous of more energy or suffering from nervous complaints would grasp. I expect they would then close their eyes and hope their self-inflicted ordeal would soon be over!

Actually, it was a very efficient machine as the "medical electrician" in charge of the contraption could frizzle quite a few folk at the same time. One person only needed to hold one handle, with the other participants all joining hands to create a long daisy chain. I wonder if the cost got less, as the chain got longer?

Electric shock was believed in Victorian times to have medical benefits and is still used by a few psychiatrists under the fancy name of electroconvulsive therapy.

One of the signs on Slavin's stall in the background of the photo says "Vital Energy", which is what the machine was claimed to impart. I suppose it did in a way, although I expect the burst of electricity only provided a very fleeting energy transfer and did not mean the patient could go home and begin running marathons!

Anybody then could call themselves a medical electrician and similarly the title "professor" did not come with any certificate. It was a common handle used by Punch and Judy men, lightning tooth extractors etc.

John Joseph Addis Slavin appears to have appointed himself a professor in the mid-1880s. Born in Manchester c.1831, he married Elizabeth Holland in 1857 when she was only 17 or 18. Slavin claimed to have been a schoolmaster for a long time before going into the electric shock business – but I can find no corroborative evidence.

TRAVELLING SHOWMAN

What I have been able to discern was that during the 1870s and early '80s, Slavin was a travelling showman. In the 1871 census Joseph and Elizabeth are recorded in Workington, with "travelling with panorama" listed as Slavin's occupation. The diorama and panorama shows that showcased paintings and photographs in unusual ways were very popular at that time and the Heywood Advertiser described one of Slavin's exhibitions in their edition of December 30th 1870:

On Tuesday evening Mr. J. E. Slavin exhibited his excellent Panorama in the Conservative Hall. The views embraced the battles and places most celebrated in the great war between France and Germany, including several of beautiful but sorely afflicted Paris. There were also good paintings of the Overland Route to India and China, Pilgrims Progress, Scriptural scenes, and at the conclusion a few comic views. The attendance was scanty.

Nine years later on January 17th 1880, the Runcorn Examiner described how in Holy Cross Schools in Corporation Street in St Helens, Slavin had presented a panorama of the Lake District and the Giant's Causeway. The entertainment had been a fundraiser for distressed Catholics in Ireland. A similar event in aid of new schools for Sacred Heart Church in Borough Road took place a year later and featured another Slavin panorama presentation.

The man was selling his electric shocks to the people of St Helens from at least 1887. We know that, as the St Helens Examiner from April 30th of that year described a court case involving the now "Professor" Slavin:

Joseph Slavin, who stands in the market with a galvanic battery, and is known as "Professor Slavin," was summoned for threatening to assault, beat, and ill-treat Bridget Gibbons, of Bickerstaffe-street, who also has a stall in the market. Complainant stated that on Saturday night last defendant came up to the stall and shouted several times, "I'll knock your neck out," &c. A crowd collected. She had not spoken to him for four or five years, and he came so suddenly that she was "completely mesmerised". He was a madman, a dangerous man, and she was afraid of him. She suffered from palpitation, was taken ill, and had to go straight to Dr. Jamison's. She had since been ill. Defendant said he was not talking to the complainant at all. She asked if him he was talking to her, and he said, "If the cap fits, you can wear it."

ALLEGED WIFE ASSAULT BY A ST. HELENS ELECTRICIAN.

At St. Helens on Monday, Joseph Slavin, an electrician, of Gladstone-st., and St. Helens Market, was summoned for assaulting his wife (Elizabeth Slavin). Mr. J. O. Swift defended. Complainant said her husband got into a passion on Saturday. He gripped her by the throat, and threatened to choke her. She got away from him, and ran into the back-yard. He then threw some water over her and drenched her. He fastened the door, and would not let her in nor give her any clothing. She went to a neighbour's house, and had not seen him since.—By Mr. Swift: She had a deal to contend with when he took those moods. She did not have any moods. She had been married thirty-five years.—Mr. Swift: Are you not willing to go home and start afresh for another thirty-five years?—Witness No, I cannot. He won't be comfortable with himself. There is nothing in the wide world to make him uncomfortable except his temper.—Mr. Swift: He says he will not throw water on you any more, and will try and make you comfortable. Won't you go back?—Witness: I don't know. It is not the water I complain about.

In that case Slavin was bound over to keep the peace but Bridget Gibbons was only a neighbouring stall-holder and did not have to live with the man – unlike Elizabeth Slavin.

In 1892 when the couple were residing in Gladstone Street, she summoned her husband to court alleging assault. Then two years later the St Helens Examiner of February 17th 1894 described a second court appearance by Joseph that Elizabeth had initiated:

Complainant said her husband got into a passion on Saturday. He gripped her by the throat, and threatened to choke her. She got away from him, and ran into the backyard. He then threw some water over her and drenched her. He fastened the door, and would not let her in nor give her any clothing. She went to a neighbour's house, and had not seen him since. – By Mr. Swift [Joseph's solicitor]: She had a deal to contend with when he took those moods. She did not have any moods. She had been married thirty-five years. – Mr. Swift: Are you not willing to go home and start afresh for another thirty-five years? – Witness: No, I cannot. He won't be comfortable with himself. There is nothing in the wide world to make him uncomfortable except his temper.

– Mr. Swift: He says he will not throw water on you any more, and will try and make you comfortable. Won't you go back? – Witness: I don't know. It is not the water I complain about. He gets himself into a violent passion, and if I don't speak he says I am dumb. – Defendant: She is labouring under a mistake. She wants to be the missus (laughter). – The case was adjourned for a month to allow the parties to come to terms, but Mrs. Slavin remarked that she would never go back.

Elizabeth Slavin's nephew was John Donegan and he lived with his uncle in Chorley Street (off Duke Street) in St Helens. However, the pair clearly did not get on well – despite being (or probably because they were) in the same electric shock business.

SUMMONS

A fortnight before the marital hearing in St Helens Police Court, Slavin had taken out a summons against his nephew in the local County Court. The case concerned a debt of £3 and the judge at an earlier hearing had ordered Donegan to repay the money at the rate of 5 shillings per month.

However, over a two-year period, Donegan had paid off less than half of his debt and so Professor Slavin had his housemate and nephew by marriage back in court demanding the balance.

But the judge adjudicating on the case felt the underlying problem was that both men were medical electricians with stalls in the market – and Slavin did not appreciate the competition.

The Liverpool Mercury of February 1st 1894 described what occurred at the hearing:

Plaintiff [Slavin] stated that the defendant [Donegan] was well able to pay the amount owing. He had been trained as an electrician, and went about to fairs and markets with an electrical machine and a weighing chair, and made a lot of money. Defendant said he did not earn a lot of money. He was a labourer at Pilkington's glassworks, and earned a 17s. 4d. per week. He could only attend markets on Saturday afternoon every month, as he was obliged to work at other times. Plaintiff remarked that his wife was defendant's aunt, and defendant had caused some trouble in the family. His (plaintiff's) wife went to Southport in consequence.

Defendant said that Mr. Slavin had forgiven him the debt, and handed to the judge a letter which he had received from the plaintiff. The letter was addressed "My dear John William," and commenced "The Rev. Father Brown has proposed an all-round forgiveness, and I have accepted it. All your county court papers are in the hands of Father Brown, and you have to call and see him." The Judge: By this letter you have promised to forgive this debt? Plaintiff: But I wish you to enforce the law and make him fulfil his engagements. The Judge: You have promised to forgive him? Plaintiff: On certain conditions which he has not fulfilled. He has not been to see Father Brown, and there has been a lot of unpleasantness about it. Defendant said he had done all he could to make Slavin and his wife happy. He had been to see Father Brown. Plaintiff: He is telling lies.

The Judge: You [Slavin] pretend to be very religious, but I don't think you show any great signs of your religion in your conduct to-day. You are very vindictive. You have forgiven this man and yet you bring him up before the court. Defendant said the reason [for the summons] was that he had applied for a space at St. Helens Market for his machine, and the plaintiff had a "standing" there. The Judge: Do you mean that you are a sort of rival? Defendant: Yes. His Honour remarked that it was clear from the letter that plaintiff had once forgiven the debt, but he (the judge) could not act on the letter. He ordered the sum still owing to be paid at 1s. 6d. per month.

ALLEGED ASSAULT BY "PROFESSOR SLAVIN," OF ST. HELENS.—At St. Helens Police Court, yesterday, before Messrs. W. Tyrer, W. Gamble, and A. H. Michell, John Joseph Addis Slavin, of Windlesham-road, who styled himself "Professor Slavin," and stands in St. Helens Market with a galvanic battery, weighing chair, &c., was charged with assaulting John William Gaunt, aged thirteen, of Charles-street. Mr. H. L. Riley appeared to prosecute, and Mr. E. W. Swift defended.—Mr. Riley said that the assault took place in the market about six o'clock on Saturday night last. Gaunt was an errand boy for the Atherton Drug Stores, and on Saturday night, when he was passing through the market, he was attracted to Slavin's stall, where he was trying to teach his boy how to manage the galvanic battery while he was away. The boy seemed unable to understand the machine, and this lack of receptivity of the boy seemed to have irritated Slavin, and he turned round on Gaunt and another boy who was there and assaulted him very badly, and kicked him.—The boy Gaunt gave evidence as to being struck on the face by Slavin with a cane, and being kicked on the

Liverpool Daily Post July 10th 1897

277

In July 1897 Slavin was accused of assaulting a 13-year-old lad in St Helens Market. John Gaunt worked as an errand boy for the Atherton Drug Stores and was passing through the marketplace when he stopped for a moment at Slavin's stall.

The electrician had been trying to teach his own son how to use the electric shock equipment but the lad was struggling to understand.

In frustration and without provocation, Professor Slavin turned round and struck John Gaunt in the face with a cane and then kicked him on his leg and thigh. Two adult witnesses corroborated the court evidence of the boy, with one saying the kicks and blows were very violent.

Slavin's solicitor told the court that the "urchins" who frequented the market caused great annoyance to his client by congregating round his stall. However, he was a man of good character, who had been a schoolmaster for a long time before becoming a medical electrician.

But the St Helens Chief Constable revealed to the Bench that the defendant had been summoned five times previously and for his attack on John Gaunt he was fined £1 14s 6d.

In the 1901 census, Joseph Slavin is shown living at 189 Windleshaw Road and still describing himself as a medical electrician. The 70-year-old's wife, Elizabeth, was shown as a *medical electrician (assist)*. No doubt that meant she helped her husband out on his electric shock stall frizzling people with more money than sense! Professor Slavin died in 1910.

The Burning of Effigies in St Helens

"Old clothes and straw were produced and effigies made and burned amid the beating of tin pans and kettles"

Elderly folk discussing the "olden days" have often used the expression: *"We had to make our own entertainment"*. That might summon up mental images of activities like piano playing – but many people in working class districts had neither the cash nor the know-how to play musical instruments.

In the pre-cinema and wireless era, free entertainment and sport could be conjured up out of virtually nothing. Huge crowds would appear at the drop of a hat at the prospect of a fight; a policeman attempting to make a difficult arrest; a sporting challenge or, perhaps, some medical emergency.

Most people then kept the front doors of their houses open in order to keep in close touch with their local community – and they could be out on the street at the drop of a hat!

In those days neighbours were more easily branded good or bad, with reports on their alleged actions related in a black and white fashion – with all those subtleties provided by shades of grey removed. That's still the case today, of course, but I think to a much lesser extent than in the past.

So, someone involved in an extra-marital relationship or what was perceived as being on the "wrong" side of a court case could expect the ire of the mob.

I'm tempted to write "angry" mob but I think the crowd's fury was at times little more than perfunctory, with newspaper reports suggesting that the participants in their neighbours' humiliation often had a jolly good time!

HOOTING AND YELLING

Neighbourly disapproval of some unpopular person often came in the form of a procession past the unfortunate individual's house – with members of the crowd beating tin kettles, pots and pans and hooting and yelling. An effigy of the victim might also be produced and burned, or destroyed in some other way.

Those picked on for such treatment would normally remain indoors while the nonsense went on outside. Often it was not spontaneous silliness but could involve some considerable planning.

On June 5th 1880 the St Helens Examiner described how a married woman had for over two months been conducting an affair with a younger man from the Kirkland Street / Lyon Street district of the town. The husband knowing of the relationship had relocated with his wife to St Ann's in Eccleston – but the affair continued and so he had thrown her out of the house.

The woman had subsequently moved in with her boyfriend and his neighbours, angry at the immorality on show in their street, decided the "gay Lothario" should receive the St Helens version of the "tar and feather". That was to cover the young man in flour and treacle.

The Examiner described what occurred:

> At noon on Tuesday a crowd assembled in Lyon-street to wreak their vengeance on the guilty pair, particularly on the man, as he was going to his dinner from his work. The necessary paraphernalia – treacle pots and flour bags – were in readiness, but he managed to elude them, and escaped to work by the back way from his house. The women were not to be dismayed in their first attempt, and during the afternoon preparation were made to carry out their demonstrations on a larger and more elaborate scale when the offender returned from his work at half-past five.

At that time about two hundred women assembled in the street, but the friends of the young man had evidently got a hint of the proceedings, and two police officers were sent for who escorted the man through the crowd. A rush was made at him, and the holders of the pot and bag succeeded in applying a few patches on the object of their dislike. The policemen prevented anything more serious taking place, but had it not been for their protection, the man with the fierce-looking moustache would certainly have presented a "ghostly" appearance on being delivered from the hands of his enemies.

One of the houses in Lyon Street became what the Examiner called a committee room, full of *"bustle and excitement"* as further plans against the couple were hatched.

These included the making of two effigies, *"one representing the masculine atom of their contempt"* and the other being *"the willing destroyer of her husband's happiness"*.

Both dummies were 4 to 5ft. in height and supported on poles, with the male effigy adorned with a black moustache, a hat, a coat and a pair of paper cuffs. The female effigy wore a cloak, hat and tie.

The Examiner described what happened next:

Two courageous women marched with these, followed by the crowd, to the window of the house where dwelt the guilty couple, and there they exhibited the effigies at the window amid the groans, yells, and shouting of the people. To give the man a reminder of the danger he had undergone, the treacle jars were exhibited at the window for his inspection. The women then marched along the streets, carrying the effigies, and threatening injury to the wayward pair. More than once the women threatened to break open the doors of the house, which were kept locked.

Unusually, it appears that the effigies in this case were not burned. However, thirteen years earlier, similar dummies had successfully been set ablaze in Haydock, when a group of miners decided that a couple living in sin needed teaching a lesson in morality.

performed. The services were largely attended.

A SCANDAL AND A SCENE.—At the Newton sessions on Saturday last, William Harrison and fifteen other young men, colliers, residing at Haydock, were charged with having conducted themselves in a riotous and turbulent manner at Haydock, on the night of the 19th September, to the annoyance of the inhabitants, and "against the peace of our sovereign lady the Queen." —The defendants, who all pleaded not guilty, were defended by Mr. Ackerley, of Wigan.—Police-constable No. 425 (Holden) said on the night of Thursday, the 19th of September, while on duty at Black Brook, he saw a great crowd of people collected there for the purpose of burning effigies. He cautioned them and advised them to go away, but they would not, and commenced to make a noise. They brought the effigies out, and he took one of them from them, but while he was attempting to rick it up he was struck on the

St Helens Examiner April 30th 1887

That led to sixteen men appearing in Newton Sessions on September 28th 1867 charged with having conducted themselves in a "riotous and turbulent manner to the annoyance of the inhabitants".

The police evidence was that on two successive nights at Haydock, a great crowd of people had assembled to burn effigies but despite being ordered to disperse, had refused to leave and a constable was assaulted. The Wigan Observer described the evidence of PC Holden:

After carrying the effigies up and down the street they set them on fire, and in endeavouring to stop them one of the burning effigies was hurled at him. After that they went away, some of them shouting that they would "kill the bobby next night." On the following night they assembled at the same place and were very disorderly. He was struck several times with stones. It was a great annoyance to the public, as the thoroughfare was stopped up, so that no person could get up or down. There were a thousand people in the crowd, and the defendants were the ringleaders of it.

SHAMELESS ADULTERY

There were so many accused men in the dock that they'd been able to club together and hire a solicitor to represent them in court.

The line of defence of Henry Ackerley was that his clients' actions were perfectly permissible because of the immoral behaviour of their victims. The Observer's report said:

The circumstances of the case were these; the man and woman who had been referred to were living in open, shameless adultery at Haydock, and he contended that the proceedings of the defendants were justifiable, being in the interests of public morality.

However, the prosecuting counsel countered that what had occurred had been in the interest solely of *"lynch law ... but that is not the law of England"*. The magistrates said they did not intend to punish the men severely but to give them a serious warning and bind them over in their own recognisances to keep the peace.

THE SEQUEL TO AN EFFIGY-BURNING.—At the Town Hall on Monday, before Alderman J Harrison, two women named Mary Jane Lawton and Margery Goulding, residents of Parr-street, were summoned on a singular charge of obstructing the street. The two defendants pleaded not guilty. P.C. Grant stated that about half-past seven on the previous Monday evening he saw the defendants creating an obstruction in Parr-street. They had a long pole, with a lot of old clothes stuffed with straw at the end of it. They carried it along Parr-street, and when they got to the end of Parr-street they set it on fire. About 200 people gathered round, and the street was completely blocked for about twenty minutes. The fire was subsequently put out with a lot of water. In reply to Superin-

St Helens Examiner April 30th 1887

It was unusual for such ringleaders to be male. Most instigators were middle-aged women with those described by the St Helens Examiner on April 30th 1887 being next-door neighbours aged 56 and 34:

At the Town Hall on Monday, before Alderman J Harrison, two women named Mary Jane Lawton and Margery Goulding, residents of Parr-street, were summoned on a singular charge of obstructing the street. The two defendants pleaded not guilty. P.C. Grant stated that about half-past seven on the previous Monday evening he saw the defendants creating an obstruction in Parr-street. They had a long pole, with a lot of old clothes stuffed with straw at the end of it. They carried it along Parr-street, and when they got to the end of Parr-street they set it on fire. About 200 people gathered round, and the street was completely blocked for about twenty minutes.

The fire was subsequently put out with a lot of water. In reply to Superintendent Johnston, witness said the old clothes stuffed with straw was intended to be the effigy of somebody, and the proceedings were calculated to cause a disturbance. P.C. Massey gave corroborative evidence. The defendants denied that they carried the pole, and alleged that they only witnessed the proceedings from amongst the crowd. They called two witnesses to that effect. The Bench ordered each defendant to pay a fine of 5s and costs.

Children were often involved in such events – but they were certainly not the instigators, with their mothers seemingly allowing – if not encouraging – them to join in the fun.

On June 20th 1885 under the headline *"Burning Effigies At St. Helens – Lively Scene"*, the St Helens Examiner described how hundreds of women and children from Parr had burnt two effigies.

One was intended as a representation of a local glassmaker and the other figure was described as being of the wife of a chemical labourer, with the pair suspected of having an affair:

On Tuesday morning several neighbours saw the two leaving the house together and going to a neighbouring public-house. They were hissed and hooted, and the protection of the police had to be sought. Later in the day the glass-maker was again seen in the house of the woman. A crowd collected, and, amid a scene of considerable excitement, old clothes and straw were produced, and so-called "effigies" of the "pair" made and burned, amid the beating of tin pans and kettles and the hissings and hootings of women and children. The man, fortunately for himself, made good his escape over the back wall, and the woman bolted the door and drew down the blinds. The crowd was afterwards dispersed by the police.

A GOOD DO AT SUTTON

In the next example, the police said they had overheard an effigy burner admitting having a fun time. Under the headline *"A Good Do At Sutton – Burning Of Effigies"*, the St Helens Newspaper of June 12th 1897 described how in St Helens Police Court, 37-year-old miner Thomas Berks of Berrys Lane, 38-year-old copper worker Llewelyn Roberts of Watery Lane and John Oates from Moss Nook had denied breaching the peace:

Police-constable Rigby stated that on the previous Monday night he saw the defendants carrying two effigies from Watery-lane across some waste land and into Sutton-road. Berks and Roberts carried the effigies, while Oates walked alongside them, shouting and making a great noise. A large crowd of men, women and children rattling tin cans etc., followed. The effigies were placed in front of the house of a Mrs. Hayes, 201, Watery-lane, where paraffin oil was poured upon them and set on fire.

There were between 200 and 300 people there shouting, "booing," and making use of very bad language. Witness tried to put the fire out, but unsuccessfully. During the evening one of the defendants got an old jacket, which he steeped in tar, and after placing it on a long pole, carried it through the streets. He shouted to a lot of men, "Fall in, men; come on let's have a _____ good do." He then set fire to the coat, and the stench which it gave rise to was most unbearable.

The trouble – or perhaps I should say, fun – lasted for four hours. But the police got little pleasure out of it and neither I should imagine did Mrs Hayes or Mrs Yates.

Reading between the lines, it appears that the latter had brought court proceedings against her husband and their neighbour, Mrs Hayes, was accused of being the other woman. The Bench bound the three men over to keep the peace for six months.

The destruction of effigies could also occur during heated industrial disputes. In February 1887, around thirty Swedish and Norwegian bottlemakers came to St Helens to work at Lyon Brothers. The glass firm recruited the foreign labour to replace workers sacked during a dispute.

There was enormous anger over the importing of the Scandinavian bottle-hands, who had to receive police escorts between their accommodation in Corporation Street and the glassworks in Peasley Cross.

On February 5th 1887, a mass rally was held at Hardshaw Fields, near Providence Hospital, to protest against the foreign labour. Around 5,000 persons comprised a procession, which journeyed through Shaw Street and along Church Street and then into Duke Street. The St Helens Examiner wrote:

> About the middle of the procession an effigy of a person was carried, presumably intended to represent a member of the firm, which caused considerable amusement, and when the procession arrived again at Hardshaw-fields the effigy was trampled under foot.

A GOOD, STIFF GLASS OF WHISKEY

I conclude this chapter with an example from September 1868 of how the creation of an effigy elevated a trivial dispute between neighbours into a court case.

Rosannah Webster and Mary Hardman had fallen out with each other and the latter's husband decided to make a comic effigy of Rosannah in straw – as the St Helens Newspaper explained:

> Having examined the article, and found it to his taste, he engaged the services of a little boy, promising, by way of inducement, to reward him with a "good, stiff glass" of whiskey. The lad, pursuant to instructions, went out to the front of the complainant's door, and began to put the straw figure through various motions, to the amusement of a number of curious neighbours.

However, Rosannah Webster was not amused and a furious row developed. Somewhat tongue in cheek the Newspaper said: *"A great deal of compliments were constantly exchanged by both women on each other's nationality"*.

Mary Hardman was bound over to keep the peace.

The Cairo Connection of
Train Driver Tom Melling

"The Reported Ghastly Discovery At St. Helens"

I expect many a person has wandered out of Thatto Heath Park and wondered about the plaques that adorn an old property on the corner of Thatto Heath Road and Cairo Street. On the wall facing the park, a small, shield-shaped plaque reads:

T. MELLING, CAIRO SQUARE, 1875

Then high in the brickwork on one side of the building – which at the time of writing serves as a hairdresser's salon – a much larger, weather-beaten plaque proudly states:

This building was erected by a donation given by the government of Egypt to Thomas Melling for his heroism displayed in driving the English mail through that country during the distructive [sic] plague in the year 1865.

A similar memorial also exists in Portico Lane in Eccleston Park on a small house known as Suez Lodge. This reads:

Built by Thomas Melling who took the first English outward mail through Egypt in 1858 and brought the last homeward mail in March 1878 when it was transferred to the Egyptian Government.

Such original information boards on 19th century properties are quite rare – although these only provide scant detail as to Mr Melling's achievements. The commemorative plaques on both buildings also fail to mention what local papers dubbed the *"ghastly discovery"*, when frightened boys fished a human skull out a pond.

That embarrassing event in 1895 was also connected to the train driver's lengthy stay in the land of the pyramids. But first some background to this unusual story…

DRIVER OF THE FIRST CLASS

Born c.1818 in Moss Bank in St Helens, Thomas Melling began his railway career as an apprentice at the Sutton loco sheds. By the time he was twenty-nine, he had become an engine driver on the Great Western Railway and his adventurous spirit then took him to

France, where Tom was presented with a certificate for being a *"driver of the first class"*.

After two years based in Paris, Tom set off to explore Egypt and soon was driving mail trains. This, of course, was at a time when very few people journeyed any great distance from their hometown, making his experiences even more remarkable.

In 1859 the loco driver transported Dr David Livingstone across the desert during the famous Scottish explorer's Zambezi River expedition. Six years later Melling drove mail-trains through Egypt at the height of a cholera epidemic.

The Moss Bank railway man became the first to conquer the desert between Cairo and Suez and a grateful Egyptian government gave Melling the cash to build a house back home in England – which he constructed in Thatto Heath.

Tom's driving skills were highly praised by Egyptian royalty. In 1867 he was presented with a gold watch by the mother of the country's Viceroy for driving a train non-stop from Alexandria to Cairo, a distance of 131 miles. That was considered a great feat at the time for there were no filling points en route where a moving train could pick up water.

Tom was also presented with another gold watch by a second Viceroy's mother, for taking her on her first train journey for prayers at Tanta, a city 60 miles north of Cairo.

By the time Tom returned home for good in the late 1870s, he had turned sixty and decided to retire from driving trains. But he still had sufficient life in him to marry a woman thirty years his junior and father three children.

HUMAN SKULL

But Tom brought back to England not just the money that he had made and the gold watches presented to him – he also returned home with a human skull!

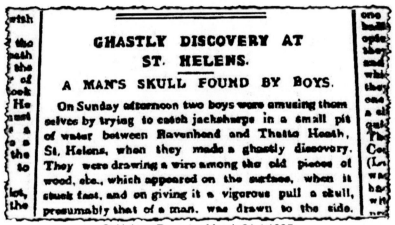

St Helens Reporter March 31st 1895

More than twenty years later, Tom's gruesome souvenir of his time in Egypt caused a scare, as the St Helens Reporter described in March 1895 under the headline *"Ghastly Discovery at St. Helens – A Man's Skull Found By Boys"*:

On Sunday afternoon two boys were amusing themselves by trying to catch jacksharps in a small pit of water between Ravenhead and Thatto Heath, St. Helens, when they made a ghastly discovery. They were drawing a wire among the old pieces of wood, &c., which appeared on the surface, when it stuck fast, and on giving it a vigorous pull a skull, presumably that of a man, was drawn to the side. Some consternation prevailed, and eventually Police-sergeant Small got possession of the skull, and conveyed it to the police office at St. Helens. The pit in question up to a few years since was wide and deep, but it has been gradually filled up, and now only a

291

portion, about 10 feet wide and very shallow, remains. One theory regarding the gruesome find is that foul play took place years ago, and that the skull became detached from the trunk, and has been forced to the top by the tipping of the dirt, &c., round the sides. Another theory is that the skull, which is entirely devoid of flesh, has been recently conveyed to the place and thrown in. The jaw is missing, and so also are a number of the upper teeth.

However, in the same edition the newspaper was able to update its readers on what had actually occurred:

It would appear that the ghastly discovery has a very simple and common-place solution attached to it. Thomas Melling, of Thatto Heath, states that he was at one time proprietor of this remnant of humanity. A number of years ago Melling was in Egypt during the time when a remarkable cholera epidemic raged, and while there he had the honour to drive the first mail train from Alexandria to Cairo, which fact is now recorded on the front of his house. He was presented with a large sum of money and other valuables by the Egyptian Government, and in addition to other things brought the skull back home with him.

Some few years ago his daughter was married to a man named Platt, of Elephant-lane, when he gave her the skull and other things. The daughter appears to have soon become tired of so gruesome an ornament on her mantelpiece, and after discovering that moths were inducing a continuance of the mortification to which human remains are naturally liable, she threw the skull into the water, where it has just been found. Probably the much-travelled skull will now find a proper and safe bestowal by means of interment.

Tom died on November 17th 1896, aged 78, and his remains were interred in the Christ Church cemetery in Eccleston. The inscription on his memorial states:

From Cairo to Suez he drove the first train,
And if he were able he would do it again;
He loved to run through Egypt's sandy soil,
And view the ancient ruins of Joseph's toil.

Newspapers all over the country covered the death of Melling, including the St Helens Reporter, who under the headline *"Death Of A Notable Engine Driver"* wrote:

On Saturday afternoon at Eccleston Cemetery, the funeral of the remains of Mr Thomas Melling, 78 years of age, of Suez Lodge, Eccleston, took place. Mr Melling was the first man to drive a train across the desert between Cairo and Suez, in 1858, and he continued on this line for twenty years without a single accident. During the last three years of this engagement he drove the Royal trains. On a special occasion, in 1867, he accomplished the whole distance of 131 miles in two hours and twenty minutes without a stoppage, and for this he was presented with a handsome and richly chased gold watch by the mother of Mahomed Said Pasha, Viceroy of Egypt. In 1859, he brought Livingstone across the desert. Mr Melling was a native of Moss Bank, near St. Helens. Deceased was the driver on the first newspaper express train between London and Birmingham previous to going to Egypt.

The 1891 census has 72-year-old Tom living in Portico Lane with his 43-year-old wife Elizabeth, 10-year-old son Thomas, 6-year-old son William and 4-year-old daughter Ann. William appears to have inherited his father's adventurous spirit – as he joined the Royal Navy as a boy. However, in November 1901 at the age of 17,

William was drowned when the cutter HMS Active was dashed to pieces in the Firth of Forth and twenty sailors died.

THE SUEZ CRISIS

Tom's daughter Ann Melling married John Kenyon in 1913 and, at some point, the couple moved into her father's old family home in Eccleston Park that still to this day bears the name **'Suez Lodge – 1879'**.

The Suez Crisis of 1956 generated increased interest in anything Egyptian and led to Ann Kenyon making the news pages of the Liverpool Echo.

Under the headline *"Suez Lodge Makes Them Stop And Ask"*, the paper reported on September 19th of that year how this curiosity was annoying Mrs Melling:

> The passers-by who pause to read Suez Lodge on the nameplate of a house in Portico Lane, near St. Helens, often stay to enquire the history of the building. Mrs. Ann Kenyon, who lives there, says she is thinking of having the plate painted over, and that, she declares, "will out an end to the questions." The house was built by her father, the late Thomas Melling, an engine driver, who lived in Egypt many years and drove the King of Egypt a century ago.

Mrs. Kenyon treasures a gold watch presented to her father for the then considerable feat of running a train non-stop on the 131-mile journey between Alexandria and Cairo: "When my father returned to this country to settle down the name of the house was linked with his work in Egypt. I am sure he could not have anticipated how many questions would crop up because of the choice of that name," Mrs Kenyon added.

Egypt has figured a few other times in the history of St Helens. A particularly curious incident was related in St Helens Police Court on September 29th 1882 when a row in Peasley Cross led to John and Bridget Gahan appearing before the Bench.

The couple were accused of assaulting their neighbour Bridget Grey by pulling her hair and striking her with a piece of ironstone slag. John Gahan was also accused of violently kicking Bridget and trying to strangle her until blood came from her nostrils.

The row had begun when the Gahans were celebrating the exploits of Sir Garnet Wolseley outside their home in Appleton Street. He was commander of the British forces in Egypt, who had been suppressing a nationalist uprising called the Urabi Revolt.

The Catholic Gahans took exception to their discussion, which led to the argument and assaults.

Acknowledgements / Credits

St Helens Archive Service

Eccleston Library, St Helens

British Newspapers Archive

FindmyPast

Most images are from the author's own personal archive

Sir Samuel Brighouse picture courtesy Lionel Taylor

Thanks to my sister Diane Charnock for her unwavering support

Newspaper sources: St Helens Examiner; St Helens Newspaper, St Helens Reporter, Chester Chronicle, Liverpool Courier, Liverpool Daily Post, Liverpool Echo, Liverpool Mercury, Manchester Courier, Manchester Evening News, Manchester Guardian, Prescot Reporter, Preston Chronicle, Preston Herald, North British Daily Mail (Glasgow), Illustrated Police News, Ormskirk Advertiser, Heywood Advertiser, Wigan Observer, Cheshire Observer, Blackburn Standard, Pall Mall Gazette, Londonderry Standard, Widnes Examiner, Runcorn Examiner, Warrington Examiner.

Book quotations: Sir James Sexton, Agitator – The Life of the Dockers' M.P. (Faber and Faber, 1936)
James Brockbank – History of St. Helens With Local Landmarks (1896)

Want More Stories Like These?

Check out *'Stories From St Helens Heritage'* **on Facebook**